Hunting America's Wild Turkeys

By Toby Bridges

With: Rob Keck, James Earl Kennamer, Will Primos, Harold Knight, David Hale, Mark Drury, Brad Harris, Michael Pearce, Jerry Martin, Ray Eye, Steve Stoltz...and other wild turkey hunting experts

D1636854

Stoeger Publishing Company

Title: *Hunting America's Wild Turkeys*
Publisher: *Jay Langston*
Project Coordinator: *Studiocrafts*
Design & Production Director: *Dominick S. Sorrentino*
Editor: *William S. Jarrett*
Design, Electronic Page Makeup & Photo Imaging: *Lesley A. Notorangelo*
Cover Photo: *Donald Jones*
Cover Design: *Stephen McKelvain*

Published by Stoeger Publishing Company
17603 Indian Head Highway, Suite 200
Accokeek, Maryland 20607

ISBN: 0-88317-228-3
Library of Congress Catalog Card No.: 00-135097
Manufactured in the United States of America

Distributed to the book trade and to the sporting goods trade by Stoeger Industries, 17603 Indian Head Highway, Accokeek, Maryland 20607

About The Author

Toby Bridges has pursued the wild turkey for three decades,
hunting this magnificent game bird in more than 20 states. Since his first hunt in the rugged Missouri Ozarks in the spring of 1972, he has not missed a single season—and not many fall seasons. He has taken gobblers with shotgun, muzzleloader, rifle and bow. Over the years he has hunted with many legendary turkey hunters and become close friends with men such as Mark Drury, Ray Eye, Rob Keck, Jim Casada, Brad Harris, Robbie Rohm, Harold Knight, David Hale, and many others. In an effort to make this book live up to its name—*HUNTING AMERICA'S WILD TURKEYS*—he has called upon these recognized experts to share their knowledge of turkey hunting.

Toby's knowledge of turkey hunting is second to none, an assertion that will be readily apparent in the manner with which he covers the various aspects of the sport. In some 30 years of turkey hunting, he has harvested more than 200 mature gobblers. As many of these grand birds were taken with a muzzleloading shotgun as with a modern shotgun. This shouldn't come as any surprise, for Toby is recognized as the leading authority on muzzleloading hunting in the country today. His experience and knowledge has led to the creation of eight books on the subject, including *ADVANCED BLACK POWDER HUNTING*, another fine book from Stoeger Publishing Company.

I know you will enjoy reading this book as much as I've enjoyed working on it.

—*William Jarrett, Editor*

Introduction

The Dynamics of Wild Turkey Hunting

WITH ■ Rob Keck, *C.E.O., National Wild Turkey Federation* ■ James Earl Kennamer, *Vice President of Conservation Programs, National Wild Turkey Federation* ■ Dr. John Lewis, *noted wild turkey biologist* ■ Harold Knight, *co-founder, Knight & Hale Game Calls* ■ David Hale, *co-founder, Knight & Hale Game Calls*

While barely a teenager growing up in west-central Illinois,

I occasionally read in magazines like *Outdoor Life*, *Field & Stream* and *Sports Afield* feature articles about turkey hunting. At the time, I'd never even seen a live wild turkey (for that matter, I'd never seen a dead one either). I had read those articles simply because they were about hunting, and I was hopelessly "ate up" with anything on the subject. Any article that dealt with hunting was for me prime reading material.

I remember thinking that turkey hunting might be fun, but I couldn't understand how it compared to chasing whitetails, climbing high for elk, or going after other big game. After all, my mother could drive down to the local supermarket and buy a turkey already cleaned and ready for the oven—all for only 29 cents a pound! At the time, Illinois didn't even allow turkey hunting, and the closest places where true wild turkeys could be found were a hundred or more miles from where I lived. The birds had become nonexistent in Illinois during the 1930s and '40s, and many hunters felt that efforts to reestablish them were a waste of time and money. So early on in life, I simply accepted the fact that I would probably never hunt wild turkeys.

How things have changed! I still live in west-central Illinois, about 80 miles north of where I spent my boyhood years. Less than a half-mile to the east, the Illinois River flows lazily southward, and only eight miles to the west, across a wooded ridge known as Pike and Calhoun counties, lies the mighty Mississippi. Now hardly a week goes by during which I fail to spot wild turkeys at least half a dozen times. Each April, through an open window of my small rural office, I can invariably hear the gobbles of maybe six or more wild turkey toms.

Yes, the wild turkey is here to stay—or at least it seems that way. Those readers who are new to turkey hunting—especially younger hunters in their 20s and 30s who may not have been around during the early days of modern wild turkey management—may not be aware of how close we came to losing this tremendously popular game bird. Indeed, the wild turkey population across the U.S. had reached its lowest level during the late 1930s. While little had been written concerning the wild turkey population at that time, professional game managers accepted the fact that these great birds had been decimated in 18 of the original 39 states (where they had once been found in abundance). America was just emerging from the Great Depression, and while few sportsmen still hunted the turkey, it's a good bet that many a farm boy intent on shooting a mess of squirrels to help feed a hungry family welcomed the opportunity to come home toting a prized turkey on his back.

Ironically, those hard times which destroyed the dreams of so many hard-working Americans led to good times for wild turkey. So much of the prime turkey habitat had been lost to a

Author Toby Bridges, who grew up in Illinois, was convinced at one time that he would never see wild turkeys in any appreciable number within his home state. Fortunately, he was wrong, for the state now offers tremendous opportunities for birds the size of this tom.

patchwork of small farms, many of them operated by tenant farmers with only 40 to 80 acres on which to eke out a living for their families. No room was left for timber, for mature fencerows, or for idle land grown over with brush and briars. Every bit of useable farm ground was cleared and planted or heavily pastured, leaving less and less for the troubled wild turkey and other game populations.

The economic chaos following the stock market crash, coupled with the terrible drought that decimated farms in the Midwest and the Great Plains, forced many small farmer in the 1930s to abandon the land and head for the cities in search of work in order to support their families. Nature slowly reclaimed many of these marginal farms, once again providing much needed habitat and nesting cover for the wild turkey.

According to James Earl Kennamer, Vice President of Conservation Programs for the National Wild Turkey Federation, "Little was known about the biology of wild turkeys, or the factors that influenced populations." It was during this period that the first books on wild turkey management appeared. One of the first to be recognized and accepted was by Aldo Leopold in 1933. His work set the stage for other, more specific studies, including, "The Wild Turkey in Virginia," written by naturalists Henry Mosby and Charles Handley. With its publication a whole new era of wild turkey research and management was ushered in.

Kennamer further notes that the Pittman-Robertson Act of 1937 also played an important role in funding early wild turkey research by increasing the excise tax on the sales of sporting goods and ammunition. When these funds were added to moneys collected through state hunting license sales, game departments could then afford to conduct the early studies and habitat improvement needed. Gradually, the restocking program brought the wild turkey back from the brink of extinction. World War II interrupted the task of restoring America's dwindling wildlife populations, so much of this work did not start in earnest until the latter part of the 1940s.

Unfortunately, some early attempts to pump up existing turkey popula- tions or reintroduce the bird back into its ancestral range were unsuccessful. For example, there was an attempt to release pen- raised "game farm" birds. The idea seemed logical: Mass-produce turkeys from wild stock by hatch- ing them under ideal con- ditions, rearing them in pens until they could take care of themselves, then releasing them in suitable turkey habitats. It was an idea that proved good in theory but not in practice. As James Earl Kennamer pointed out, "Using the pen-raised method slowed the wild turkey comeback in North America for almost two decades. Further- more, this technique used

untold millions of dollars that might have been spent in more wild turkey trap-and-transplant programs, which have proved immensely successful."

Kennamer further stated that one turkey restoration survey, comparing the success of pen-raised releases to that of birds trapped in the wild, indicates how costly these early efforts were to game departments in both time and money. In this study of 30,000 or so wild-trapped turkeys released on some 968 sites, viable wild turkey populations were

In most states today, wild turkey biolo- gists carefully monitor the number and quality of birds harvested.

dangers, not to mention a great deal about food sources, the geography of their home ranges, and their social behavior, such as vocalization and flocking. A pen-raised turkey hasn't had a chance to learn these important survival mechanisms."

In the same survey cited above, pen-raised turkeys released in six states were found to be diseased. Following the failure of these efforts, 23 of the 36 participating states passed legislation within a few years banning the release of farm-raised turkeys. The release of pen-raised turkeys is now illegal in nearly every state. Still, advertisements can be found in certain outdoor magazines claiming that eggs, poults and adults on sale came from "truly wild" turkeys, all suitable for releasing into the wild.

Shared use of land for both wildlife and agriculture purposes has generally benefited the wild turkey. Grain crops provide sufficient food sources even during years with poor mast crops.

established on 808 of them, occupying more than 200,000 square miles of range. Conversely, of more than 300,000 pen-raised birds released on 800 sites, total failures occurred on 760 of them: Only Michigan reported any measure of success with pen-raised turkeys. Still, of the 882 birds released on 12 Michigan sites, only three releases were successful. Even then, many felt that the birds were never really "wild;"

Note: *If you've ever thought about rearing turkeys for the purpose of releasing them into habitat where there are no turkeys...DON'T! One study of about 100 pen-raised wild turkeys reveals that they carried at least 33 species of parasites and three other potentially harmful diseases. If released into the wild, these birds could spread diseases that could set wild turkey management of a particular region back years, if not decades.*

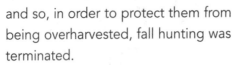

and so, in order to protect them from being overharvested, fall hunting was terminated.

"A major factor in the poor success of game-farm birds," James Kennamer points out, "is the absence of wild turkey hens to teach skills to developing poults. Wild hens teach their poults the proper response to predators and other

The area around my home in western Illinois was one of the last sites in the state to receive a transplant of trapped wild birds. The timbered ridges ringing every creek valley nearby have always been ideal turkey habitats, so their survival there was never a question. The problem stemmed from the fact that several well-intentioned but impatient hunters had pen-raised and released a large number of so-called "wild strain" turkeys. However, before the Illinois Department of Natural Resources spent the time and money trying to restock the area with wild-trapped turkeys, it first wanted to make sure that the inferior pen-raised birds had all been removed from the region. Even after the last of these pen-raised birds had all been shot, no other wild birds were released for the next five years as a preventive against pen-raised turkeys being bred with true wild strain birds. Today, that same area is alive with wild turkeys.

One highly significant development in wild turkey restoration was the development of the *cannon net*, which was first used successfully to capture waterfowl. Trapping enough birds for release into another area had always been a problem for game managers. Early devices resembled huge box traps, generally made from logs. The birds were attracted by corn, then trapped once the doors slammed shut. The system worked in a way, but only accounted for a few turkeys. Drop nets, which are nothing more than huge nets used to cover established feed areas, worked better than traps. But the netting—which usually stretched only five to six feet off the ground—was always visible, hence the turkeys were often reluctant to feed all the way under. When a flock of hungry birds moved completely under the net, however, a single trapping could result in several dozen or more birds.

Cannon nets, which generally measure 30 feet by 60 feet, can be completely concealed by grasses, corn stalks or other ground cover or foliage. Along the length of this net are three or four cannons or rocket-like projectiles that propel the net up and over a flock of birds drawn in by the lure of corn or some other bait. The trapper sits in a nearby blind and waits until the birds

are all well within the coverage of the net, at which point the trapper electronically detonates the cannons or rockets, sending the two-inch mesh net across the flock.

The cannon net makes it possible to capture large numbers of wild turkeys at a reasonable cost and with a minimum amount of man-hours, especially compared to the time it took to build those large wooden box traps. Where an over-abundance of birds is involved, several trappings enable game departments to acquire enough turkeys needed to move many wild birds quickly into restored habitats. By 1959, wild turkey

The National Wild Turkey Federation (NWTF) has built public interest in the wild turkey and turkey hunting in general. It has, for example, helped reintroduce this great game bird to much of its ancestral habitat, plus areas where it was previously not found. (Russ Lumpkin, NWTF photo)

numbers had been restored to around 500,000 nationwide. The increased number of turkeys allowed game managers to escalate their trapping and restocking efforts for three decades beginning in the 1960s. By 1990, the estimated wild turkey population in the U.S. and Ontario, Canada, had jumped to nearly 3.5 million turkeys, and by the fall of 2000 the number had approached 5.5 million of the big birds.

Join The NWTF

Among the organizations that have played a significant role in wild turkey conservation and education has been the National Wild Turkey Federation. Established in 1973, this nonprofit organization has been dedicated to conserving America's wild turkey resources and preserving our turkey hunting traditions.

Starting with only 1,300 members, it boasts now more than 300,000 individuals from all 50 states, plus Canada and a number of other foreign countries. Rob Keck, the chief executive of this fast-growing organization, comments: "With that growth has come impressive strides in wildlife management as the National Wild Turkey Federation has forged dynamic partnerships across the country. Together, the NWTF's conservation partners and grassroots members have raised and spent more than $115 million on projects benefiting wild turkeys throughout North America."

The NWTF brings to its members opportunities to share in the management of the wild turkey through different habitat improvement programs, all of which can be carried out on privately owned properties. These landowners are provided with the latest information on wild turkey management; they can receive advice and assistance to improve the quality of the habitats located on their lands; and they are able to purchase the seeds, seedlings and other management products at low prices. All across the country, members of more than 1,800 NWTF chapters have rolled up their sleeves and are

hunting. For example, its JAKES Program ("_Juniors Acquiring Knowledge, Ethics and Sportsmanship_") brings turkey hunting to youngsters 17 years of age and under. Its mission is to inform, educate and involve youth in wildlife conservation and wise stewardship of our natural resources. Another NWTF program seeks to get more women involved with wild turkey conservation

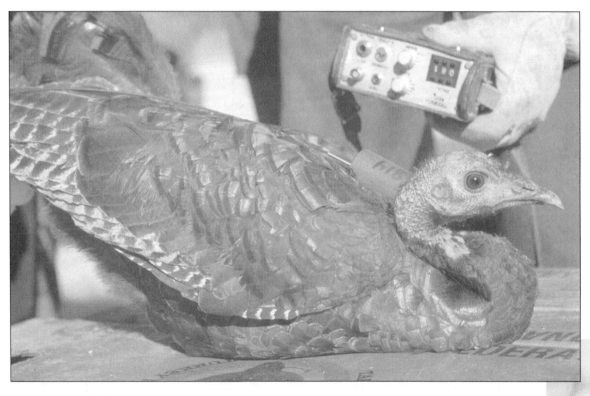

This hen has been fitted with a radio telemetry transmitter, allowing biologists to more fully understand wild turkey movement. (NWTF photo)

pitching in to help with the regional habitat programs. Most of this work is done on privately-owned N.W.T.F. member properties, but much takes place on public lands as well. In one year alone, NWTF planted more than 150,000 seedlings nationwide and ordered more than 4.5 million pounds of seeds—enough to plant 90,000 acres of habitat.

The NWTF organization has done much indeed to promote quality turkey

and hunting. The goal of these and other NWTF programs is to ensure enough wild turkeys for our hunters as we head into the future.

Back when the National Wild Turkey Federation was established, about 1.5 million wild turkey hunters existed in the country. Today, more than 2.6 million turkey hunters are actively engaged in the sport, and they hunt every U.S. state except Alaska. Wild turkeys are even found now in 10 states where turkey experts had failed to recognize as ancestral ranges. Several subspecies have been introduced into areas located hundreds—if not thousands—of miles from their original ranges. As an example, the Rio Grande turkeys of the southern plains are now found in portions of Oregon, Washington, Idaho and Utah, California and Hawaii. And where the ranges of several subspecies now meet and overlap, hybrids reflect the features or characteristics of two or even three different subspecies.

The wild turkey hen has a remarkable ability to lay and hatch large

Dedicated wild turkey biologists work year around to study today's growing flocks. (NWTF photo)

clutches. In fact, hens have been known to lay a full nest of eggs (usually 10 to 15), lose all of them to predators, then rebound by laying a second or, when necessary, a third clutch of eggs. I've spoken with experienced turkey hunters who claim they've seen hens with what must have been a second hatch for the year. The poults were just too small to come from the spring breeding period. In reality, what these hunters most likely saw were poults reared from a late clutch of eggs that may not have been laid until mid-June. Many wild turkey releases consist of nine to twelve hens and three or four gobblers. From this small nucleus of wild turkeys a resident flock of 200 to 300 birds can result in only four to six years.

Back in 1972, I had the good fortune to have as a "guide" on my first wild turkey hunt a man who later became known as the "Father of modern wild turkey management"—Missouri's wild turkey biologist Dr. John Lewis. During that hunt, I managed to tag my very first wild turkey, after which John shared with me a few thoughts and discoveries concerning the restoration of the wild turkey in Missouri. It was a "learn as you go" process. Failures were duly recorded, and successes were outlined in detail. What surprised this pioneer in turkey management more than anything else were the areas in Missouri where turkeys had prospered. At the time, most turkey managers felt that huge, unbroken tracts of hardwood timber (such as those found across the southern Ozarks) were required in order for

turkeys to do well. For that reason, one of the very last areas to receive transplants of turkeys trapped in the wild were the rolling farm and timber lots of north-central Missouri. Restocking efforts there didn't begin until the mid-1960s. But by the early 1980s, this region harbored the densest turkey populations in the state, with an estimated 45 to 60 turkeys per square mile (most prime Ozarks habitat held only 15 to 20 turkeys per square mile). Thanks to John Lewis and countless others, the

Thanks to the efforts of game departments around the country, the wild turkey can now be hunted in every state except Alaska. (NWTF photo)

wild turkey has now been reintroduced into every ancestral range, plus habitats in which professional game managers insist the wild turkey was never found in the past.

In the U.S., hunters generally pursue four subspecies of the wild turkey: Eastern, Florida, Rio Grande and Merriam's. A huntable population of eastern wild turkeys has been reintroduced and established in Ontario, Canada. And to the west along the U.S. border, small pockets of Merriams and Rio Grande turkeys can occasionally be found on the Canadian side. To the south, in Mexico, the Gould's and the colorful ocellated wild turkey may be encountered. The northernmost range of Gould's now crosses over into the southeastern corner of Arizona and the southwestern corner of New Mexico. But because of the small number of birds found in the U.S., no hunting is allowed. However, the game departments of these two states, along with Mexican game officials and the NWTF, are working together in an attempt to establish new flocks of Gould's in the U.S.

The Mating and Breeding Periods of the Wild Turkey

The Eastern subspecies found in the U.S. represent close to three-quarters of the country's total wild turkey population. Except for the Florida subspecies, it is the only one of the four found east of the Mississippi River drainage, with

healthy populations in Louisiana, east Texas, eastern Oklahoma, Arkansas, Missouri, eastern Kansas, Iowa, southeastern Nebraska, Minnesota, and in small pockets in both North and South Dakota (on the western side of the Mississippi). Thanks to modern transplanting efforts, there even exists now a strong flock of Eastern birds residing in the state of Washington.

Next in numbers are the Rio Grande subspecies, which are abundant in South Texas, but with strong flocks found throughout Texas and into Oklahoma and Kansas. Pockets of the Rio Grande are also in evidence in Nebraska, South Dakota, North Dakota, New Mexico, Colorado, Utah, Idaho, Washington, Oregon, Nevada and California, plus several Hawaiian islands. The Merriam's subspecies, which ranks third in overall numbers, enjoy a fairly wide range across the western U.S., from the mountains of western Texas, up through New Mexico, Arizona and southern California, then northward into southern Canada. Although the NWTF does not recognize established flocks of Merriam's turkeys in Oklahoma, several hunters I've known have harvested these birds in the far western edge of the state. The Florida subspecies—often referred to as the Osceola turkey—is the least populous of the four U.S. subspecies, with fewer than 100,000 birds found on the Florida peninsula.

In Oklahoma, Kansas, Nebraska, South Dakota, North Dakota, Wyoming, Utah and California, strong populations of so-called hybrid wild turkeys have been found. These are not true hybrids, since they can and do reproduce, but they are more accurately crosses between two or more subspecies. In some regions, notably Kansas and Nebraska, these crosses have occurred naturally as the Rio Grande and Eastern turkey ranges expanded and overlapped. In some regions these crosses are the result of subspecies introduced purposely in order to make another stronger, or more fertile breed. While many of these birds may not display the distinct markings associated with one or more of the subspecies, they are still considered wild turkeys and should be treated as such.

Biologically speaking, the four subspecies found in the U.S. vary little. Depending on their latitude, the start of the breeding period may be as late as mid-May or as early as late January, with temperatures and weather conditions often being the determining factors. In the Midwest, winter flocks start braking up sometime in mid-March to early April. During the winter, it often seems that most males, especially immature gobblers (or jakes) have left the brood flocks, which are made up primarily of hens. I've seen flocks of jakes numbering nearly 40. Once, while hunting the tail-end of a south Texas whitetail season in January, I spotted a flock of nearly 200 adult Rio Grande gobblers!

Wild turkey restoration has become a major media event in many areas. Here in Tennessee, National Wild Turkey Federation C.E.O. Rob Keck (center) and country music artist Porter Wagoner (holding turkey) prepare to release a bird in front of the news media. (Russ Lumpkin, NWTF photo)

Gobblers get the urge to breed well before the hens, so it's not uncommon to hear lots of gobbling in my region as early as the first of March. A few turkey hunters in Florida have told me they often hear the toms become very vocal in mid-to-late January and then get really fired up in February. While hunting seasons can be a month or two away in most of the country, this early gobbling peak is a great time to find gobblers. During this period, though, don't always count on them being exactly where you heard them come hunting season. When the hens don't react to their early gobbling, these same toms could be miles away in their search for receptive hens.

Many state game departments have now made it illegal to call in wild turkeys before the season opener. During this early gobbling period, hens rarely leave

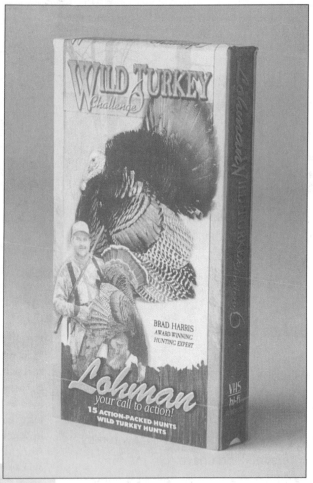

Excellent turkey hunting videos, such as this example from Lohman, have done much to educate today's hunter on the proper ways to hunt the wild turkey.

out of frustration because the hens have refused to respond to the males' gobbling. Noticeable tension begins building among the gobblers who had blocked together so peaceably through the winter. Large gobbler bands break up into small groups of two to four, and often a lone gobbler will roam the woods looking for a hen to breed. When finally the hens begin to get into the swing of the breeding season, they will respond to the lusty gobbles of a wild turkey tom. Once they've gone to the male, the gobbling usually stops instantly. Now the male begins to strut back and forth seeking to impress his female companion. It's a courting ritual that is quite common to all subspecies of the wild turkey. It also explains why a hunter will often move in on a vociferous gobbler—one that has answered every yelp, cluck or purr from his turkey call—only to encounter a sudden dead quiet. No matter what the hunter does, he can't get another gobble out of the bird. More than likely the gobbler in question has been joined by a real hen, and he's not about to blow it all by advertising his location to other gobblers in the area.

their young from the previous year to go to a gobbler. When a tom's gobbles fail to get a response from the hens, they become "easy." A few strokes on a box call will very often bring an anxious gobbler running in hopes of finding an eager hen. Even where it's legal to call before the season opens, serious turkey hunters frown on the practice. There's no sense in educating these birds—it only makes the hunting tougher for everyone.

With the approach of the actual breeding period, gobblers become less tolerant of one another. Some serious butt-kicking may take place, perhaps

Once a hen has been bred, she'll usually lay her first egg a few days after mating, returning to the same nest each day to lay another single egg. This will continue for about two weeks, or until a full clutch of 10 to 15 eggs has been laid. At the end of this period, often just before or immediately after the last egg has been laid, the hen will begin the incubation by sitting on the nest overnight. In 26 to 28 days, the first poults will hatch. Although it may have taken two full weeks to lay this nest of eggs, most will hatch within the same 24-hour period. While a hen will often continue to mate with gobblers right on through the egg-laying period, she can also store sperm in her oviducts for nearly two months. In reality, though, mating with just one gobbler is usually enough to fertilize an entire clutch of eggs.

While turkey hunting one day, I came across a nest filled with 19 eggs. Could one hen have laid all those eggs, I wondered. The gobblers having gone silent, I found myself a concealed position about 50 yards away and waited for that hen to return and lay an egg, or sit on the nest. About an hour later, two hens—not one—approached the nest. One, obviously a young hen from the previous year, waited off to one side for about 30 minutes while the older one tended to the nest, cleaning out debris before settling down to lay an egg. Almost as soon as the mother hen left, the younger one stepped in and repeated the process, deposited her egg to the already sizable clutch, then left. After the two hens had disappeared, I eased over to the nest and flipped the leaves off the eggs and counted them a second time. Now there were 21 eggs. I often wondered if those two hens took turns incubating the eggs, or would share the responsibility of rearing such a large brood.

At the height of the mating period—usually around the second or third week of April (in west-central Illinois and central Missouri, where I hunt Easterns)—the gobblers often grow very quiet within a half-hour or so of flying down from their roost. The reason is simple: they're with the hens. Once the hens return to their nests to lay their daily eggs, the gobblers will often go on the prowl in search of other hens. Lonesome toms will often respond to hen calls late in the morning, or especially in the afternoon. That's when they can be quite

The odd coloration of this South Dakota Merriam's is a "smoky gray" color phase wild turkey. Berdette Zastrow harvested this tom with a Knight muzzleloading shotgun.

patterns. At only one week, the young birds are dusting with the mother hen, and at two weeks some of them can already fly short distances. At three weeks, most poults are able to fly up to roost in low trees, thus greatly improving their chances of survival. Once a poult can roost off the ground, it's out of reach for most predators. After 3 months or so, poult plumage and coloration begin to help one make a distinction between male and female. During this period, the young turkeys begin to develop definite pecking orders, normally headed up by the male poults. The mother hen is still the dominant turkey. Young jakes eventually leave the brood group and join other young males, forming a kind of juvenile bachelor group. As winter draws near, many such brood groups band together to form winter flocks. Both juvenile and adult gobblers form social groups of their own, separate from each other as well as from the adult and young hens.

Since wild turkeys establish definite feeding, roosting, nesting, strutting and social patterns, an observant turkey hunter can easily define those areas where such daily routines take place. He does this by listening and noting the signs while moving quietly through turkey habitat. But even as established as these patterns may be, never count on a turkey to do the exact same thing day

Predators like this big bobcat taken by the author's son, Adam Bridges, pose a real threat to young poults.

vulnerable. Several states now allow hunting up to noon only. This gives the turkeys time to go about their business undisturbed during the afternoons.

Hens and their young poults spend much of the late spring and early summer in or near grass- or weed-filled open areas where grasshoppers and other small insects are found. Within two days after hatching, the poults begin to display some characteristic feeding, movement and behavioral in and day out. "Make no mistake," warns Harold Knight, a legend among turkey hunters, "a wild turkey gobbler, especially one that's three years old or older, is a sharp bird. A hunter has to be sharp to have any real chance of harvesting him. A hunter has to be persistent and versatile, because no two hunts are ever the same. In all the years I've hunted turkeys, I can't remember two hunts that were exactly alike. They've all been different."

Harold believes that the differences between one turkey hunt and another represent at once a major challenge and a great reward. He enjoys hunting each day, especially in places where new turkeys are found, each with a different personality and habits. About the time a hunter feels he's got a hot call or introduced a tactic the turkeys can't resist, that's the time he'll run into a tough old gobbler who slams the door in his face. "Each day is like a new chess match," Knight explains. "You make a move, then the turkey makes a move. The game is never played out the same way twice."

As David Hale, a partner of Knight's in their business (Knight & Hale Game Calls), comments: "I've hunted deer and elk and a lot of other species around the country, and a turkey will humble you quicker than anything. I mean, you can think you've got everything going your way, then you'll run up on an old gobbler that'll beat you so bad it hurts. He'll drag you down on your knees and leave you totally confused as to what to try next."

"And that's good! That's what makes turkey hunting so enjoyable," David continues. "You need those defeats to make the successes meaningful. A lot of times you learn more from when you're beaten by a turkey than when you beat him. When a gobbler gets the best of me, I enjoy going back the next morning and trying something different. I enjoy thinking about how to hunt him, planning my next day's strategy, then getting back in the woods and giving it a try. I think this anticipation from one day to the next is a big part of it."

Anyone who has hunted turkeys for any length of time can probably recall a tough gobbler or two who kicked their butts royally. From each of these tough birds, however, we all learn a little more about the sport we love. There's nothing wrong about not pulling the trigger on a cagey ol' bird. In a way, they are our mentors. As my good friend and fellow outdoor writer, Wade Bourne, once wrote, "Turkey hunters are noted for a special enthusiasm about their sport; there are few casual participants. Those who try it and who like it usually jump in with both feet. This is why turkey hunters bear reputations for being more hard-core than, say, deer hunters."

Winning and losing those duels at dawn are all part of turkey hunting. Hopefully, the information and advice shared by some of today's top turkey hunters who've contributed to the chapters that follow will make the process of winning and losing much more appreciated. ■

Table Of Contents

Chapter 1

Identifying the Different Subspecies and Where They Live

WITH ■ Rob Keck, *C.E.O., National Wild Turkey Federation* ■ Mary C. Kennamer, *Wild Turkey Biologist* ■ Mark Drury, *Founder, M.A.D. Calls* ■ Bill Farley, *Owner, Farley's International Adventures* ■ Michael Pearce, *Outdoor Writer*

According to the National Wild Turkey Federation,

approximately 5.5 million wild turkeys live in the U.S. and southern Canada, representing a dramatic increase over an estimated 1.3 million only 30 years ago. Huntable populations of this great game bird are now available in every state except Alaska. Turkeys have been reintroduced to all of their original home ranges, so that one wild turkey subspecies or another now exists in all habitat where wild turkeys were traditionally found.

Today's numbers still fall far short of the tremendous wild turkey population that existed during the early settlement of North America. Modern conservation programs, combined with the efforts of individual citizens and conservation-minded organizations, have done much to bring the wild turkey back from the brink of extinction. And with the growing number of wild turkeys and turkey hunting opportunities has come a steady growth in the number of wild turkey hunters, which in the year 2000 numbered more than 2.6 million.

Indeed, interest in turkey hunting has nearly reached cult proportions. Each spring, small rural restaurants from coast to coast are often filled with camouflaged hunters convening hours before daylight. An uninformed eavesdropper who happened to overhear the pre-dawn conversations of these turkey hunters might think we'd been invaded by aliens. Turkey hunters have developed their own lingo and terminology, their conversations filled with terms like "the bird hung up," or "I cut to him real hard," or "he spit-n'-drummed so loud, I knew he was close." Only another turkey hunter would have a clue to what was being said. Modern turkey hunters also do a lot more traveling in order to experience turkey hunting in other types of terrain or habitat, or to

hunt an entirely different subspecies. More and more hunters now pursue what is known as the "Grand Slam," which entails harvesting all four subspecies in North America.

There exists in the far southeastern corner of Arizona and the southwestern

The author's then 13-year-old son, Adam, poses with a 26-pound Eastern tom.

corner of New Mexico a fifth subspecies of the wild turkey, the "Gould's" (see also Introduction). Only a few hundred of these birds are found north of the Mexican border but they are not hunted in the U.S. A very large population can be found south of the border, causing a growing number of avid turkey hunters to make the trek. Even farther south, ranging from the Yucatan Peninsula and

south into Belize and Guatemala are the colorful "Ocellated" turkey. Because of the remoteness of the region where these birds are found, only a handful of turkey hunters annually pursue this jungle variety of wild turkey. Add the Ocellated turkey to the aforementioned five northern subspecies and you have a wild turkey hunter's variation of a "World Slam." A full description of these six species and subspecies follows. Each defines the bird's characteristics, the habitats they prefer, and where hunters may seek the best chance at harvesting one or more of these wild turkeys. Sharing their thoughts on hunting these big birds, including some of their favorite hunting areas, are five recognized experts.

EASTERN (Meleagris gallopavo silvestris)

"The Eastern wild turkey is the most widely distributed, abundant and hunted turkey subspecies of the five distinct subspecies found in the United States." So claims wild turkey biologist Mary C. Kennamer, who further comments that this subspecies tends to range farther north than others, and that adult males are some of the largest of the subspecies. Typically, a mature gobbler ranging north to south will weigh on average between 20 to 22 pounds on the heavy side and 15 to 18 pounds on the light side (the farther north one hunts, the bigger the birds).

In the steep, rocky Quachita Mountains of west central Arkansas it's considered quite a feat to harvest a tom

approaching 20 pounds (most adult gobblers average closer to 18 pounds). Only 150 miles north, in the Ozarks of southern Missouri, I've taken several beautiful birds that tipped the scales at close to 24 pounds. But for a real heavyweight Eastern gobbler, I'll head for northern Missouri or southern Iowa, where I've harvested some of the best birds of my life, including a monstrous 29-pounder. Here even a run-of-the-mill Eastern gobbler weighs 24 pounds, but to win one of the "Big Bird" contests sponsored by sporting goods stores in that area, it takes a bird topping 30 pounds. Another great place to hunt for a 25-pound-plus Eastern tom is in the river country of western Illinois. Today's Eastern wild turkey population comes to about four million birds. The Eastern subspecies ranges

from northern Texas northward to the Canadian border, then east all the way to the Atlantic Coast. These birds are also found throughout southern Ontario and have been transplanted successfully in several western states, mostly Washington, Oregon and California.

Distinguishing characteristics of the Eastern subspecies gobbler include long tail feathers tipped with a chocolate brown band and upper tail coverts covering the base of the tail feathers, which are also tipped chestnut brown. A gobbler's body feathers are commonly characterized by a rich, almost metallic copper-bronze color, which in bright sunlight can be brilliantly iridescent. Breast feathers of the Eastern gobbler are tipped in black. According to turkey biologist Mary Kennamer, "The primary wing feathers have white and black bars

This Eastern jake already sports a six-inch beard; if he reaches the age of three he could become a true trophy gobbler.

Michelle Bartimus, marketing manager of Knight Rifles, proudly displays the Rio Grande gobbler she took with a Knight TK-2000 muzzleloading shotgun.

breast, flanks and sides are typically brown-tipped. The average weight of an adult Eastern wild turkey hen ranges from around 8 pounds in the South to over 12 pounds in the North and Midwest. Among the leading producers of the Eastern turkey in the south are Alabama, Georgia and Mississippi with 250,000 to 400,000 birds in each state. In the Northeast, the top Eastern turkey states are New York and Pennsylvania, with about 250,000 birds each. And in the Midwest, Missouri is by far the number one choice among Eastern wild turkeys with an estimated population exceeding over 400,000. In fact, Missouri is second only to Texas in overall population; but of the 600,000 or so turkeys that inhabit Texas, probably less than one third are Easterns, most of which belong to the Rio Grande subspecies. States like Missouri meanwhile, are evenly covered with huntable numbers of wild turkeys, whereas Illinois and Iowa, which may not compare in overall statewide turkey populations, still offer tremendous hunting because of their high turkey densities within smaller geographic areas.

When trying to choose where to hunt in the Midwest, champion turkey caller and hunting video producer Mark Drury admits, "Where do I start? I love Missouri, Iowa, Illinois, Kansas, Wiscon-

extending from the outer edge of each all the way to the shaft. Secondary wing feathers have prominent white bars and are edged in white, producing a whitish triangular area on each side of the back when the wings are folded."

Eastern wild turkey hens are less dramatic in coloration as well as size. Overall, the feather coloration of a hen's body is similar to that of a gobbler, but with more brownish tint and less iridescence. The feathers on her sin and Minnesota. Most years, I hunt each of these states and consider them to be as good as it gets, with heavy-weight birds that gobble aggressively from March 'til May. You couldn't ask for better."

MERRIAM'S (Maleagris gallopavo merriami)

The Merriam's subspecies is often referred to as the "prettiest" of all the wild turkeys found in North America. The gobbler's dark body coloration and almost bright white tail feather tips result in striking contrasts. According to the NWTF, the suspected historic home range of the Merriam's subspecies was restricted to Arizona, New Mexico and Colorado. But now, the subspecies is found in most western states, thanks primarily to stocking efforts undertaken by game departments. "Adult males are clearly distinguished from the Eastern," claims Mary Kennamer. "For example, Merriam's gobblers are known by the nearly white feathers on the lower back and tail feather margins. Merriam's closely resemble the Gould's turkey, but its tail margin is not usually quite as pure white, nor is the lighter margin of the tail tip quite as wide."

Ms. Kennamer also points out that the Merriam's size is comparable to the Eastern turkey. Its feather coloration, though, tends to be blacker, with blue, purple and bronze reflections. One

The highly adaptable Rio Grande turkeys can be found in a variety of habitat other than the cactus-covered hills of the deep Southwest. These seemingly barren ridges of Utah are now home to huntable numbers of transplanted Rio Grande turkeys. (Russ Lumpkin, NWTF photo)

thing is for certain, the white—or nearly white—feathers found on the Merriam's back and tail feathers cause the bird to really stand out, especially when one of these strutting gobblers stands in front of a dark background. Much like the Eastern, its breast feathers are black-tipped, while the hen's breast feathers are buff-tipped. The white markings, or bars, on a hen's wing are more extensive than those of the gobbler, giving the former a whiter appearance on its folded wing.

Originally, the Merriam's wild turkey was found primarily in the ponderosa pine regions of the western mountains. But today these birds are found at much lower elevations, with large flocks a common sight along lowland creeks and rivers, in cultivated fields, pastures and barn lots as far east as northeastern Nebraska. Among Merriam's favorite hot spots are the broken ridges and draws of north central Nebraska, along the Niobrara River. Brad Arrowsmith operates an 18,000-acre cattle ranch right on that river. His domain starts out with big hayfields bordering the Niobrara, then slowly transforming to oak-covered ridges as the elevation rises to the east. Once a hunter reaches the high ground four or five miles from the river, he's standing in ponderosa pines so huge it takes three or four men to reach around the trunks. On any given mid-to-late-April morning, it's not uncommon to hear 30 to 40 different gobblers. For those readers who are interested, Brad Arrowsmith does outfit a limited number of turkey hunters each spring.

He can be reached at HC 88, Box 61, Basset, NE 68714.

Mark Drury also picks Nebraska as a favorite spot for Merriam's. "About 90 miles north of Omaha are two Indian reservations," he explains. "The Omaha reservation at Macy and the Winnebago reservation just to the north. Both offer excellent hunting. Situated right along the Missouri River, I do believe that those two reservations hold the eastern-most viable populations of Merriam's. What I like especially are the thousands of acres of rolling timber in which these birds reside. It's sort of like northern Missouri, only the gobblers have white tail tips. Having 20 to 30 birds gobbling every morning is truly impressive." Mark's second choice for Merriam's is the canyon country of southeastern Colorado, near Trinidad. "The scenery there is awesome," Mark exclaims," and the birds call quite well, too. One outfitter he recommends is Trophy Mountain Outfitters, which operates on 125,000 acres of private land.

For a classic mountain hunt for Merriam's, Rob Keck (C.E.O. of the National Wild Turkey Federation) picks the northeast corner of Wyoming, in the area around Devil's Tower (America's first National Monument). The region consists of a nearly unbroken series of pine-covered ridges, with an occasional streamside hay field. Much of this region is privately owned, but scattered throughout it are several hundred thousand acres of the Black Hills National Forest, along with lands administered by the Bureau of Land Management.

Merriam's turkeys were introduced into the area about 50 years ago and are now doing quite well. Any hunter who is willing to cover some ground and get far back from the roadways will find undisturbed hunting and very cooperative toms. When you can locate such birds, Rob says, a dozen or more gobblers will often break and literally run to the call. What a sight!

RIO GRANDE (Meleagris gallopavo intermedia)

The Rio Grande subspecies of the wild turkey is the second most populous among North America's native turkeys. Originally, this bird was native to the central plains states southward across much of Texas and into northeastern Mexico. The Rio Grande, with its adaptable nature, has been introduced successfully into habitats that vary greatly from their historic range. For example, pockets of Rio Grande turkeys are doing quite well in places like Hawaii and northern Idaho. Recently, Rio Grande turkeys have expanded their ranges on their own, with noticeable northward movements. "It is similar in general appearance to the other subspecies of the wild turkey," Mary Kennamer says, "and similar in body size to the Florida turkey—about 4 feet tall, but with disproportionately long legs."

One distinguishing factor in identifying an adult Rio Grande gobbler is the yellowish-buff colored tips of its tail feathers and tail coverts. Depending on where a Rio is harvested, the shade of this buff-tan coloration may vary considerably, but it is always lighter than the tail fan of an Eastern and darker than the tips of a fanned out Merriam's tail. The overall body coloration of an adult Rio Grande gobbler, with its distinctive copper hue, is generally paler than that of other subspecies. In general, the average weight of a "good" Rio

Rob Keck (right) and his hunting partner Gene Goodwin display a fine pair of Wyoming Merriam's gobblers, taken from the Black Hills region of the state.

Grande gobbler is around 20 pounds, while a typical hen averages about 10 pounds. The breast feathers of a Rio gobbler are black-tipped, while those feathers from a hen will display a pale, pinkish buff-colored tip.

When it comes to hunting the Rio Grande, south and central Texas usually get the nod as "best place to go" from knowledgeable turkey hunters. For one thing, nearly half of the Rio Grande turkeys found in the U.S. are Texas residents. Mark Drury agrees. "For Rios, far and away my pick would be South Texas." He also says that lots of birds gobble quite well and are extremely responsive to calling. He pinpoints areas 50 to 100 miles south and west of San Antonio as the hot spots for lots of

A typical western Merriam's habitat offers a constant water source, riverbottom hay fields and pine-covered ridges.

action. Most years, Mark will easily fill all of his tags, then help others to bag six to ten more during an extended hunt. While the hunting is usually good through most of the six-week season, Mark likes the first week to ten days, claiming that a hunt any later could mean having to deal with some very hot weather.

I can well remember a hunt I made into that region a few years back, about half-way between San Antonio and San Angelo. I was hunting with Toxey Haas and Ronnie Strickland (Mossy Oak Camouflage), plus several highly respected outdoor writers, including Jim Casada, Michael Hanback and Wade Bourne. Our hunt took place during the third week of the season, and when we pulled into camp I could hear a mature gobbler hammering back at every noise we made in camp. Although the season was officially open, our hunt didn't actually begin until the next morning, but I couldn't stand one more gobble from that loud-mouthed tom. I quickly slipped into my camo, threw a few shells in my pocket, grabbed my Rohm Brothers box call and a Mossberg 835 Ulti-Mag pump turkey gun and went after that bird. Everyone sat out in the yard of the camp and listened to me work that tom for another 20 minutes before I had him standing at less than 15 yards. One well-placed shot and our hunt was off to a great start. During the next three days, our group of nine hunters tagged another 17 adult Rio Grande gobblers.

FLORIDA OR OSCEOLA (*Melaegris gallopavo osceola*)

This subspecies of the wild turkey has the smallest range of all North American turkeys. The Florida—or Osceola as it is often called—is found only on the Florida peninsula, with none

Noted outdoor writer Gary Clancy shows off a mature Merriam's gobbler, distinguished by the snow-white tips of its tail feathers and tail-feather coverts.

In several regions of the country, such as the Niobrara River of northern Nebraska (shown), cross-breeding of various sub-species takes place. Here both Rio Grande and Meriam's can be found, along with crossed hybrids.

appearing in the northernmost 24 counties bordering Georgia and Alabama (home of the Eastern subspecies). The farther south one hunts, the greater the chances of taking a true "Florida" strain wild turkey. Biologist Mary Kennamer explains how to identify an Osceola gobbler. "It's similar to the Eastern wild turkey, but smaller and darker in color with less white veining in the wing quills. The white bars in these feathers are narrow, irregular and bro-

The overall coloration of a true Florida subspecies gobbler also displays more green and red iridescence than is found on an Eastern bird, and it's less bronze than its northern cousin. Osceola gobblers stand nearly as tall as an Eastern bird, but they are definitely slimmer in stature, making the legs appear noticeably longer. Osceola gobblers are much sought after by turkey hunters, if only because it's required to complete a coveted "Grand Slam."

ken. . . .they don't extend all the way to the feather shaft. The black bars predominate the feather. Secondary wing feathers are also dark. When the wings are folded on the back, there are no whitish triangular patches one sees on the Eastern."

On the other hand, they are one of the more difficult trophies to harvest, not so much because they're smarter or more elusive than any of the other subspecies in the U.S., but because of their limited range and fewer opportunities for hunters. Today, an estimated 80,000 to 100,000 Osceola turkeys inhabit approximately 70 percent of Florida's land mass, the vast majority of which is privately owned.

GOULD'S (Meleagris gallopavo mexicana)

Along the border between the U.S. and Mexico, where Arizona and New Mexico come together, the fifth subspecies of wild turkey—called Gould's—is found. Unfortunately, only a few hundred birds have wandered north of the border and are therefore not hunted in the U.S. Large populations of this subspecies are, however, found southward into central Mexico, offering ample opportunities for turkey hunters. The largest of all wild turkey subspecies, the Gould's appearance is much like the Merriam's. It stands taller, has longer legs and larger feet and central tail feathers than any of the other wild turkeys found in North America.

As Mary Kennamer notes, "Gould's differ by having distinctive white tips on the tail feathers and tail rump coverts, which usually separate to display an "eyelash" appearance. Lower back and rump feathers have copper and greenish-gold reflections, not like the faintly iridescent, velvety black ones found on Merriam's. Gould's body plumage is said to be somewhat blue-green in coloration. Adult females have a less pronounced metallic greenish and reddish sheen and are more purplish."

The Sierra Madre Occidental mountain range in northern and central Mexico

is home to most of the Gould's turkeys. And while actual population numbers have not been established, it's safe to say that much of this range produces levels that are high and stable. This is

rough terrain featuring steep ridges and canyons, with birds often found as high as 9,000 feet. Most hunters who head for old Mexico for a shot at this unique subspecies will find themselves hunting at elevations of 4,500 to 6,500 feet. Although most of the Gould's range lies no farther south than that of the Florida wild turkey, Gould's gobbling activity usually takes place much later, beginning in April and on into May.

Bill Farley, an avid turkey hunter, proudly claims this near 30-pound Gould's gobbler from the Sonora region of northern Mexico.

According to the NWTF this delayed gobbling by the subspecies coincides with plant green-up in the Gould's higher and often more arid habitat. Those who have hunted the Gould's say this bird's gobble has a considerably lower frequency than that of the Merriam's or Rio Grande turkeys, and that the toms can be very talkative and extremely "call-able."

The birds inhabit areas very similar to some Merriam's in the mountains of Colorado, New Mexico and other western states."

"Our hunts for the Gould's," Farley continues, "originate out of either Hermosillo or Obregon in the state of Sonora, or Chihuahua City in the state of Chihuahua. Their habitats can be either extremely rough, making

A confessed turkey hunting addict, Bill Farley describes the Gould's turkey hunts he has led in the states of Sonora and Chihuahua in the Sierra Madre mountains of northern Mexico. "The habitat is generally mountainous with distinct types of turkey habitat, from typical rolling hardwood timber to very rough, steep and mountainous terrain.

them difficult to hunt, or they might often occur in quite accessible, rolling country. Most of the areas hold large numbers of birds with hunting success running very high, generally 100 percent in most years. If additional permits are available, a hunter can often obtain an opportunity to harvest a second gobbler."

Mark Drury hunts the Eastern variety of wild turkey in typical Midwestern habitat.

IDENTIFYING THE DIFFERENT SUBSPECIES AND WHERE THEY LIVE **33**

Turkey hunting expert Jim Casada packs out a northern Missouri gobbler.
This region, the last to receive wild bird transplants during the early 1960s,
is now home to Missouri's greatest wild turkey densities.

"Physically, the hunt can be demanding," Farley concludes. "I have seen birds in some of the toughest terrain I've ever hunted. Most guides, while experienced with the birds' habits, terrain and roosting preferences, are not the most adept at calling. They are, however, usually competent enough to get the job done, but it's helpful if a hunter is a capable caller." Farley goes on to point out that the turkey hunting season in this region typically runs from April 1 to the middle of May. He rates the last two weeks of April and the first week of May as the prime time during a normal year. Rainy weather is normally not a factor. However, he warns that mountain mornings early in the season can be cold, but that temperatures usually warm up fast once the sun is up.

According to Farley, "Hunting in Mexico can be a unique experience. The country is filled with tradition, the habitat is breathtaking, and the people are extremely accommodating. One factor which can be quite intimidating to foreign hunters is the presence of the Mexican military, something I've experienced on every trip I've made there. But I've never had a real bad experience. You must, of course, deal with the military while going through customs; but if your outfitter has done his job properly, the experience should be positive and brief. On odd occasions, you may be asked to pull over at a checkpoint to produce some paperwork, and they may go through your belongings, but that's all part of visiting a foreign country."

OCELLATED
(Meleagris ocellata)

Worldwide, only two different species of wild turkey actually exist. In North America, there's *Meleagris gallopavo*, which consists of the five different subspecies, *silvestris* (Eastern), *merriami* (Merriam's), *intermedia* (Rio Grande), *osceola* (Florida) and *mexicana* (Gould's). In addition, there's the ocellated turkey (*Meleagris ocellata*) of southern Mexico and portions of Belize and Guatemala. The most "huntable" population of ocellated turkeys is found on the Yucatan Peninsula, in the ancient lands of the Mayan Indians. Like the ornamental dress of the natives who once inhabited this jungle country, the ocellated gobbler can best be described as exotic. Hunting this species is as close to a true life adventure as turkey hunting can get.

If you prefer to judge a trophy turkey by its beard length, the ocellated variety is not for you, for neither the gobbler or hen grow beards. But if you're into spurs, then this could be your bird. Adult ocellated gobblers commonly grow spurs that measure more than two inches in length, while a one-year-old tom will often sport $1^{1}/_{2}$-inch spurs. There's no mistaking an ocellated turkey when you see one. Its appearance is considerably unlike its North American cousins. The body colorations of both adult males and hens have a distinct bronze-green iridescence. In some areas, the hens may display a duller hue that is more green than bronze.

The bluish-gray tail feathers of both sexes are quite colorful, with distinct,

eye-shaped iridescent blue spots near a gold tip shaped like a chevron. The upper tail coverts display bright blue spots with a similar shape. The secondary wing coverts are a bright copper color, which explains the unusually bright coloration of the ocellated turkey. Both males and females have blue heads with wart-like orange, red and yellow growths (or nodules), which are more pronounced on the head of a gobbler. The gobble of an ocellated tom is unlike the gobble of any other turkey. To some who've heard it, the

Toby Bridges took this Rio Grande gobbler in typical Texas "hill country" habitat.

sound is more like a call than a gobble. In the NTWF's "Wildlife Bulletin No. 6," this gobble, or call, is described as something like a "whump-whump-whump...pum-pum-pum-peedle-glunk."

Bill Farley (Farley's International Adventures) has hunted this exotic turkey species and shares a few observations and thoughts. "This species is generally the last obtained by most avid turkey hunters seeking a "World Slam," and is the most beautiful of all turkeys and definitely worth seeking. Our hunts take place in the Campeche region of southern Mexico. The season starts about the last week in March and runs through the end of April. Typically, the larger gobblers start singing earlier, but as the season progresses more gobblers are heard. Overall best time would probably be the middle of April. . . .These birds are not large in size, ranging from around nine to twelve pounds, with 1.5" to 2"spurs. The size of the bird is the reason why most of our clients hunt them with a 20 gauge, since most want them mounted and don't want to damage the bird anymore than necessary."

Bill Farley adds, "These birds are hunted in the jungle, so this is not a traditional turkey hunt in terms of calling gobblers. The foliage is extremely dense and the birds aren't readily seen. The harvesting of a gobbler usually depends on ambushing the birds at known waterholes, feeding areas, or where they roost. These locations are found through extensive scouting by the guides, who listen for the birds as they quietly sing. Bird populations seem to be healthy and all of our hunters either take a bird of have the opportunity to. The economics of hunting these birds for sport has been nothing but positive for these birds. They have been poached for years, and the placing of a value on them through sportsmans' dollars seems to be having an impact."

An ocellated turkey hunt isn't for everyone. Farley's clients stay in two-man walled tents, enclosed in mosquito netting. All meals are served in a thatched roof lodge, which also serves as a lounge in the evening. These amenities, along with the jungle, the Mayan ruins, or the chance sighting of a jaguar, make a hunt into the Yucatan an adventure to remember.

HYBRIDS

The expanding turkey populations and range often translate into the overlapping of two or more subspecies of North American turkeys. Where this occurs, sooner or later we will begin to come across turkeys of crossed breeding. When one subspecies readily breeds with another, the resulting "hybrid" crosses are fertile and create an entirely new mixed subspecie. In several regions of the country, game departments have purposely brought in an outside subspecies in order to create such a hybrid that is better suited for a particular habitat, climate or what have you. But most such crosses happen naturally without human interference.

When I'm lucky enough to obtain a permit, one of my favorite turkey hunting areas is along the Republican River of south-central Nebraska, near the town of Arapahoe. Years ago, the Nebraska Game and Parks Commission stocked Eastern wild turkeys there. After several years, these efforts were deemed unsuccessful and another stocking was made with Merriam's, which took hold. Then, lo and behold, the commission discovered several small pockets of Eastern birds. Within a few years, it became evident that a hybrid cross had become predominant. To compound the situation, the Rio Grande turkeys began to expand their range northward out of Kansas. Soon it was difficult to find a gobbler with the true markings of any of the three different subspecies.

I remember one particular morning ending up with 11 adult gobblers strutting around me at one time. No two birds looked exactly alike. In some, I could see the Merriam's/Eastern /Rio Grande cross. Only one bird had all the markings of a true Merriam's, and that's the one I packed out with my tag attached to its leg.

Michael Pearce, a good friend and occasional hunting partner, once told me, "Rio Grande and Eastern crosses are so common in central Kansas (where he lives) that biologists feel there are few, if any, purebred Rio Grandes left in the area. On some occasions, Kansas has intentionally encouraged such interbreeding by introducing a few Eastern toms into a stagnated flock of Rio Grandes. Most times such hybridization has led to a turkey population explosion."

Personally, I could care less about the color on the tips of a tom's tail, or if it's a true Eastern, Merriam's, Rio Grande or Osceola. If that bird is wild and it gobbles, I'll hunt it—and I'll love every minute of it! ■

Chapter 2

Who's Calling Whom?

WITH ■ Jerry Martin, *Hunting Advisor, Bass Pro Shops* ■ Ray Eye, *World Champion Caller* ■ Steve Stoltz, *World Champion Caller* ■ Mark Drury, *Founder, M.A.D. Calls* ■ Rob Keck, *C.E.O., National Wild Turkey Foundation* ■ Preston Pitman, *World Champion Caller*

The going was easy as outdoor writer Phil Bourjaily and I

made our way quietly across a field that had only two weeks before been choked with waist-high weeds. An unplanned brush fire had burned off several hundred acres of this weedy growth, along with old ground leaf cover amid a sizable tract of hardwood timber. A 10-mile-an-hour wind in north-central Missouri had created havoc for local firefighters, but it proved to be one of the hottest turkey hunting spots I've ever enjoyed. Within a week, spring rains and warm April temperatures had brought on a fresh new carpet of two- to three-inch high green growth. Every turkey within several miles was now using the burn. Just the night before the Missouri season opener, I had watched through binoculars as 11 adult toms had strutted around a sin-gle hen near a timbered edge. I knew exactly where Phil and I would begin our season early the next morning.

Under the cover of darkness, we eased to the backside of the field,

placed a couple of hen decoys 20 yards out into the open and settled down next to a pair of huge oaks standing less than five yards apart. As daybreak slowly approached, the woods came alive with the singing of cardinals, fol-lowed by the first gobble of the morn-ing. Soon the woods were filled with the calls of more than a dozen different birds. Now the sound of beating wings told us that some of the birds were on the ground. As I softly stroked the pad-dle of my Rohm Brothers box call across the thin sounding rail, the barely audi-ble yelps were greeted by a crescendo of deep, throaty gobbles. As I started to repeat the calls, I was immediately cut short by the gobbling of more than a dozen toms and the squeaky, high-pitched yelping of a lone hen—right there among all those gobblers.

I called again, this time a little louder, and the hen, not caring to have ano-ther female in her midst, immediately squawked back at me in an irritated way. I hammered right back at her in an even more agitated tone, throwing in a couple of sharp cuts at the end. Not to be outdone, the hen came back at me, yelping louder than ever. For the next 20 minutes or so, that ol' hen and I carried on something fierce. Whatever calls she made, I duplicated, throwing in a

That experience convinced me that there isn't a soul out there who truly understands what turkeys are saying to each other with all the different calls they make—if indeed there are any meanings for such sounds. Depending on whom you ask, the "language" of a typical wild turkey consists of 20 to 30

Many game call manufacturers offer a wide selection of turkey calls, most of which duplicate the sounds of the wild turkey hen.

few more for luck. All the while, those toms never quit gobbling. It was, without a doubt, the loudest morning I'd ever spent in the turkey woods. Several times Phil and I caught sight of the tips of fanned out tails over the curvature of the hill, only 50 yards away. But not one of those toms ever ventured close enough for us to get off a shot. To make matters worse, when that old hen left she took all the toms with her.

different calls. Why this large discrepancy in the number of different calls? Primarily, it's because "experts" rarely agree on much of anything. One may recognize four or five purrs, clucks and yelps, while another hears only one or two. There's no better way to understand these different sounds than to hear them for yourself in the turkey woods. Trying to describe them is nearly impossible. Nevertheless, let's take a look in the following pages at the most recognizable sounds made by both hens and gobblers, plus a few other calls that may be nothing more than a turkey with an attitude—like the old hen I encountered in that burned out field in northern Missouri.

Ray Eye, a world renowned caller, recalls, "As a boy, I learned that the first

In the real world of turkey biology, it is the hen that responds to the sounds of the gobbling tom.

Not only has Ray Eye become one of the most recognized turkey hunters in the U.S., he has used his knowledge of what turkeys sound like to win several calling championships. If you don't have the time to study turkey sounds the way Ray Eye did, he recommends attending a calling contest. "There's no better place to hear good calling," he advises,

step in calling a wild turkey is simply being able to sound like one. Time after time, I'd hear a gobbler who had ignored my calls open up to the first calls of a hen. At the time, I wanted to make those sounds more than anything in the world, so I went to great lengths to learn how to talk with turkeys. I'd crawl on my belly through wet leaves and muck to get within hearing distance of a flock of turkeys. I'd follow them all day, then go home and mimic them all night."

"You can hear caller after caller giving their best shots at imitating every call in a turkey's vocabulary."

Don't expect to master every turkey sound in the first year or two, or even to recognize every sound that turkeys make. Many successful turkey hunters spend an entire life pursuing this great game bird, relying on five basic sounds to call and locate turkeys. Those sound or calls are the *yelp*, the *purr*, the *cluck*, the *cut* and the *gobble*. In the real

world of the wild turkey, it's the gobble of a mature tom that attracts the hen during the spring mating season. It's the hen, by the way, who goes to the gobbler, not the other way around. Fortunately, since not all gobblers go by the book, the sounds of a receptive hen can sometimes bring a gobbler running. That explains why a caller can often reproduce the sounds of a hen and induce a gobble or two. No matter, the gobbler will stay right where he is, waiting for that hen to come to him. It's simply a matter of who's calling whom! Knowing what sounds to make—and when—can greatly improve the odds of luring a gobbler close enough for a shot. Likewise, knowing which sounds or calls to avoid can help prevent a gobbler from running off.

YELP

Turkeys rely on several different variations of the "yelp" to communicate with one another. In a sense, it can be considered the basis for most of the calls made by the wild turkey hen—and to some degree even the gobbler. Many experts believe that it is the "feeling" the turkey puts into a yelp, or series of yelps, which convey the true meaning of the bird's call. The mating yelp, tree call, assembly call, lost call or simple feeding yelp can all sound quite similar to a hunter's ears and yet have a totally different meaning for the turkeys—even though the basic sound remains the same. The sound we all try to reproduce with the many different calls we carry in our pockets sounds something like the word "calk." The tone, volume, rhythm and feeling we

Two young toms, having responded to hen yelps made on a call, are lured even closer by the sight of the decoys.

put into each of these calls determines which call we're trying to make and whether or not it has the desired effect on the gobblers.

The plain, or mating, yelp of a hen is generally anywhere from three to six or seven moderately loud yelps in succession, with slightly less than a second's pause between each yelp. Depending on the hen, these yelps may be soft or clear in tone, or they can be raspy and broken (which usually denotes an older

One of the easiest calls to learn and use is the "box call," which has been around for more than a century.

Consider the mood of the hen and try matching it with your own delivery. Change the cadence, volume and speed of your calls through listening and practice. And with just one call you can imitate a variety of hens."

The tree call—or tree yelp—is the first call a hen makes at daybreak. It's usually a little softer, quieter and slower than most yelps made once a hen is on the ground. It's a calming yelp, one that's audible only to birds close by. If

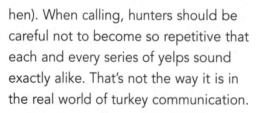

hen). When calling, hunters should be careful not to become so repetitive that each and every series of yelps sound exactly alike. That's not the way it is in the real world of turkey communication.

Rob Keck, a former World Champion caller himself, believes there's no better way to learn the different yelps of a hen than to go out into the woods and listen to the real thing. "You can improve your calling," Rob assures me, "by adding excitement and inflection.

a turkey hunter is close enough to hear the soft tree calls of a hen, he's close enough. Another champion caller, Preston Pitman, explains further: "The tree call is the first sound a hen makes when she's sitting on the limb before flying down. It's an extremely good call to use, just to let a gobbler know you're in the area (imitating a hen, that is). In fact, that's what she's doing first thing in the morning. She's trying to find out where everybody is, so when they do fly

This muzzleloading shotgunner is ready for action, well camouflaged and relying on the sweet sounds of a good box call.

Turkey hunting expert Jerry Martin, shown with a Rio Grande gobbler, often relies on a "gobbler yelp" to bring reluctant toms within range.

down, they're all together. Sometimes that's the only call you'll have to make, because a gobbler is liable to hit the ground right there in front of you."

While many turkey hunting experts warn against "calling too much," one of the more effective calls is the so-called "lost yelp," which is sporadic and usually quite repetitive. As its name suggests, the lost yelp is the call of a hen or jake who has gotten separated from a flock or family group. A bird will often wander the woods, or stay in one place and continue to call for hours, or until other birds show up. Generally speaking, the lost call tends to have very little pattern to it, although a common cadence is two or three yelps of moderate loudness—ten seconds of silence followed by a long drawn-out series of yelps, perhaps as many as 10, 15 or 20. The final yelps often grow increasingly louder, with a sense of urgency thrown in.

The lost call or yelp isn't one I use on a regular basis, but it's a call that has accounted for several good gobblers. When a warm spring makes my eyelids weigh a ton apiece, I'm not above taking a short mid-morning nap. It beats walking back to camp, plus I'm right where I want to be—in the turkey woods. Before nodding off, though, I've found it's a good idea to do a ten- or fifteen-minute sequence of lost yelps, stopping only occasionally to listen for a gobble. More than once, I've opened my eyes to see a good gobbler standing or strutting within shotgun range.

Many turkey hunters don't realize it, but gobblers also make a yelping sound. My good friend and hunting partner, Jerry Martin (Hunting Advisor for Bass Pro Shops), once described a gobbler's yelp as longer, louder, coarser and spaced farther apart than the ones made by a hen. The first time I actually heard that sound, I knew exactly what it was. It's commonly almost twice as long as the yelp made by a hen. Instead of being spaced nearly a second apart,

Jakes often yelp much like a hen, but their yelps are coarser and lengthier.

gobbler yelps are often 1½ seconds apart. While a year-old jake yelp may be nearly as clear in tone and high-pitched as a hen's yelp, the yelp made by an older gobbler is generally much louder and more raspy. So if you're ever calling to a gobbling tom, and suddenly the gobbles end and you hear what sounds like an older hen yelping as it approaches, get ready. It just might be that same gobbler. The gobbler yelp is usually associated more with fall and winter hunting, but it's not uncommon for a springtime tom to yelp as much as he gobbles.

CLUCK AND PURR

The "cluck" and "purr" are two different sounds, but often in the turkey woods one call is made concurrently with the other. As a result, many turkey hunting experts refer to the "cluck and purr" as a single call. Most of these sounds are so soft, you'd never hear them unless they were easing past within a few yards. While feeding, turkeys nearly always "cluck and purr" as they scratch away the leafy ground cover in search of acorns, insects, tubers or what have you. It's a sound of contentment, often with a few very soft yelps thrown in.

Many respected authorities agree that these soft sounds are a way for turkeys to maintain contact with each other as they move through an area. Where the foliage is so thick that many birds could lose sight of one another, they can still hear the clucking and purring of the other birds. This helps them to avoid straying away from the flock. The "cluck and purr" is a great way to keep calling to a gobbler you haven't seen yet, keeping him on course until he's within range.

PUTTS

Too often, the "putt" is associated only with danger and alarm. Like yelps, though, turkeys have several putts they use for different reasons. I've actually had both gobblers and hens come

Slate or glass surface "friction calls" produce excellent yelps, purrs and clucks. The tone is changed by working a different surface area, or by using a striker or peg made of a different material.

While hunting with his uncle, Rob Keck (right)
took this great tom using friction calls.

through the woods bobbing their heads in jerky movements and "putting" with sharp but relatively soft tones. One highly regarded turkey hunter with whom I've shared several great hunts once told me that this sound is something like a "Where are you?" putt. I tend to agree with him. These birds are not alarmed; they're simply looking for the source of the calls that lured them there in the first place.

During one of his excellent turkey hunting seminars, champion turkey caller Ray Eye once commented that some hunters associate putting with alarmed turkeys. But turkeys will putt—or "pop," as some call it—under a vari-

Diaphragm calls come in a wide range of tones according to the number of latex reeds that are formed or cut.

ety of conditions, such as when they're spooked. But they also make the same sounds when excited for other reasons, like anger or pleasure. Many times I've "putted" loudly, trying to get a gobbler to raise his head from a full strut for better shot placement. While I usually get the job done by putting loudly and excitedly several times, rarely will the tom stop at once and lift his head. As

with so many other sounds made by wild turkeys, the "putt" is a tone, not a call unto itself. It's the sequence and volume that go into a series of "putts" which give the call a particular meaning.

CUTTING

"Cutting" has grown in popularity in recent years, especially with a box call or the special "cutter" mouth calls. It's simply a drawn out series of loud, aggressive putts, or pops. The best way to describe its rhythm is "extremely erratic and broken." Many experts believe that "cutting" is a social call used to locate other turkeys. When a hen becomes impatient in her efforts to locate a gobbler, she'll often walk through the woods cutting loudly. That's why the cutter is such a deadly call for spring toms. Not many late morning or afternoon gobblers can resist the calls of such a receptive hen.

Dominant hens will commonly challenge each other by means of aggressive cutting. The old hen described at the beginning of this chapter immediately began cutting back at the calls made by my box call. She wanted me to know that the hen she thought I was had trespassed onto her territory and wasn't welcome.

CACKLE

The "cackle" is most often associated with hens flying down from the roost. While the true purpose of this call is basically unknown, many experienced turkey hunters feel that it's natural for some turkeys to make a sound of some sort as they leave the roost. Over the years, I've watched many birds fly down and have come to the conclusion that only a few actually "cackle" on their way to the ground. Ray Eye describes

before rushing in and flogging the daylights out of my Feather-Flex hen decoy. If there's one thing I've learned about wild turkeys, it's never to say with any conviction that they'll do this or that. It's much safer to say there are birds out there who are waiting to make a liar out of anyone who will make such state-

Mark Drury prepares to make a few calls on one of M.A.D. Call's aluminum-sur-faced friction models.

cackling as a string of snappy, excited calls that begin low, rise in volume and rhythm, then drop off again. He feels that a "cackle" is actually a short, excited cut rather than a yelp. I've heard others claim that hens only cackle while in flight, but I can recall several instances in which hens on the ground rose almost straight up, flapped their wings and cackled. One such hen went through this antic a half-dozen times

ments. No two turkeys sound the same, nor do they share the same mannerisms.

GOBBLE

The one call a wild turkey hunter lives to hear is the throaty gobble of a mature wild turkey tom. There are mornings when the first owl hoots are greeted by the gobbles of a dozen or more of the big birds. And there are mornings when you can't raise a single

Author Toby Bridges poses with an outstanding Illinois gobbler he brought down after more than an hour of excited hen calling.

gobble. The only reward for the efforts of an entire morning may be to hear one single, far-off gobbler. Hunting turkeys is a richer sport because of the deep, rolling rattle that lets us know when we've captured a tom's attention, and when he's getting closer. Without the gobble, turkey hunting would lose much of its excitement.

Why do tom turkeys gobble? It's widely accepted that the primary reason is to allow the gobbler to attract hens during the spring breeding season, and to establish dominance as well. Ray Eye claims that the real reason for all that gobbling from March through early June is because that's the time of year when gobblers are most excited. Ray adds that he has heard toms gobble throughout the year. I can recall one cold December morning in southern Nebraska when the gobblers were exceptionally loud-mouthed. There was nearly a foot of snow on the ground and the temperature was hovering around the 20° mark. Hardly the time of year or weather for wild turkey gobblers to surface. Still, as the morning sun slowly lifted above the tree line, hundreds of mixed Merriam's, Rio Grande and Eastern wild turkey hybrids grew louder and louder as the warming sun rose higher and higher. Shortly before 8 a.m., the birds all flew down from the roost. Through my binoculars I watched one group of 50 or so adult gobblers feeding, when suddenly several big toms began pushing each other with their breasts to claim a small pile of corn that had spilled from the grain

truck. Soon a real fight broke out. Dozens of other birds rushed up to watch, including several jakes and a few other adult toms who came running from the river bottom brush to join the melee. Before I knew it, more than 75 gobblers had arrived in the field, purring loudly and strutting to show their dominance, and gobbling as if it were late April.

I've also heard birds gobble, for whatever reason, right in the middle of summer and occasionally in the fall. Even so, spring is the "official" gobbling season. Most of the activity begins as soon as the days grow longer and temperatures begin to rise. Through most of the northern habitat, the toms begin to sound off in March, while farther south the initial gobbling period can begin as early as late January or early February. The gobblers are ready, but the hens may be a month or more away from actually mating. Many respected experts on turkey hunting believe that the reason for such early gobbling periods is so the gobblers can sort out the pecking order.

Gobbling in most regions of the country actually enjoys two peaks. The first generally takes place during the two to three weeks prior to the actual breeding period, a time when hens begin to show interest in the males who are courting them. The second peak usually takes place during the weeks following the breeding period. While toms will continue to gobble on through the breeding period, the amount generally drops off quite dramatically. Gobblers are spending a

great deal of time then with the hens; instead of gobbling to attract a hen that's already in sight, the big birds turn to strutting and displaying their puffed up bodies, fanned tails and brightly colored heads. Their purpose is to hold the attention of the hen (or hens) with whom they are trying to mate. This explains why a red hot gobbler will often hammer back at every sound a hunter makes on a call, then suddenly go completely silent. The gobbler has

the birds are still on the roost—until about an hour to an hour and a half after fly down. Once a gobbler goes to a hen, there's nearly always a notice-able lull in gobbling activity. Later in the morning, from around 10 o'clock on into early afternoon, the toms often head for traditional strutting areas. There they will often spend hours strutting back and forth, gobbling now and then to attract any hens who may still be searching for the company of a gobbler.

simply mated with the real thing, which means almost every call the hunter tries now will fall on deaf ears.

Most gobbling takes place early in the morning, from about 30 to 45 min-utes before good daylight—often while

This can be one of the most productive times to hunt the wild turkey, provided the hunter isn't too discouraged when his calls were ignored earlier, or when every gobbler in the country seems to have left during the lull which followed.

Too often hunters are sitting back at camp or at home when the best hunting beckons.

Many experienced turkey hunters recognize 20 to 30 different calls made by wild turkeys. Calls not cited in this chapter include the assembly call, the kee-kee run of young birds, the fighting purr or rattle, the hatching yelp, the hush call, cooing, and a few others. Some have a legitimate place in turkey hunting, but to learn them a hunter must spend more time in the turkey woods.

The real meaning of the calls we've studied is usually found in the mood or manner in which the turkey makes the call. A purr can mean contentment, anger or excitement, depending on the tone, volume and cadence. The same is true of the yelp and a few other sounds. Moreover, real turkeys often engage in a series of different calls. As for the turkey hunters themselves, it's not necessary to know every call a turkey makes, or even what the call might mean. Learn the basics—the yelp, purr, cluck and maybe even the cut—and you'll hang your tag on a few gobblers. As noted turkey hunter and video producer Mark Drury points out, "My three favorite calls during spring turkey season begin with yelping. My favorite call by far is an excited hen yelp. My second favorite is probably a soft "cluck and purr" call. And Number Three is the cutting of a very aggressive hen, which I especially like for locating a gobbler.

World Champion caller Steve Stoltz tends to agree with Mark Drury's choices. "My best three hunting calls are, first, cutting. I love to cut because I know it's going to get a gobbler excited. My second favorite is the plain hen yelp, especially when some excitement is involved. And third is the "cluck and purr"—a great call for bringing 'em in that last 50 yards." ■

Chapter 3

Mastering The Call

WITH ■ Dick Kirby, *Quaker Boy Calls & World Champion Caller* ■ Chris Kirby, *Grand National Champion Caller* ■ Mark Drury, *President, M.A.D. Calls & World Champion Caller* ■ David Hale, *Co-founder, Knight & Hale Game Calls* ■ Brad Harris, *Public Relations Director, Outland Sports* ■ Robby Rohm, *Grand National Turkey Calling Champion*

The ground literally vibrated from the old tom's thunderous

gobble. The first-time turkey hunter gasped for breath and the muzzle of his shotgun shook from excitement. To calm him, I leaned slowly in his direction and whispered a few words of encouragement. Then suddenly we saw it, all fanned out and looking as big as an ostrich. The bronze-colored gobbler strutted out of the brush into a small opening along the wooded ridge. As the big bird moved behind a huge oak some 20 yards away, my colleague shifted the muzzle of his Remington Model 870 12-gauge pump in that direction. A few seconds later, the bird stepped from behind the tree, taking a few more steps while I "putted" loudly on the diaphragm call. Up came the gobbler's head, and with the roar of his three-inch magnum smoothbore the world gained one more successful turkey hunter. His counterparts in every state but Alaska can now enjoy the opportunity to hunt spring turkeys. Thanks to the efforts of the NWTF and the various state game

departments, this magnificent game bird has been brought back from near extinction to almost unimaginable population levels. In fact, the wild turkey has been reintroduced to all of its original native ranges, plus a number of other regions where the wild turkey had never existed before (such as Hawaii). Any hunter with the time and money can now open the spring season as early as the first of March in the far south and hunt his way northward for almost three-and-a-half months!

This abundance of wild turkeys now offers a growing number of new turkey hunters a chance to get into the spring woods, preferably accompanied by an experienced hunter and caller. While most won't have that luxury, there are fortunately several outstanding turkey hunting videos available from proven turkey call makers, including Quaker Boy, Primos, M.A.D. Calls and Hunter's Specialties. They will advise the proper use of various calls, how to locate turkeys and lure them into range, when to call and when not to, and much more. The variety of such products available to novice turkey hunters is truly amazing—especially where calls are involved—from the simple box call to such new innovations as aluminum or glass-faced friction calls and carbon strikers, which can be operated even in a light rain. Turkey hunters who are consistently successful must strive to master each call and reproduce with accuracy all the various turkey sounds. It simply takes practice—and lots of it.

One notable turkey hunting expert told me, "More gobblers have been called into the gun using the basic hen 'yelp' than all of the purrs, clucks, whines, cackles and other hen sounds combined. I would rather be the best yelper in the woods than be only so-so with all the others. The hunter who can make all the calls effectively definitely has an ace up his sleeve."

Dick Kirby, a world champion turkey caller and founder of Quaker Boy Calls, adds, "The art of calling wild turkeys is the ultimate challenge for today's sportsman. Learning to reproduce the wide variety of calls made by wild turkeys is not difficult and can be very rewarding." The earliest form of turkey call, Kirby opines, was most likely an early hunter simply using his own voice to copy the sounds of the wild turkey, especially the easy calls like the hen "yelp." In fact, a few experienced hunters still rely on nothing more than their own vocal cords to call turkeys. I

have on several occasions called gobblers in simply by yelping at them with my mouth. More than once I've gotten bow shots at young fall birds merely by whistling a "kee…kee…kee" call after having stumbled onto the birds, flushing a small flock in all directions.

One of the oldest forms of turkey callers is the *suction* call, which was originally made from a simple hollow reed, a piece of thin cane, or the wing bones of a wild turkey. Generally speaking, a "wing bone" call is made from

One of the oldest known forms of turkey calls is the "suction call," often made from the hollow wing bones of a wild turkey. Here the author demonstrates how to use a suction call made from pieces of cane.

The box call—an old favorite of many turkey hunters—is easy to master.
The hunter shown is using the call to locate a gobbler.

three bone sections taken from the wing of either a gobbler or a hen turkey. After the sections have been removed from the wing, they are boiled lightly and cleaned of all flesh, then thoroughly dried. The end section has the largest diameter, into which the next smallest diameter is inserted until it fits flush with the end piece. Once that's in place, the section with the smallest diameter is inserted through the larger end opening and pushed through the middle section until it protrudes from the other end. In several of the wing bone calls in my collection, these three sections have been cemented together with a light application of epoxy glue (I suspect early man used a natural glue made from various plants or animals).

A completed wing bone call usually measures six to ten inches in length, depending on whether the bones were taken from a gobbler or a hen. High quality calls are considered works of art, and in the hands of an expert they can sound amazingly realistic. Dick Kirby points out that a call made from the wing of a hen is much smaller than one made from a gobbler's wing. As a result, the hen wing bone call produces sharper or higher tones, sounding like the calls made by younger turkeys. Veteran callers like Kirby have even learned how to produce the "kee...kee...kee" calls of older poults during the fall season. On the other hand, the larger, heavier gobbler wing bone call sounds more like an adult hen, with deeper, more raspy sounds.

Dick is also quick to point out that suction-type calls are difficult to master, but are, in the hands of a pro, quite deadly.

Other than a few small custom makers who continue to craft suction type calls from actual wing bones, cane and other tubular materials, not many of these calls are produced commercially

these days. For years, I used an old "Turpin Yelper" made of wood, rubber and plastic that produced great tones. Still, it proved difficult for me to master. When I sucked lightly on the small diameter tip, it tickled my lips, making it even harder to produce a series of yelps. But the yelps that did work properly were sharp and crisp.

Most of the calls on the market today are basically of two types: they are either operated by air or friction.

Most hunters work the "box call" by holding the box in one hand, then drawing the paddle (or lid) across a thin sounding rail.

Here the box call is worked by holding the paddle stationery, then working the sound rail across the chalked paddle.

An air-operated call requires a flow of air, its tones produced by the vibration of a latex rubber reed(s). Sounds made from friction-type calls are caused by rubbing two surfaces against one another. Personally, I like the friction type. It's easier to master, especially using an old

box or slate call. One call I always carry in my vest or jacket pocket when heading out for another day in the turkey woods is a Rohm Brothers box call made with a poplar box and a cherry wood paddle. I call it the "Stradivarius of box calls." It has been the undoing of nearly a hundred gobblers over the nearly 20 years since Robby Rohm presented it to me on a Missouri hunt.

According to Robby, there exist only five basic calls a hunter needs to know to bag a turkey. While the hen "yelp" has probably brought more gobblers into gun range than any other call, he feels that the hunter who can learn to "cluck, cut, putt and purr" has mastered the basic language of the wild turkey hen. And this Grand National and U.S. Open calling champion can do it all on the simple box call!

While box calls from different manufacturers vary slightly in length, width, height, depth, and even in their shape, the basic design has remained unchanged since the first calls of this type were produced—and they've been around for more than a century. In use, the call's paddle is moved across a thin lip on the box. To create friction between the surfaces, the bottom of the paddle is rubbed lightly with an oil-free chalk. Most blackboard chalk is treated with a special oil or grease to eliminate those spine-tingling, high frequency screeches. This also eliminates the sharp tones that make a good box call effective on a love-sick gobbler. Many call makers sell chalk for box calls, or you can buy a piece of carpenter's chalk so long as it's oil-free.

Different hunters develop their own styles for holding a box call. The most common method is to hold the bottom of the box in the left hand (assuming it's a right-handed person), with the free end of the lid (or paddle) pointed at you. With the other hand, the lid or paddle is lifted out to one side of the box, then drawn across the lip or rail of the call, creating a yelp. I prefer to hold the paddle in my left hand and grasp the box with my right hand. Holding the call upside down, with the free end of the paddle pointed away from me, I stroke the box across the paddle. This method allows more control and a broader range of calls.

World champion caller Chris Kirby advises that, when making the basic yelp with a box call, never lift the lid from the rail, even when it is pulled back to make a series of yelps. Chris learned a great deal about turkey hunting from his father, Dick, including a love for good friction-type calls. Seldom will you find father or son competing in the turkey woods without a box or slate call within easy reach. When a paddle or lid is lifted from the rail to make successive yelps, it becomes more difficult to maintain the angle of the lid with the rail, causing the rhythm to break. Box calls come in two basic variations: two rails and a single rail. Boxes with a rail on each side of the box provide the hunter with the versatility of two completely different tones, but they're a little more difficult to learn. When the

hunter switches from one side to the other, the angle of the lid must be reversed, which explains why one-sided box calls can be a lot easier for beginners. In fact, the Quaker Boy "One-Sider" call has the angle built right into the lid. The caller simply pulls the lid across one side until it hits the blocker rail.

Brad Harris (Director of Public Relations for Outland Sports) offers the following tips for calling with a box call:

YELPS: Learn the proper way to stroke the call, remembering that it takes practice. Relax your wrist and maintain a short, rhythmic motion. Give a full stroke across the lip and the rest comes naturally. If the box call has two sides, one side is usually high and the other, low. The tone can be changed according to which side the lid is worked

The slate call has recently become a popular caller. Before it can produce the sweet-sounding tones it's known for, the surface must be lightly sanded.

When working a slate call, the peg (or striker) is angled slightly away from the body and drawn toward the caller.

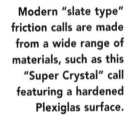

Modern "slate type" friction calls are made from a wide range of materials, such as this "Super Crystal" call featuring a hardened Plexiglas surface.

on. When yelping, use three to eight notes in any given series.

CLUCKS, PUTTS & CUTTING: Calls like the "Lohman Double Thunder" make clucking, putting and cutting easier and more effective. It has a pre-cut groove in the lid and left side of the box. Place the thumb of the left hand in the notch on the lid, with the crease of the first knuckle resting in a notch of the lip. This holds the lid to the right, against the right lip. To produce the desired sound, strike the handle of the lid with the right hand. Light taps spaced properly produce excellent clucks. On the other hand, harder, erratic hits produce the alarm putt of a frightened turkey. Quick, hard and broken hits on the handle create the excited cutting of a hen.

To make these same sounds on a Rohm Brothers box call (held in the reverse position), I can easily produce a "cluck" by placing the lip of the box against the chalked surface of the paddle or lid, applying a slight amount of pressure, then popping it free. The entire movement takes less than half an inch. To create an alarm "putt," I do the same thing, only a little harder and louder, with five or more erratic putts. To create the excited "cutting"—which says to an ol' gobbler, "Hey, where are you?"—I lift the box away from the lid and then

strike it against the chalked surface five or six times in a broken series of pops (repeated three or four times).

Another effective call using a box call is the "purr." Holding the lid in my left hand and the box in my right hand, I gently slide the lip or rail across the chalked surface of the lid. When combined with several light clucks, a few purrs tell an old gobbler that everything is okay. When using a softer wood like

butternut or poplar, the sound of a box call is softer. The harder the wood, like walnut, the sharper and crisper the tones. One call was made for me especially out of sassafras, a softer wood that creates very soft but raspy tones. Another call (made of walnut) produces sharp tones that can produce a gobble a mile away.

David Hall (Knight & Hale Game Calls) discounts the value of the box

The "Triple Threat" from Quaker Boy offers three totally different surfaces and sounds: traditional slate (upper right), glass (bottom) and aluminum (upper left).

calls. "They're probably the easiest call to use," he says, "and they produce extremely natural sounds. But they have some drawbacks. One is their versatility, or lack of it. They're mostly limited to basic yelps, clucks and purrs. Granted, somebody who's used a box for years can get more out of it than that, but the average caller can't. You can still be a successful hunter with these basic calls, though."

Different tones can be made on slate-type friction calls by using a different type peg or striker made of wood, carbon, plastic or ceramic.

In recent years, the small "push or pull button" box calls have won widespread popularity. They are easier to operate, with less chance of being spotted by an oncoming gobbler. Most calls of this type barely measure 2" by 4" and can be easily held in the palm of one hand and operated by one finger. Most such calls can even be attached to the bottom of a shotgun barrel, with a string running back to the hunter,

"Another drawback of a box call" David continues, "is the fact that you have to use both hands to run it. This can get chancy when a turkey's in close. You can try to shield it with your knees or set the box on the ground and run it with one hand. Either way, you risk the turkey spotting you."

allowing the call to be operated with a free hand even as the hunter sights down the gun barrel. With practice most anyone can learn to duplicate most of the basic calls.

David Hale relies heavily on calls of this design. "I take two push-pull calls on every hunt," he says, "so I can make fighting purrs. Harold Knight and I popularized this calling method, and I guarantee it's no gimmick. It may not work on every turkey every time, though. There's a time to use it and a time not to. However, simulating a fight between two rival gobblers can be extremely effective. It'll excite and bring in some old gobblers who can't be called by any other way."

Fighting purrs are aggressive, rapid and excited sounds made by holding a push-pull type call in each hand and operating the two calls simultaneously—just like two gobblers threatening to kick the living daylights out of each other. David Hale says that it's the equivalent to one whitetail buck grunting aggressively to another. When used properly, the fighting purr can be one of the hunter's best techniques. He claims that it has been one of the most productive calls he and his hunting partner, Harold Knight, have used.

At one time, a slate call could only be found in the pocket of a seasoned turkey hunter. For some reason, beginners felt the slate-type calls were too difficult to master. They leaned more in favor of the old box call. Nothing could be further from the truth, however; in fact, some slate calls available today rank among the easiest calls to learn. Many of these calls don't have a slate surface at all; instead, the working surface of many popular calls of this type is a thin piece of Plexiglas or aluminum. Like the box call, this one comes in a variety of sizes and configurations. Most are of the "single" or "double" surface design, which generally means the caller has only one surface to work with, or a working surface on each side of the call.

Master slate caller Dick Kirby advises: "When calling with a slate call, begin by holding the call parallel with the floor or ground. The striker, or peg, is held straight up and down (90°) to the surface, then angled away from the body at about a 15° angle. Hold it about the same as you would a pencil.

Hand-operated friction calls, such as the one shown from Lohman, can be worked with one finger; or they can be mounted onto the bottom of a gun barrel and operated by pulling a string.

To make a "cluck," move the tip of the peg and let the tip "pop" toward you. To make a "purr," pull the tip of the peg in a nearly straight, half-circle or C-shaped line toward the caller."

Dick adds, "The tip of the peg should never come off the slate surface. The farther out you move toward the edge, the higher the pitch. As you come in (toward the center), you're going to get deeper and deeper yelps."

Calls like the "U 101 Carlton Black Widow" double glass call (from Hunter's Specialties) make it easier than ever to produce the right tones. Printed on the

surface of this friction call are the patterns, or striker paths, a hunter follows to produce the various turkey sounds. A free 30-minute instructional video makes learning even easier. The size of a slate call and how it's built greatly influences the tones it produces. A small 2½-inch to 3-inch single surface slate—especially one that's relatively flat without a "sound" chamber behind

its surface—will produce soft, mellow tones when compared to a double-sided 4-inch (or larger) slate type call with a resonating "sound" chamber between the two surfaces. To produce the clear, crisp tones of a hen, many slate-type companies now make their calls with a half-inch deep sound chamber located behind the calling surface. Many are now built with an internal baffle that amplifies the calls.

Different working surfaces also create totally different tones. Whatever the maker calls the surface of a glass-slate type call—whether glass, Plexiglas or crystal—it will produce the softest yelps, purrs and clucks. Next in line is the true slate surface, which is valued for the variety of tones it produces. Most slate surfaces produce mellow yelps with only a slight rasp. But if it's volume or frequency you're looking for, concentrate on the metal surface calls such as the M.A.D. "Super Aluminator."

The "Quaker Boy Triple Threat" offers three deadly calls all wrapped up into one. This friction call offers the versatility of three different calling surfaces: traditional slate, aluminum and Plexiglas. By shifting the striker an inch or so one way or the other, the caller can in an instant switch from the high frequency sounds of an aluminum surface to the mellower tones of slate to the super soft purrs, clucks

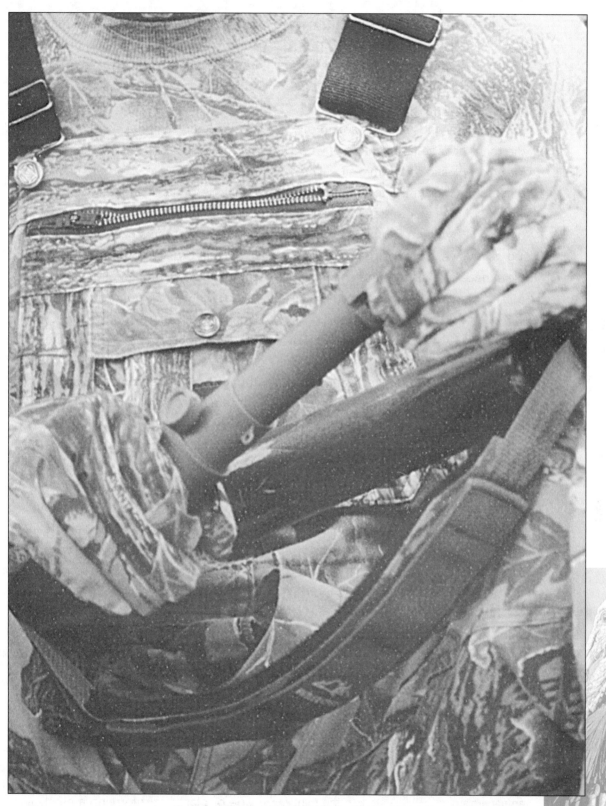

Another easy call to use is Lohman's "Pump-Action Yelper;" in only a few minutes of practice with this call most novice hunters can reproduce authentic hen yelps.

and tree yelps of a glass surface. These and other features make the Triple Threat one of the most complete turkey calls available today. "When different types of pegs are used on a slate call." Dick Kirby reminds us, "the sound of the tones change. Pegs made of wood, Plexiglas, plastic or ceramic all create different pitches in the tone."

One of my favorite slate calls is one made by Rohm Brothers measuring nearly five inches across. This single surface call has a sound chamber behind the calling surface. I carry mine in a quart-size plastic Ziplock bag. I also carry a two-inch square of "Scotch Brite" to keep the calling surface working, along with two different strikers, or pegs. One is made of hard locust wood, the other, a ceramic peg with a hard maple top. When I want soft, seductive yelps, clucks and purrs, I always rely on a locust peg. The grain of the wood peg grips the surface of the slate, making these calls almost effortless on the big Rohm Brothers slate. If I want to reach out farther with my calls, this slate can produce more volume. For louder, higher frequency yelps, especially when trying to produce excited cutting on the call, I opt for the ceramic peg.

"The main disadvantage with these calls," claims David Hale, "is that they require both hands, but you can learn to work around that. Also, a slate's no good if it gets wet, but a glass call with an acrylic striker will still work in the rain."

Dick Kirby, on the other hand, points out another problem hunters may encounter with slate-type friction calls. "When you use a slate or glass call," he warns, "you have to make sure it's clean. To do that, use a regular scouring type pad or fine sandpaper to clean and scuff the surface."

The easiest surface to take out of action is true slate. Even the oil from a few fingerprints is enough to eliminate the friction between the slate surface and the tip of the striker, which is necessary in order to produce those rich tones. Too much of an oily substance can actually ruin a good slate call. If any kind of heavy oil sits on the surface for too long, it can penetrate the slate and take lots of sanding to remove. Mostly, though, oily fingerprints and other light contaminates can be cleaned off the surface by a few quick strokes with a scouring pad. According to Kirby, the tip of the peg or striker must also be cleaned regularly, using the same scouring pad used to clean the slate. By keeping both the call and peg clean, a good slate call can produce sounds which many feel are the sharpest, truest sounding turkey calls.

By far the most widely used turkey call today is the "mouth diaphragm" call. Like most other types of turkey calls, it too comes in a wide range of designs. Even so, most share the same physical characteristics: thin latex rubber reeds stretched across an aluminum or plastic U-shaped frame. The majority are trimmed with a moisture-proof tape or plastic skirt forming a nearly airtight seal between the tongue and roof of the mouth. While the number and

combinations of reeds—and how they are cut or shaped—has led to a seemingly endless selection of diaphragm calls, they fall into two basic categories: either "clear tone" or "raspy tone." The sharp, clear tones of the former are usually produced by calls with straight-edged reeds. The raspy sound is commonly the result of a notch, V-cut, or a flap cut into at least one of the reeds. The small size of a mouth diaphragm call makes it possible for a hunter to carry a wide variety of calls in a case that slips right into a shirt or jacket pocket. Another major advantage of a call that fits handily into the roof of a caller's mouth is that it keeps both hands free for other important things—like taking aim on a gobbler and pulling the trigger!

As widely used as these diaphragm calls are, many hunters cannot use them. For some reason, there's a natural gag reflex that simply won't allow these callers to position the call in the mouth in such a manner that the taped skirt rides on the rear portion of the palate. Most proficient mouth callers agree that if a hunter can learn to put one of these calls in his or her mouth, they can learn to use any one of them. There seems to be a considerable difference in the size of these calls, depending on the manufacturer. The novice mouth caller may have to buy several before finding one that fits comfortably in the mouth. Fortunately, a few call makers offer several different frames.

Most calls can be improved even more by bending an aluminum frame far enough so that the call fits the curvature of the palate—but be sure the call has an aluminum frame. I tried this once with a call made of plastic and it simply broke the frame and ruined the

Many hunters insist the tube call is among the hardest to master; they still rely on it, however, because of its great sound.

call. So when bending the frame, be sure to keep the front edge of the latex reed(s) reasonably taut. If the latex is too floppy, the entire sound of the call will change. Also, if a taped skirt is too large, some of the excess can be trimmed with a pair of scissors. Be careful not to trim away too much, though, or the call could be lost. Most first-time mouth callers make the mistake of trying to "blow" the call. Surprisingly, it doesn't take much air to produce the sounds of a wild turkey hen. In fact, most calls are made with the same amount of air it takes to speak. With lots of practice, one diaphragm call can produce the wild turkey's entire vocabulary.

Mark Drury, founder of M.A.D. Calls, advises that learning to call with a diaphragm may not be all that difficult, but to be truly proficient requires lots of practice. He shares the following advice for those who want to try a mouth call for the first time, or who simply can't produce the right sounds.

1. *First, the long reed on any call should be on top, with the short reed on the bottom. Place the call on the tongue much like a piece of candy, with the reeds facing forward. Then position the call into the roof of your mouth. To get the necessary air seal on the taped skirt, simply say the word "huck" while holding the tongue against the call.*

2. *Start with a simple high-pitched sound made by a constant flow of air across the reeds, then exhale. Keep trying until you've produced something like a high-pitched squeal. To make a combination of higher and lower tones, drop the tongue slightly to reduce pressure against the call. Once you've made both higher and lower pitched sounds, begin to shorten the gap between them. Soon you'll produce the basic two-toned "yelp" of a wild turkey hen.*

Dick Kirby (Quaker Boy Calls) takes a similar approach to helping novice mouth callers. He also advises beginners to use a word similar to "huck," pushing the call into the roof of the mouth with the tongue, creating an airtight seal between the taped skirt and

This small diaphragm call fits into the roof of the mouth, leaving both hands free for aiming and shooting.

the roof of the mouth. Instead of relying on a simple exhale of air across the reeds, Kirby instructs callers to say simply "Chee-Uck." The resulting sound will be a yelp. At first, the sounds may not be the same as the calls made by worldwide champions like Dick's son, Chris Kirby. But with continued practice almost anyone can learn to make the most productive call in turkey hunting: the basic hen yelp. As Chris Kirby attests: "The cluck is a sound you'll hear turkeys make more than any other. It's a real simple sound, and the way you do it with a mouth call is to keep your tongue tight against the roof of your mouth, with the call between. Then release a normal breath of air and, with your lips together, say "puck," followed immediately by a quick burst of air flow across the reeds."

Most experienced mouth callers start with a few light clucks, followed by a series or two of yelps, followed in turn by several more clucks. This sequence adds a sense of realism to the calling, for turkeys seldom move through the woods without making any sounds at all. Hens are nearly always clucking as they feed, working along the edge of a field, or socializing with other turkeys. The cluck should not be confused with the putt, especially the alarm putt. Both sounds

are made in basically the same manner. It's the volume and rhythm involved that differentiates one from the other. Clucks are generally more subtle, while putts are usually loud and excited. After all, the putt is the turkey's way of warning others of danger. A few loud putts can cause a strutting gobbler to poke his head up for a look around, and that usually leads to a better shot. According to Dick Kirby, "If you've never heard

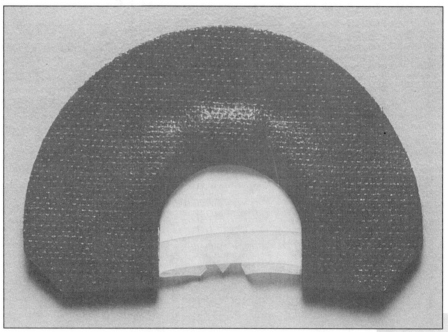

Determining the tones produced by any mouth-operated diaphragm call, such as M.A.D. Calls "V" Enom, depends on the number of reeds and how they're formed and cut.

a turkey give an alarm putt, then you haven't hunted turkeys very long."

One effective call that's relatively easy to make on a mouth diaphragm is the simple purr. It's like when you were a kid playing in the tub. You placed your lips down into your bath water and pretended to be an outboard motor by blowing bubbles in the water. The purr is made in basically the same manner. Lightly place your tongue against the bottom of the reeds and, with your lips

pressed together lightly, make that same motorboat sound. I've called in countless gobblers using little more than a few clucks and purrs. It's the best combination I've come across for inducing a reluctant gobbler to close the distance from 60 to 30 yards.

"Cuttin' is a call my dad and I both use a lot," says Chris Kirby. "All cuttin' amounts to is just real excited, faster rhythm clucks. When you're calling and an old hen cuts you off with some excit-

ed cuttin', and you begin to cut back at her, it's like two old ladies yelling at each other. More important, it gets gobblers really excited."

Like clucking, cutting can be much more effective when a few yelps are thrown in here and there. It's not uncommon for a real hen to become jealous at the sound of another hen calling to "her" gobbler. Some of my most memorable hunts involved getting into a calling duel with a real hen,

which inevitably leads to a lot of cutting. Whatever calls the hen makes, I try to duplicate, adding a note or two extra. More than once, I've witnessed an irate hen approaching in search of the intruder, often with a gobbler following right behind her. The fact is sometimes when you call the hen, you get the gobbler!

Another effective mouth-operated call is the *tube call*. As the name implies, it's a simple plastic (or wooden) tube with a latex rubber reed stretched across one end. The call sounds are made by placing the edge of the reed against the lips and by controlling the amount of air entering the tube. As with the suction wingbone-type calls, tube calls can be extremely hard to master. When operated by a very experienced caller, however, they can produce unbelievably mellow tones that are impossible to duplicate on any other type of call. By using a combination of lip contact, tongue movement and fast—but short—bursts of air, a good tube caller can gobble like the real thing. There are easier ways to reproduce the gobble than by using a tube call, however. One of the easiest is to use a double-sided box call fitted with a rubber band around the box and paddle. This enables the caller to shake the call vigorously back and forth, causing the paddle to ride back and forth against the two sounding rails. The result is a gobble.

Still easier to use is the rubber "shaker" type call, featuring a latex reed at the opening of a hollow cavity. The caller simply shakes the soft rubber call back and forth, or pumps it quickly like an accordion. As the air crosses the reed each time the call is shaken or pumped, a gobble is created. With a little practice, almost anyone can produce extremely realistic gobbles. Unfortunately, some are so realistic that they attract other turkey hunters as well. Should you decide on adding a gobble to your repertoire, do so only when (and where) other hunters are not within calling distance.

These five basic calls—the yelp, the cluck, the purr, cutting and the putt—will, when mastered, produce fine birds for the beginning turkey hunter with consistency. They are not the only sounds turkeys make, however. The longer you're in the turkey woods the more new sounds you'll hear, such as the *tree call*, the *fly down cackle* and the *gobbler yelp*. David Hale once told me that reading about how to call turkeys is equivalent to hearing someone describe a beautiful painting. You must see it first-hand to fully appreciate it. To know what a particular turkey call should sound like, you must first hear the sound and the rhythm of the call. To simplify the procedure, turkey hunters are fortunate to have at their disposal

two shortcuts: an instructional video and audio tape. Several companies, including Quaker Boy, Knight & Hale, M.A.D. Calls, Lohman, Primos, Hunter's Specialties and others all offer such tapes for beginning callers to share. Neophytes will then know exactly what the different calls actually sound like. Rhythm is as important as tone, and mastering the rhythm on different types of calls often requires subtle differences in dexterity. To readers who are just getting started in turkey hunting, a few words of advice: don't try to master the mouth diaphragm, box call, tube call, slate call or wing bone-type call at once. Begin with one of the easier calls—the push-button call or a good box call—and learn the basics before moving to another type. Never be afraid to experiment, though; it's the only way you'll ever learn to use a variety of calls.

"One of the biggest mistakes beginners make," David Hale warns "is having some success with one particular call, then sticking with it to the exclusion of all others. You might beat on a bucket and call up a turkey once, but that doesn't mean you can do it again. Not all turkeys like cutting or loud, fast yelping. You need to know how to make a variety of calls on different callers. That gives you several options. You're more likely that way to find something that really lights up a bird's fire. Don't get hung up on just one call or hunting method. Adapt your calling technique to each situation."

A box or vest full of turkey calls represents quite an investment. During

most seasons, I rely on about 15 or more calls for most of my hunting, but I'll often carry another 10 or so as back-up calls, plus another 8 or 10 mouth diaphragm calls to get me back in tune before the season opens. A single diaphragm call isn't all that expensive—about five bucks—but go through a dozen or so each season and you've made quite an investment. With a little

that nearly every time the call is used, its surface, whether slate or glass, must be rubbed lightly with an abrasive scouring pad or fine sandpaper to create the friction which, in turn, produces the sounds. Likewise, the tip of the peg or striker needs to be dressed regularly with the same pad or sandpaper to prevent it from becoming slick and polished.

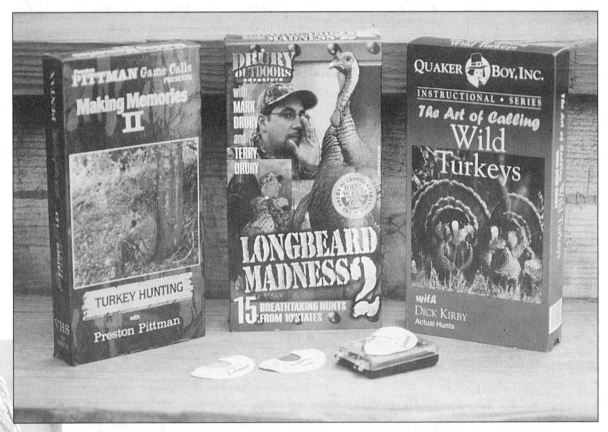

attention and proper care, these calls can last longer while continuing to produce sounds that lure an old gobbler within easy shotgun range.

Earlier, we covered the daily maintenance of a slate call. Other than keeping it dry and protecting it from lubricants (which can ruin the sound of a call), a hunter needs to keep in mind

A quality wooden box call should be cared for as if it were a musical instrument. It should never be exposed to wet, rainy weather or else the wood may swell and split, or the box will fall apart at the seams. If you know you're headed for a hunt in rainy weather, be sure to slip a favorite box call into a Ziplock plastic bag, and carry a spare piece of chalk in the bag as well. The bottom of the paddle must be chalked to produce those rich tones, but experts agree that too much chalk can deaden the tones. A heavy layer of chalk will literally pull moisture right out of the air, reducing the friction between the paddle and the sounding rail. It's also important to remember where **not** to carry a call; i.e., in the back pocket of your coveralls or vest. I've sat on several, reducing them in the process to expensive kindling.

The two biggest enemies of any call with a latex reed are heat and sunlight. When you come in from a morning hunt, don't leave your mouth calls, tube calls or even shaker gobble calls in the front seat of your truck, especially on the dash. Mouth diaphragm calls will last much longer when time is taken to wash them off in a cup of mouthwash, then rinsing them with cool clean water and patting them dry with paper towels. To keep the latex reeds from sticking together, slip a flat toothpick or a small, flat plastic paper clip between each reed. To prolong the life of these calls even further, store them in a call case, or the small plastic box they came in, and place them in the refrigerator. Most experts agree it's next to impossible to preserve a used diaphragm call from one year to the next; but with a little maintenance the same call can be used extensively for as long as four- to six-week seasons.

One last bit of advice: Don't wait until a week or two before season to begin practicing on your calls, or start mastering a new type of call. Get these calls a month or two before the hunt and spend as much time with them as your family and friends will tolerate. Then, when opening day rolls around, you'll sound a lot more like the real thing. ■

Chapter 4

Favorite Shotguns and Loads

WITH ■ Mark Drury, *President, M.A.D. Calls/Drury Outdoors* ■ David Hale, *Co-founder, Knight & Hale Game Calls* ■ Harold Knight, *Co-founder, Knight & Hale Game Calls* ■ Mike Jordan, *Public Relations Director, Winchester-Western Ammunition* ■ Bob Rott, *President, Hasting's Chokes*

Spring comes but once a year—and so do the opportunities

to hunt hard-strutting, hard-gobbling toms. After waiting nearly a year to hit the spring woods once more, including months of planning, weeks of scouting, and doubtless more than a few unsuccessful mornings in the turkey woods, the success of an entire season can hang on the effectiveness of a single shot. Even those lucky few who can take a month off and hunt in three or four different states each spring know within a few seconds how critical their shotgun and load patterns are in determining whether they go home empty-handed or with a gobbler in tow.

Thanks to the growing interest in hunting wild turkeys, expanded turkey hunting opportunities and the swelling ranks of turkey hunters in this country have brought with them a greater selection of shotguns built especially for wild turkey hunting. Most come with shorter barrel lengths, factory-applied camouflage finishes, and tight choke constrictions for dense patterns at 30, 40 and

50 yards. To produce the energy levels needed to down big wild turkey toms with consistency, 12-gauge models come with either 3 or 3^1/$_2$-inch magnum chambers (a few have been chambered for the 3^1/$_2$-inch 10 gauge loads).

David Hale recalls: "When I started hunting turkeys back in 1965, I used an old 12-gauge Damascus twist double-barreled shotgun. I didn't know I wasn't supposed to shoot 3-inch magnum shells in it, so I loaded it up with 3-inch BBs and went hunting. Somehow, I managed to kill the first gobbler I shot at with this combination. Looking back, I was lucky to hit the turkey with shot that large, and it was also a wonder that I didn't blow the barrel clean off that old gun. Truth is, I was totally ignorant about what kind of shotgun and shells were best for turkey hunting. I was also limited to hunting with whatever was available, and the only gun in my closet was that old double-barrel shotgun."

David now does most of his turkey hunting with a 3¹/₂-inch 12-gauge Mossberg 835 Ulti-Mag pump shotgun designed expressly for turkey hunters. It sports a short 24-inch barrel, full camouflage finish, and a tight patterning extra-full screw-in choke. Loaded with a 2-ounce payload of No. 6 shot in a 3¹/₂-inch shotshell, David considers this the ultimate turkey hunting shotgun. Until going to this gun and load, he had preferred hefty magnum loads of No. 4 shot in a 3-inch magnum Remington Model 870 pump gun. After using the heavier shot charge of the 3¹/₂-inch shotshells, however, he discovered that the smaller shot size delivered patterns much denser out at 30 to 45 yards. David explains, "I've switched to No. 6s, at least when I'm hunting in the woods, and for the first time in my life, I'm comfortable with this shot size. Not only does it have the zip to reach out to 45 yards, it also delivers more shot out there. For me, the 3¹/₂-inch No. 6 load has definitely replaced the 3-inch No. 4."

Harold Knight (Knight & Hale Game Calls) chose a 3-inch magnum Remington Model 870 as his first "serious" shotgun for hunting the wild turkey. He bought that gun back in 1963 and over the years harvested more than 200 gobblers with it. Several years after acquiring the shotgun, Harold re-choked it with an extra-full constriction at the muzzle for tighter patterns at extended ranges. "Now that was a tight shooting shotgun!" he exclaims. "I could now consistently kill turkeys with it at 55 yards."

While he still occasionally uses his old Remington, Harold also switched to the 3¹/₂-inch Mossberg 835 Ulti-Mag. He reckoned that early in the season, when there's not much foliage on the trees and undergrowth, both hunter and turkey can see greater distances, which meant the hunter had to take shots at greater distances. For that reason, Knight tends to stick with No. 4s when hunting in early season hardwoods, or when the edges of a field or pasture offer shots out past 40 yards.

The "magnum" turkey load (right) packs more pellets and punch than field loads, but it also produces far more recoil. When sighting or checking the impact of a turkey shotgun, first shoot with lighter loads, then switch to a few of the magnum loads for verification.

Once the foliage begins to fill out, and the turkeys must come closer in search of the source of his calls, Harold switches to No. 6s for much denser patterns.

Compared to veterans like Harold Knight and David Hale, the author is something of a newcomer to the sport of turkey hunting. I didn't go on my first wild turkey hunt until the spring of 1972. I was the guest of Dr. John Lewis, who at that time was the head turkey biologist for the state of Missouri. The second morning out, John called in four gobblers, while I dumped one of the birds at about 30 yards with the same 30-inch barreled Remington Model 870 Wingmaster I used for trap shooting. The shotgun was chambered for 2¾-inch shotshells only, but it patterned "high brass" 2¾-inch Winchester Super-X No. 4s quite well.

Today, I still shoot turkeys with a Remington Model 870 pump shotgun; in fact, I shoot two of them. One is a Model 870 Special Purpose with Mossy

Both guns perform best with Winchester or Federal buffered 2-ounce loads of No. 5 or No. 6. Each shotgun still produces several good gobblers come spring. However, I prefer the slightly longer 28-inch barrel over the shorter barrel found on the Special Purpose "Turkey" model. Even when the same choke tube is used for both guns the slightly longer barrel consistently produces tighter patterns and better center density. At 30 yards, the Express model with a .665" extra-full

Oak camouflage and a 24-inch barrel. The other is a 28-inch barreled Model 870 Express pump with spray-painted camouflage. Both guns feature a super-tight, extra-full screw-in-choke and 3-inch chamber. Both have double beads which can be aligned much like a front and rear sight for more positive aiming.

Hastings screwed-in choke produces 100 % of the pattern inside 30 inches at 30 yards. When the Special Purpose model with its shorter barrel is fired with the same load and through the same choke tube, about 96% of the pattern prints inside a 30-inch circle at the same distance. With a 2-ounce load of No.

6s, the longer barrel generally places about 70 and 80 pellets into a turkey head silhouette at 30 yards. The shorter barrel at best puts around 60 pellets into the "kill zone." The difference is insignificant, for any gobbler who strolls within 30 yards of either gun won't walk away—unless, of course, the shooter's aim is off.

Screw-in chokes—especially the extended tubes designed for turkey hunting—have done much to improve shotgun performance. According to Bob Rott (president of Hasting's Chokes), the nominal bore diameter of a true 12-gauge shotgun barrel is .729 inches. A standard "full" choke constriction at the muzzle measures around .695". At 40 yards, a full-choked barrel should keep up to 70% of the shot load inside a 30-inch circle. By comparison, a "modified" choke is supposed to place 60% inside the same circle, while an "Improved Cylinder" barrel or choke should print 50% patterns.

Bob Rott agrees that the tightest practical choke possible in a 12-gauge bore is .640", but he is quick to add that "tighter is not always better." Keep in mind that the actual bore diameter of your Grandpa's single-barrel 16 gauge shotgun is .662", while a 20-gauge bore measure only .615". So when a .640" screw-in choke is threaded into the muzzle of a 12-gauge turkey shotgun, the bore is constricted somewhere between the true bore sizes of a 20- and 16-gauge shotgun. But that doesn't

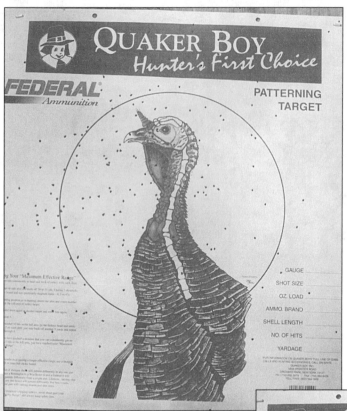

Sparse 30-yard patterns such as this may not deliver the punch needed to down a big wild turkey gobbler cleanly.

This 30-yard target was shot with a Hastings .665" "extra-full" tube threaded into the barrel of a 12-gauge 3-inch Remington Model 870 shotgun.

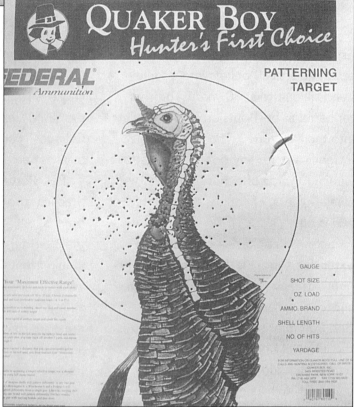

necessarily mean a choke that tight is going to produce the best gobbler-taking patterns. Veteran turkey hunter and world champion turkey caller Mark Drury (M.A.D. Calls) explains: "You can over-constrict the bore, which can result in shot deformation, poorer patterns and decreased downrange energy. When the pellets of a turkey load hit the sharp angle of such a radical choke constriction, the spheres of lead are redirected toward the other side of the bore and can result in a crisscrossing effect, which can really open up a pattern."

Long before gunmakers truly understood how a constriction at the muzzle tightened shot patterns, a few makers of early muzzleloading and breechloading shotguns toyed around with what has come to be known as a "jug choke." This device wasn't really a constriction of the bore at all; in fact, it was just the opposite. A "jug choke" was nothing more than a short section of the bore honed slightly larger than the true bore size of the shotgun. This system redirects outbound pellets traveling along the inside of the barrel wall back toward the center. In some instances noticeably better patterns were produced than with a cylinder bore barrel, but nothing like the patterns produced by matching a modern magnum shotshell load with the right screw-in choke.

Bob Rott shares the view that the best patterns are usually produced by chokes with a longer, more gradual

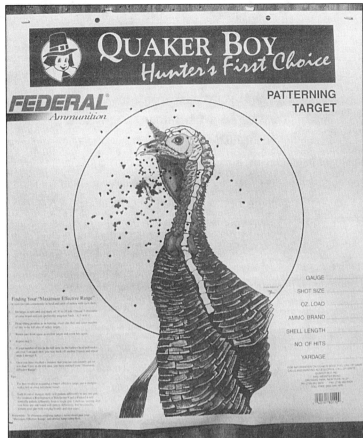

taper. He points out that the gradual inward slope of a long choke causes less deformation of the shot. That partially explains why the extended tubes are found on most of today's turkey hunting shotguns. The .665" choke tubes found on my Remington 870 pump guns measure exactly 3 inches in length, with their shotgun bores reduced from .729" to .665", or a 64 thousandths of an inch reduction of the bore. The result is a pattern at 10 yards that looks like a huge slug had ripped right through the pattern paper. This makes shot placement difficult on a bird that charges straight in and practically lies in your lap before you can even get sighted on him.

A hasty shot taken from only 15 yards with an extra-full chocked 3-inch 12-gauge. Turkey hunting requires precise shot placement with good dense patterns.

One of the most practical turkey shotguns I've come across was an over/under 12-gauge whose barrels were shortened to 22 inches with screw-in chokes installed. For most hunts, the owner would install an "Extra Full" .680" flush-mounted tube in the top barrel and a .700" "Improved Modified" choke tube (also flush-mounted) in the bottom barrel. Shooting both barrels with 2-ounce, 3-inch Federal Premium No. 6s, the hunter was ready for any shot from 10 to 50 yards. I once guided this hunter for four days in northern Missouri where he filled both of his tags, one at about 12 yards, the other close to 15 yards. Both were taken with the "Improved Modified" barrel.

With all of the exceptional turkey hunting shotguns currently available, it's amazing to me that hunters will spend $500 to $1000 customizing their guns into "modern" turkey hunting shotguns. In extreme cases, expert barrelsmiths have been known to "back bore" a barrel several thousandths of an inch larger than a true 12-bore, thereby reducing chamber pressure on the shot wad as it travels down the bore. In many instances, the bore size gradually returns to its original dimension several inches before reaching the choke, thereby serving two purposes. First, it adds several more thousandths of constriction to the bore. And second, it forms a step in which the plastic wad is pulled back from the shot load, which then travels through the choke tube without interference from the wad. Properly done,

back-bored barrels will generally shoot a little tighter than a standard barrel. Still, the hundreds of dollars spent having a barrel bored this way hardly justifies the 5% or less number of additional pellets placed in the "kill zone" of the pattern paper.

Mark Drury has played an instrumental role in the development of a specialty screw-in turkey hunting choke now marketed by his company. This extended tube has been dubbed the M.A.D. Max, and it's been designed to perform much like a back-bored barrel. It's available to fit most modern shotgun barrels already threaded to accept screw-in chokes. Like the Hasting's and a few other chokes, this one extends out past the muzzle. In fact, it adds more than 1½ inches to the length of the barrel. What makes this tube different from a simple extended choke are the parallel rectangular ports that run lengthwise around the outside of the choke tube. Once the compressed gas of the burning powder charge has pushed the wad and shot column through the choke, pressure behind the wad is released through these ports. This allows the lighter plastic wad to decelerate immediately while the shot charge travels on through what's left of the choke. In many cases, it's the wad that creates those holes in the center of your pattern—exactly where an ol' gobbler's head is likely to be. Custom ported chokes like the M.A.D. Max can put a dozen or more extra pellets into the kill zone, and for a fraction of what a custom back-bored barrel will cost ($75-$100).

After a morning of good calling and precise shooting, the author proudly throws a downed bird over his shoulder.

As we've seen, the wad plays an important role in shotshell performance. Its tough plastic base forms a gas seal needed to tap the push created by the burning powder charge. The walls, sleeves or petals of the shot cup, meanwhile, protect the lead pellets from wear as the shot column travels down the bore at high velocity. A poorly designed wad can, however, keep on pushing hard once it exits the muzzle. The result can be a donut-shaped pattern, with few

When a turkey's head is as well-centered with a dense pattern as this one, the bird should be laying on the ground. (Mark Drury photo)

Several years ago, I acquired a bag of "Turkey Ranger" 12-gauge plastic wads from Ballistic Products (Corcoran, MN) and tried my hand at reloading some of my own "hot" turkey loads. While I did manage to come up with loads that performed as well, if not better than, most factory "magnum" turkey loads, I also discovered the importance of wads that dropped back quickly from the shot charge. These one-piece wads come with a shot cup but without any slits. When loaded into 3-inch hulls with a 2-ounce charge of No. 5 shot without first making slits in the walls of the shot cup, the loads continued to blow slug-like holes in the pattern paper all the way out to 30 yards. Even when four evenly spaced $1/4$" slits were cut into the side of the cup, the wad still blew huge holes in the paper at 20 yards. The shot that did make it out of the cup printed a definite ring

pellets landing in the center. Likewise, a wad that doesn't feature sleeves or petals designed to slow down the wad and allow the shot charge to travel on to the target will continue to hold the bulk of the shot charge all the way out to a 20- or 30-yard target, where it will impact like a rifled slug.

with very few pellets in the center. But when full $1/2$" cuts were made in the cup, the wad began to excel. My old Remington Model 870 Express with a .665" Hasting's choke tube easily printed 100% patterns at 30 yards, with around 90% of the pattern inside a 20" circle.

"Many shooters do not realize the effect the shell itself has on load dispersion," comments Mike Jordan (Public Relations Director, Winchester Ammunition). "But the fact is, whatever the type and amount of shot used, the other components combine with the powder to demonstrate how a load performs and the kind of pattern it throws." Mike also points out that, when fired from the same gun and through the same choke, the patterns made by hard shot are better than those with softer shot. It's been found that smaller shot sizes generally don't pattern as well as larger shot sizes of equal hardness and quality. According to Mike, a larger gauge will almost always pattern better than a smaller one when shooting the same payload. In other words, a 2³/₄-inch 3¹/₂-dram 12-gauge load with a 1¹/₄-ounce load of shot prints a better pattern than a 3-inch magnum 20-gauge with the same amount of shot and powder. The primary reason involves shot deformation of the longer shot column in a smaller 20-gauge bore.

More than one turkey hunting expert has made the switch to the 3¹/₂-inch magnum gun, which generally allows shooters to fire shot loads weighing ¹/₄ to ³/₈ ounce heavier than is possible from a 3-inch magnum load. Here again, a longer shot column results than when shooting 1⁷/₈-ounce or 2-ounce loads out of a 3-inch magnum gun. Patterns fired from a 3¹/₂-inch gun simply do not produce center density as well as a good 3-inch gun. The 3¹/₂-inch shot-

guns, remember, were developed originally for the waterfowlers, enabling them to shoot larger payloads of steel shot for ducks and geese. These guns were never intended to be used with lead shot loads. Personally, I don't like the extreme recoil of a 3¹/₂-inch 12-gauge shotgun, and for that reason I've stayed with the 3-inch guns. Every time I've had an opportunity to compare the patterns fired with my gun with those shot with a 3¹/₂-inch with the same choke constriction, my 3-inch turkey guns have almost always produced patterns with better center density—and that's what really counts. As Mike Jordan sums up: "Point of impact is the most important factor regarding barrels and loads. The barrel must shoot where you are looking, and this is much more important than load or choke choice or any other parameter."

The two Remington Model 870 pumps I hunt with have slightly different points of impact. The shorter-barreled Special Purpose gun tends to print "dead on" at 30 yards. So when I'm hunting with that gun, I always hold directly on the head in order to center my pattern on the target. The other gun—a Model 870 Express—prints just a little on the high side. When taking aim on an ol' gobbler out at 20 to 30 yards, therefore, I'll align the beads right where the wattles and feathers meet. Again, this centers the head in my pattern.

Earlier, I mentioned how both of these guns were fitted with a rear center bead, allowing me to align it precisely

Turkey hunting expert Mark Drury packs out another fine tom.
Note the "red dot" sighting system mounted on his shotgun.

with the front bead, much like aligning the front and rear sight of a rifle. The patterns produced by the .665: Hasting's chokes found in each of these shotguns are extremely tight, even out at 20 yards, which is where I shoot most of my turkeys (not out at 40 or 50 yards). At 10 yards, my pattern is usually only 8 to 10 inches wide, which doesn't leave much room for sighting error. Fortunately, both guns shoot well from center left to right; I have only to allow for the slightly higher or lower center density of the patterns thrown by each.

One advantage of having adjustable sights, a low-powered scope, or one of the red dot sighting devices mounted on a shotgun for turkey hunting is that they allow shooters to sight the <u>center</u> of their patterns exactly where they need to go. Too often when a shotgun is aimed like a rifle, using only the front bead as a sight, the pattern will print high or low, right or left of the point of aim. The shooter who knows this and remembers how to contain his excitement during a hunt can compensate when taking a shot. But when a gobbler comes running right in, it's often too easy to forget all these things and blow an otherwise easy shot.

Mark Drury hunts with a Remington Model 870 pump in 3½-inch magnum, shooting with maximum velocity and shot load magnum shotshells. Depending on whether he's hunting the open timber of the Midwest or South, or the open prairies out West, he'll have either an extra-full .665" or an extra, extra full .655" choke tube installed. With those loads and muzzle constrictions, recoil can be quite uncomfortable. He now relies heavily on a low-powered scope or a red dot sighting device when making a precise shot on a gobbler. That means the gun must be sighted in from a bench rest—like a rifle. When shooting at paper, recoil is always more noticeable, especially when it takes five to ten shots to adjust sights or scope while placing the center density of the pattern at point of aim.

"I start out with light loads when sighting in my shotgun," reports Mark Drury. "Such loads save my shoulder from recoil and allow me to refine my aiming point and pattern without getting slammed by the heavy recoil of magnum turkey loads. This is especially true when sighting in a low power scope or red dot type sight. Once the pattern is printing where I want it at 30 yards, I'll switch to the loads I'll actually be hunting with and make the little adjustments necessary so that my shotgun is hitting right on."

Young hunters are especially sensitive to recoil. Some gas-operated, semi-auto shotguns are a little easier on the shoulder. That's because some of the gases are used to operate the system, thus softening recoil. Youth hunters often begin their turkey hunting careers with a 20-gauge, which is fine except when the toms absolutely refuse to come in closer than 30 yards, beyond the effective range of a 20-gauge shotgun. When my son, Adam, decided he wanted to try turkey hunting, he was only 13 years old. He's 6"3" now, but

back then he was on the small side for his age. But he wanted desperately to use my Remington 870 turkey gun, and that's what he started with.

We began by sitting down at the bench and patterning the shotgun with light field loads on paper targets at 25 yards. That was as far as I allowed Adam to fire a shot. After a half dozen rounds, each one on a new sheet of paper, the youngster pretty well understood how to hold the pattern to center. Next, Adam and I went into the woods near our home and we sat down next to a tree, just as we would do come opening day of the turkey season. I took a half-dozen bright red Coca-Cola cans, walked out 15 to 25 yards from where Adam sat, and slipped them over the tips of some branches I had cut, about three feet off the ground or about the height of a gobbler's head. Then I handed him one light load at a time and instructed him how to take aim at a can and squeeze off a shot. After he had put 20 to 30 pellets into a can each round, I knew Adam was ready to go turkey hunting.

Well before daylight on the first day of the season, Adam and I headed up a ridge covered with hardwood. We took only one shotgun (my old Remington) because I didn't want the boy to become fatigued before the hunt began. I also wanted to slip a 3-inch magnum shotshell in the chamber without his knowing it. My thinking was that if we got a bird in close enough for a shot, the young hunter in his excitement would never notice the extra recoil.

Come the first good light, we had not one, but four gobblers responding to my calls, each one coming toward us from a different direction. We knew that the bird almost directly across from us would be the first to reach the small clearing where we waited. Well before the bird might become aware of our presence, I slowly turned Adam in the direction of the oncoming turkey and told him to rest the forearm of the pump gun on his left knee. Suddenly, the bird walked into view 20 yards away. Like a real pro, my young son waited until the turkey had moved behind a big oak before he adjusted the muzzle of the shotgun. A few seconds later, the tom walked out from behind the tree, his neck stretched skyward looking for the hen that had lured him there. I was just about to whisper "shoot" when the big 12-bore roared and the gobbler fell. The next thing I knew, Adam had picked himself up off of the ground and ran out to claim his first wild turkey tom. Then he looked me right in the eye and blurted out, "My gawd, Dad, what in the hell did you put in that gun?" He soon forgot about the recoil of the 3-inch magnum shotshell, being more intent on putting his tag on the leg of a dandy 25-pound trophy gobbler.

When I first began hunting the wild turkey years ago, I thought it took something really big—like No. 2s or BBs—to down a bird the size of a wild turkey. Today, shot sizes that big are outlawed in most states, due primarily to safety reasons. Unfortunately, more hunters are shot accidentally during

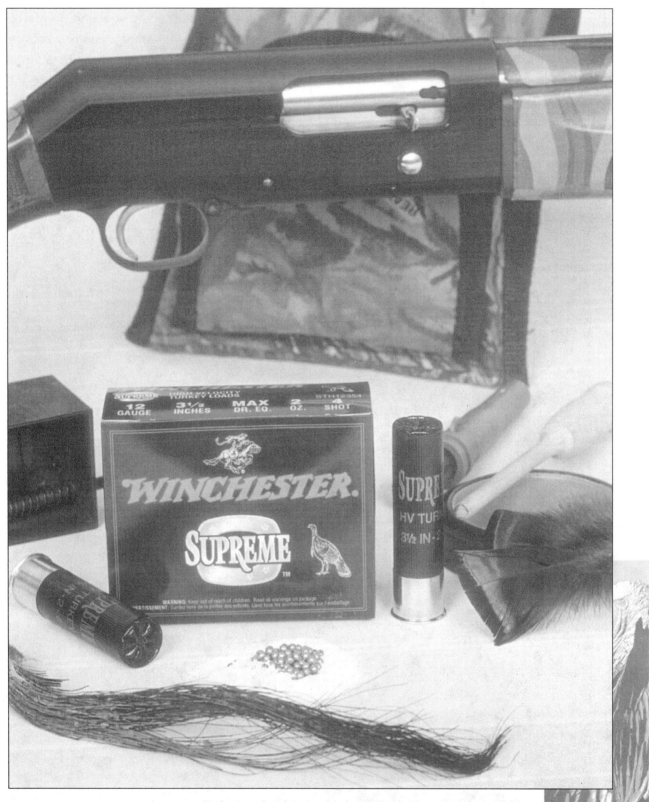

Today's turkey hunting loads are the best ever made available. Shown is Winchester's "Supreme" High Velocity Turkey load.

Mark Drury examines his "M.A.D. Max" extended shotgun choke tube, which was developed specifically for the turkey hunter.

turkey season than in any other. There are two reasons for this. One, the turkey hunter is imitating turkeys in order to attract turkeys, some of whom turn out to be other hunters., Second, the turkey hunter, when he is fully decked out in camouflage, can be extremely difficult for other hunters to see. The slightest movement—whether a hunter works a box call, adjusts his position, or even turns his head to observe an oncoming hunter—can be enough to trigger a shot. Moreover, larger shot sizes, like No. 2s and BBs, fired from less

than 50 yards away can have lethal consequences.

The most commonly used shot sizes for hunting the wild turkey are now No. 4s, 5s and 6s. It takes only two or three pellets in the neck vertebrae or the brain to bring down the largest wild turkey tom. Turkey hunters once shunned shot sizes as small as No. 5 or 6, but today they are the most widely used. Having used high velocity and buffered magnum shotshells, hunters have discovered that even 5s and 6s have more than enough energy to do the job out at 40 yards. These shot sizes, which translate into a lot more pellets to the ounce, create denser patterns. A two-ounce load of No. 4s contains 270 pellets, a two-ounce load of No. 5s contains 340 pellets, and the same payload of No. 6 shot contains

shots are often on the long side, I usually chamber a two-ounce load of No. 5s for my first shot, backing it up with two two-ounce loads of No. 4s. In the event that I roll a bird that tries to get back up, the larger shot size stands a better chance of breaking a wing or leg, thereby eliminating a wounded gobbler who tries to fly or run off.

Mark Drury believes that practicing with a shotgun is as important, if not more so, than practicing with your calls. He recommends spending enough time shooting the gun on pattern patter until you know exactly how well it performs at 10, 20, 30, 40 and even 50 yards. Both Harold Knight and David Hale agree, adding how important it is to simulate taking a shot at a gobbler from a sitting position with the gun propped up on your knee. And Mark

PELLET COUNT – LEAD SHOT

Shot Size (ounces)	1 1/8	1 1/4	1 3/8	1 1/2	1 5/8	1 7/8	2	2 1/4
#6	253	281	309	337	366	422	450	506
#5	191	212	234	255	276	319	340	382
#4	152	169	186	202	219	253	270	304

450 pellets. The chart above indicates how many pellets are in a given load.

I now shoot more No. 5s than any other shot size. Occasionally I'll also hunt with 6s, especially in areas where heavy timber is dense with late season foliage and shots are likely to be well within 30 yards. When hunting out west, where much of the country is open and

Drury strongly urges every hunter to experiment with different brands of ammo and shot sizes to see which ones work best in a particular shotgun. "Every shotgun has a mind of its own," he advises. "So try different chokes, different guns, different loads. Sooner or later, one of these combinations is going to work for you." ■

Chapter 5

Should Rifles Be Allowed For Turkey Hunting?

WITH ■ Henry Ball, *Custom Center-Fire Riflesmith*

For the avid wild turkey hunter, there's nothing quite like

luring an old gobbler so close that the soft, damp ground beneath you actually vibrates whenever the big bird rolls off a deep gobble. For most of us, it's the challenge and excitement of getting the tom in close that makes the sport so appealing. There are days, though, when even the best of us can't seem to get a bird within 75 or 100 yards. No matter what you do, that wise old gobbler won't cut the distance to where your shotgun pattern can put enough tiny pellets into the head and neck to ensure a clean kill. I'll bet that more than one of my readers has on such occasions thought to himself: "Boy, if I had my ol' centerfire deer rifle, that turkey would be in real trouble!"

A number of states still allow the use of a rifle for hunting wild turkeys, but due to safety concerns they're on the decline. In several states, rifles can be used only during the fall season. The trusty ol' shotgun, meanwhile, is the only firearm legal during most spring seasons, when the foliage is usually the thickest and more hunters are in the field. Sadly, the spring turkey seasons commonly produce a higher number of hunting accidents and fatalities than any other type of hunting—and that's with shotguns at relatively close range. If centerfire rifles were allowed throughout the country during these seasons, the number of accidents and deaths would, according to many hunting experts, rise sharply. For much the same reason, most states now disallow the use of shot sizes larger than No. 4. This discourages hunters from taking shots past 40 to 50 yards, where they might have trouble identifying the source of the turkey calls as another hunter.

As deadly accurate as a trusty ol' whitetail rifle may be for deer hunting, it's likely a poor choice for shooting a smaller, light-skinned and frail wild turkey. Keep in mind that soft-point

Many western states allow centerfire rifles for hunting the wild turkey. Rob Evans poses with a Merriam's gobbler taken with his favorite deer rifle.

SHOULD RIFLES BE ALLOWED FOR TURKEY HUNTING?　　**91**

ammunition—i.e., a 130 grain spitzer or the .270 Winchester or a similar 150 grain bullet for the ever popular .30/06—was designed to expand quickly and transfer a quantum amount of energy to a 100- to 200-pound animal for a quick, clean kill. When pushed along at 2,600 to 3,000 f.p.s., these same projectiles may literally explode upon striking a 20- to 25-pound wild turkey gobbler, not to mention a fall season hen that weighs only half as much.

Many popular "big game" calibers, such as the 7mm Remington Magnum, can totally destroy a wild turkey gobbler.

and still deliver exceptional accuracy out to 150 or 200 yards without completely destroying all edible portions of a turkey or ruining a fine trophy.

Downloading a big game cartridge for use on turkeys isn't really the complete answer. Even when the velocity of a medium bore-sized deer rifle is reduced by a third, expanding soft-point—especially hollow-point—projectiles open too fast and create excessive damage to turkeys. The best route is to handload with non-expanding

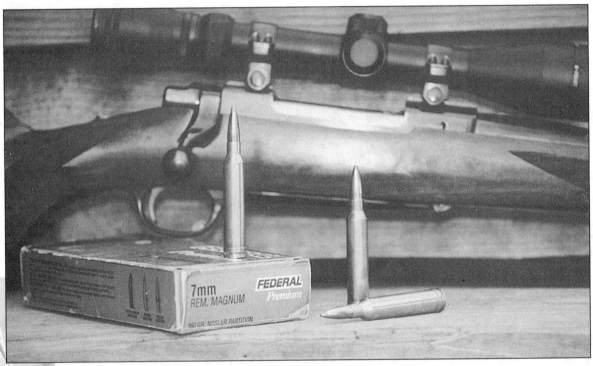

Even slower-moving deer cartridges like the antiquated .30/30 Winchester or .35 Remington may push a heavy 200-grain bullet at 2,200 f.p.s. or so and still produce far too much destruction to warrant their use on wild turkeys. Most centerfire big game cartridges, though, can be handloaded down, or armed with a more appropriate bullet,

"Full Metal Jacket" type bullets. Sierra, Speer, Hornady and other bullet manufacturers offer a good selection of such bullets, especially in .22 (.224" diameter), 6mm (.243" diameter) and .30 (.308" diameter) caliber. These bullets are often favored by fox, coyote and bobcat hunters who require a bullet that will exit a furbearer without blowing a huge hole in its pelt. If a full metal jacketed bullet can drop something as tough as an old coyote, they should work fine on a big gobbler.

If I were to put together a centerfire rifle expressly for shooting wild turkey, my first choice would be a bolt-action centerfire in .223 Remington caliber; in fact, I already own one for varmint hunting. The rifle is a Remington Model 700 stainless steel BDL model with a black synthetic stock. I chose the standard weight barrel model because I pack the rifle for great distances while walking ridge-top fields in search of coyotes and foxes. Although I've never shot a turkey with this rifle, I know it would be ideal. This slick, lightweight centerfire, topped with a good three to nine power variable scope, has been sighted to hit an inch high at 100 yards with factory Winchester 55 grain, full-metal-jacket match ammunition for semi- and fully-automatic rifles like the Colt AR-15 or military M-16.

At the muzzle, this metal-encased projectile travels at just over 3,200 f.p.s. The rifle is sighted to hit about an inch high at 100 yards, placing it dead-on at around 150 and less than two inches low at 300 yards. At 200 yards, the light bullet drives home with around 650 ft. lbs. of energy. At 300 yards, there's still close to 450

ft. lbs. of leftover energy, more than enough to do the job.

A 55 grain Sierra .224" diameter GameKing FMJ bullet handloaded for the .22-250 Remington with 39.5 grains of Hodgdon H380 leaves the muzzle at around 3,650 f.p.s. Sighted dead-on at 150 yards, a rifle-toting turkey hunter holds right on from 50 to 200 yards. If the hold was right, the bullet would not impact much more than an inch one way or the other from point of aim. At 250 yards, the bullet should hit 3 inches low, while at 300 yards it will impact at about seven inches low.

One problem with shooting such light bullets at long ranges is how easily they are affected by the wind. In the West and Southwest, where rifles are most likely allowed for hunting turkeys, a "calm" day for locals may be when the wind is blowing at 20 m.p.h., while

The key to hunting wild turkeys with a rifle is precise shot placement. With the rifle sighted to print dead on, the hunter must hone his shooting ability in order to place the bullet exactly where it should go.

Rob Evans displays an outstanding Rio Grande gobbler he
took in Texas using the same rifle he was packing for deer.

Modern in-line ignition rifles, such as the Savage Model 10ML, are now proving as accurate as many modern centerfire hunting rifles. With the right loads, they are equally effective on turkeys at 100 to 140 yards.

a windy day is one that's howling along at twice that. Under these conditions, the tiny 55 grain bullets can be blown off a foot or more at 200 yards.

When faced with shooting turkeys at 200 yards, especially under windy conditions, a heavier full-metal-jacketed bullet (the 80 grain Hornady .243" diameter, for example, or a 150 grain .308" diameter FMJ-BT bullet) may prove better choices. When loaded with 38 grains

of Hodgdon "Varget" for a .243 Winchester with a 24-inch barrel, the 80 grain Hornady FMJ bullet leaves the muzzle at around 3,300 f.p.s. When sighted to hit on at 150 yards, the load downrange is less than nine inches low

at 300 yards. At 250 yards, it prints 4 1/2 inches below point of aim.

A great choice for the old .30/06 or .308 Winchester would be the Hornady 150 grain FMJ-BT in .308" diameter. In the popular '06, this bullet can be hand-loaded to produce a muzzle velocity of around 3,000 f.p.s., using near maximum loads of powders like Hodgdon H-4350 or Alliant Reloader 19. In fact, a 61.5 grain charge of H-4350—slightly less than a "maximum" load—produces a muzzle velocity of 3,000 f.p.s. Sighted to hit on at 150 yards, this load prints the 150 grain Hornady FMJ-BT shy of an inch high at 100 yards, and only about two inches low at 200 yards. Loaded into a .308 Winchester case with a powder charge that reaches a muzzle velocity of around 2,800 f.p.s., the same bullet produces an additional drop of an inch at 200 yards.

At these velocities, either the 80 grain Hornady loaded into a .243 Winchester or 6mm Remington, or the 150 grain FMJ-BT loaded into a .30/06 Springfield or .308 Winchester, will buck the wind better than the 55 grain .224" diameter full-metal-jacketed bullets from a .22 caliber centerfire. Despite the slightly larger holes produced by these projectiles, damage to the turkey is minimal. The full jacketed bullets do not expand and there is little transfer of energy to the game, making pinpoint shot placement crucial. Any hit into the internal organs, skeletal structure and nervous system, though, should guarantee that your turkey will be laying on the ground when you retrieve it.

Custom riflesmith Henry Ball, co-owner of Bill's Custom Guns (Greensboro, North Carolina) produces some of the finest shooting high-velocity wildcats I've ever had the privilege of shooting. Henry says that since most shots at

shoot flat enough to allow a near hold-on sight picture all the way out to about 150 yards. The result is far less destruction than with expanding jacketed bullets fired at normal velocities."

Ball feels that lots of fine old single-shot and lever-action rifles are still chambered for near obsolete cartridges like the .25-20 Winchester Center Fire and the .32-20 Winchester, which were never considered powerful rifle catrid-

The mild recoil and accuracy found in a modern in-line and saboted bullets, especially with reduced loads, make them ideal for hunting turkeys (where legal).

turkeys with a rifle are usually made well inside 150 yards, the rifle hunter who doesn't mind casting his own lead alloy slugs should enjoy good accuracy and excellent results with reduced loads, especially with such old favorite calibers as the .30/30 Winchester or the venerable .30/06 Springfield.

In Henry Ball's own words, "Hard cast lead 150 grain bullets pushed along by enough powder to produce a muzzle blast of about 1,800 f.p.s. will

ges anyway. These old timers, according to Henry, can be loaded with light, hard-cast lead bullets of 70 to 120 grains with eight to ten grain charges of IMR-4227; producing velocities of 1,500 f.p.s. (or less). These old rifle can then take medium-sized game like the wild turkey out to 100 yards without destroying some fine eating.

As for the rimfire .22s, can they take turkeys cleanly as well? There's no doubt in my mind that, in the hands of a good marksman, a deadly accurate .22 rifle loaded with a high velocity Long Rifle round delivers plenty of knockdown for taking turkey. A 40 to 45 grain bullet at 1,300 to 1,400 f.p.s. can develop around 150 to 180 ft. lbs. of energy. When placed perfectly, it will do the job. Better still is the .22 Winchester Rimfire Magnum, producing around 350 ft. lbs. of energy using a 40 grain bullet.

Most game departments which still allow rifle hunting will not permit the use of a .22 rimfire. At best, a rifle chambered for the .22 LR is a 50-yard maximum turkey rifle, which means that a shotgun would probably be more effective. The .22 Winchester Rimfire

Magnum, with its 2,000+ f.p.s. muzzle velocity, flatter trajectory and muzzle energy (twice that of the .22 Long Rifle), is arguably a good 100-yard turkey gun. So even if your state allows rifles for use on turkeys, check the caliber requirements before heading out with any rifle—especially a .22 rimfire.

I've always dreamed of hunting spring turkeys with one of my favorite

smallbore .32 or .36 caliber muzzleloading "squirrel" rifles. One long-barreled percussion .36 caliber frontloader built for me by my good friend Ted Hatfield, has accounted for nearly a thousand bushytails since I first began shooting this muzzleloader back in 1983. My favorite load is good for around 900 f.p.s. and hits with about the same energy as a hot .22 LR cartridge. Anything hotter is simply too destructive on game as small as squirrels. But the rifle is deadly accurate. I can usually head shoot almost any squirrel—gray or fox —that lets me get within 25 yards.

When the 39-inch long barrel is loaded with a full 25 grain charge of slightly coarser FFFg black powder and the same diameter soft lead ball, the velocity surges to around 1,400 f.p.s., while generating some 300 ft. lbs. of energy. A load like that is ideal for turkeys inside the range I recommend with the frontloader's basic open sights. In other words, I'd take a shot at a gobbler out to about 50 yards, confident that the rifle and load will do the job.

During the early 1990s, I headed for south Texas to hunt whitetails on the famous Kennedy Ranch. I had always wanted to shoot a turkey with one of my scoped modern in-line percussion rifles, so I worked up a load for a Knight MK-85 with a 24-inch barrel using saboted .45 ACP "hard ball" bullets. The .50 caliber muzzleloader easily printed the saboted .451" diameter 230 grain Speer TMJ (Total Metal Jacket) inside two inches at 100 yards. Shooting a full 100 grain charge of Pyrodex

"Select," the non-expanding projectile left the muzzle at nearly 1,700 f.p.s. The rifle had been sighted to print "dead on" at 100 yards. During the first two days of the hunt, I glassed no less than 300 adult Rio Grande Gobblers, but none came within 200 yards of the truck. Sooner or later, I knew I'd get a shot at a bird, and so I kept my muzzleloading "turkey rifle" handy.

Early the third morning, I spotted more than 100 large gobblers easing down a grassy arroyo with heavy brush offering me a sure-fire sneak to a spot slightly ahead of the birds. I grabbed my Knight MK-85 and got into position. The first birds passed about 130 yards in front of me, followed by a group of about 20 angling toward me. Using the gnarled trunk of an oak for a rest, I held right at the juncture of the wing butt and squeezed off a shot. To say the gobbler never knew what hit him would be putting it lightly. The 230 grain full-metal-jacketed .45 slug had taken out the tom's spine, so there was no flopping or running, nor any ruined meat.

More recently, I've been shooting a non-expanding muzzleloader projectile known as the DEVEL bullet. What makes this saboted .45 caliber projectile unique are its composition and configuration. Produced by a small bullet-making operation known as Leved Cartridge Ltd. (Georgetown, Texas), the DEVEL is made from a copper-tin composite resulting in a somewhat lengthy bullet for its 175 grain weight. In fact, the projectile is nearly as long as the 300 grain Hornady XTP jacketed hollow point,

even though it's only about half the weight. When loaded ahead of the same 100 grain charge of Pyrodex "Select" I used to take my Texas Rio Grande, this bullet leaves the muzzle of a 24-inch frontloader barrel at more than 1,800 f.p.s. The 230 grain hard ball bullet I used on that big tom drops around six inches from 100 yards out to 150 yards. With the same powder charge, the light DEVEL bullet tends to drop only four inches at 150 yards, making it easier to hold right on while placing the bullet with accuracy, especially with a muzzleloader sighted to print about two inches high at a hundred yards. Bear in mind, the DEVEL bullet is totally non-expandable, having been designed for hunting whitetails and other big game.

How is this possible with a non-expanding bullet? First, the nose of the projectile features five distinct flutes running back along the ogive. A raised fin separates each of these flutes, which merge at the nose to form a five-pointed star. The theory here is that upon hitting flesh and bone, the flutes will create shock waves hydraulically, much like an expanding bullet. And since this bullet does not deform when loaded or fired or upon impact, it becomes an extremely accurate projectile.

In 1999, Savage Arms (Westfield, Massachusetts) took muzzleloading to an entirely new performance level with its Model 10ML. At last, a muzzleloader had been designed to shoot safely with a cleaner-burning, harder-hitting smokeless propellant. This futuristic muzzle-

This old Marlin Model 39 lever-action .22 is a good tack driver but a poor choice for turkeys because of its inadequate energy levels.

loader can still be loaded with older black powder or Pyrodex, but its best performance is assured with powders like IMR-4227, Accurate Arms XMP 5744, or Vihtavouri N110. I've found the Savage Model 10ML and saboted DEVEL bullet to be an ideal combination. With a 45 grain charge of Accurate Arms' XMP 5744, the light 175 grain bullet leaves the muzzle at more than 2,300 f.p.s. At 100 yards, this combination has repeatedly printed one-hole groups with considerably better results than with a variety of high quality centerfire rifles I've used.

Sighted to hit on at 100 yards, the load described above drops a mere one inch at 150 yards, which is as flat as muzzleloader trajectories can get. What this means to a muzzleloader intent on hunting both deer and wild turkey is that he can now rely on the same rifle and load. And while the fluted nose of a non-expanding DEVEL bullet will not cause major destruction to game as light as a wild turkey, it still delivers enough punch and energy transfer to drop game as large as a whitetail.

This chapter was never intended to persuade readers to hunt turkeys with a rifle of any kind. First of all, it's illegal in most states. However, if there's

a rifle hunt in your future, consider the information covered in these pages before running out and blasting away at a gobbler with your favorite deer rifle. Part of the enjoyment of turkey hunting lies in the eating. A gobbler brought down with a .270 Winchester, .30/06 Springfield or 7mm Remington Magnum and soft-pointed expanding ammo won't offer much in the way of table fare.

If it were legal and I had a permit, would I shoot a gobbler at 150 yards with a centerfire or muzzleloading rifle?

This brace of bushytails was taken by an expert marksman firing a small bore muzzleloading .32 caliber Dixie "Squirrel Rifle."

You bet I would! That doesn't mean I prefer hunting turkeys under such circumstances. Frankly, I enjoy the challenge and woodsmanship required to call a wary tom to within shotgun range—just as I do with a bow and arrow. ■

Chapter 6

How To Bag A Gobbler With A Bow

WITH ■ Ray Eye, *World Champion Caller*

Turkey hunting is challenging enough, so why would anyone

make even an attempt to bag one of these elusive birds with a bow? I ask myself that same question every time I go after a gobbler with only a bow in hand. The truth is, I've pursued a spring gobbler with a bow just once in my life, but I have bow-hunted during the fall months for more than 20 years now. Actually, I spend only a small amount of my time hunting turkeys with a bow. Most of the time, I'm going after deer and just happen to have an archery turkey tag in my pocket.

Most bow-tagged turkeys are harvested by bowhunters who do the same thing. While waiting in an elevated tree stand for deer, they seize an opportunity to take a shot at a turkey who happens to wander a little too close. In many states, though, serious bowhunters who actually pursue wild turkeys are blessed with long fall seasons. As often as not, the fall archery turkey seasons run the same as the archery deer season. In my home state of Illinois, for example, I can hunt turkeys with a bow each fall for nearly 3½ months, beginning on October 1. During the fall seasons, hunters aren't usually restricted to shooting gobblers only. Hens also become fair game, increasing the opportunity for shots.

When it comes to bowhunting for turkey, Ray Eye comments, "You simply can't get good shots off at every bird that comes into range—so you need lots of chances. That's why I suggest most newcomers to the sport look to the fall seasons—the later, the better." Ray further points out that most of turkey movements revolve around a major food source, one that grows near where they are most apt to roost. All this activity enables the patient bow-hunter to set up a blind and wait in ambush. During this time of the year—late fall and early winter—flocks can get large. It's not uncommon to see several hundred birds moving together. That many sets of sharp eyes can make it extremely difficult to get a bow drawn without being spotted. "The hardest part of getting a bowshot at a turkey, Eye concludes, "is simply drawing the bow. Unless everything is just right, these birds will spot the motion and spook."

or the trunks of large trees to mask his movements. A favorite setup of his is to sit with a large tree at his back and another located a few yards in front of him. That way, he can hunker down and draw without being seen by any birds who are behind or in front of him. When a turkey steps out from behind the tree in front of him, he's fair game.

The author shot this wild turkey gobbler—an Ozarks bird—while hunting whitetails back in the mid-1980s. It was his first tom taken with a bow.

Many turkey hunters armed with bows find that a blind of some sort—either made from brush, cornstalks or other natural materials, or camouflage material—provide enough cover to get an arrow back to full draw. Ray Eye, however, likes to use the lay of the land, heavy brush,

Several seasons back, I bowhunted for whitetails along the edge of a soybean field. Late each afternoon, more than a hundred turkeys would ease their way along the edge of the field on their way to roost. They'd scratch through piles of shaft looking for remnant beans,

HOW TO BAG A GOBBLER WITH A BOW

Most wild turkeys harvested by bowhunters are shot from elevated tree stands by those in search of whitetails—provided they can draw their bows all the way without being spotted.

but most of their feeding took place in a cornfield half a mile away. The open soybean field, however, offered nice, easy access to the timbered ridge where the birds roosted just about every night.

While the turkeys always entered the woods about a hundred yards from my tree stand, I noticed that each evening, in late December, they passed within 25 yards of an old blown-over oak with lots of limbs. That downed tree itself, I knew, wouldn't offer enough cover to get a bow to full draw without spooking the birds. So I took a piece of surplus military camouflage netting and draped it over several large limbs close to the ground, then climbed in behind it, leaving a two-foot opening in front of where I sat. I now had a window through which to watch and shoot a gobbler. That first evening, I watched more than a hundred turkeys file past me at 20 to 30 yards, including four nice gobblers who brought up the rear of the procession. An easy 20-yard shot sent a 22-pound tom flopping and rolling. My razor-sharp broadhead had found its mark, and the bird struggled only 50 yards or so before the thrashing ended.

"Shooting from a sitting position can be difficult with a bow," Ray Eye confesses. "I prefer to rest on one knee with the bow vertical in front of me." Another important element in taking a wild turkey with a bow, he feels, is to learn when exactly to make a move—and then make it quickly. Ray often uses a recurve bow, which he shoots instinctively, enabling him to get off a shot with lightning speed. He doesn't have to worry about holding the bow at full draw or aligning sights. He simple gets ready for the shot, and when it's time to act he brings the bow to full draw and instinctively looks down the arrow. When everything looks right, he releases. His style, similar to the "snap-shooting" favored by the late Fred Bear, happens so fast that a turkey does not have time to react.

This style has worked well for Ray Eye, enabling him to take many a turkey with a bow. It's a style that works well for him—but not for me. I have to take a much more deliberate aim, just as I would when making a shot on a deer or any other big game animal. I want that arrow to hit precisely where I'm aiming. To my mind, there's a lot more to bow-bagging a wild turkey than shooting a sharpened stick through a body covered with feathers. I opt for a moderately fast compound bow with at least 65 percent let off, but I prefer 80 percent. It allows me to come to full draw, refine my anchor point, steady my sight pin on the turkey and, when necessary, hold the bow at full draw for up to five minutes. I can't do that with a recurve, not even one with a light 40-pound pull. When I do go after turkeys with a bow, it's the same one I use for hunting whitetails, which I shoot almost year-round.

Over the years, I've gravitated toward a shorter single-cam bow, one that can launch a full-length 31-inch aluminum arrow at around 230 or 240

f.p.s. Often, a bow that's a little faster can be beneficial, especially in open country where shots are made at 30 to 40 yards. A faster bow—when shot with lighter, carbon-type arrows and broadheads—shoots flatter, hence compensating for slight misjudgments of distance. Most bows, which can launch a carbon arrow at 260 to 280 f.p.s., allow a hunter to rely on a single sight pin from 10 to 30 yards. The impact of the arrow at any point in between may vary by only a few inches, which is important when shooting for the small vital areas of a wild turkey. Precise shot placement when bowhunting these birds is extremely important.

Shotgunners have long realized that the best place to hit a turkey with a hefty load of No. 4, No. 5 or No. 6 shot is in the head and neck areas. These are the only parts of a wild turkey where the tiny pellets can penetrate deep enough to reach vital areas—in this case, the neck vertebrae and the brain. For bowhunters, the head and neck make tough targets. For one thing, rarely will a turkey stand perfectly still, like some statue, allowing the archer to refine his sight picture sufficiently to hit the head with an arrow. A turkey's head is always moving, twisting and turning, bobbing back and forth, looking for danger, food or other turkeys. The shotgun hunter who throws a dense 20-inch diameter pattern can catch the head and neck with almost any part of that pattern and still down a turkey cleanly. The bowhunter who shoots a single

broadhead tipped arrow shaft must be right on target.

So exactly where do you shoot a turkey with a bow? It all depends on which direction the bird is facing. Remember, a turkey's heart and lungs ride high in the chest cavity. When a gobbler is looking straight at you, try placing the arrow slightly above the base of the beard and below the waddles at the bottom of his neck. When a hen is the target, place the arrow three to four inches below the bottom of the neck. The arrow should strike the internal organs and catch the spine as well upon exit.

A favorite strategy of mine when hunting wild turkey with a bow is to place the arrow squarely through the upper center of the back. The vital spot to aim for is like an oblong circle measuring about three to four inches in width by six or seven inches in length. That vital spot is located between the wing butts. An arrow that travels through this area should catch vital internal organs and often the bird's spine as well. It's a shot I go for whenever turkeys pass beneath my elevated deer stand. If a turkey is working past me broadside, I'll stick the arrow in at the butt of its wing. A square hit from this angle should pass through the chest cavity and perhaps break one or both wings, ensuring the turkey's inability to fly off. It may run like hell—but it won't fly off.

A strutting gobbler offers other really tough shots for bowhunters. Once he's all puffed up, it becomes even more

Noted bowhunting authority Rob Evans shows off a fine Nebraska
Merriam's gobbler taken with a single well-placed arrow.

Like many successful archery turkey hunters, Rob Evans generally relies on the same broadhead he uses when hunting deer.

difficult to determine where the vitals lie. The feathers on the back stand up to make the tom look taller, so there's a tendency to shoot too high on a broadside bird. Keep aiming at the butt of the wing, though, and your arrow will stay in the ball park. Another great shot on a strutting bird is to wait until it turns directly away from you, then hold for the base of the tail. A square hit here will take out the spine and some of the vitals. Also, when a strutting gobbler faces away, it can no longer see the hunter come to full draw, make sight adjustments and release the arrow. This shot is a favorite among bowhunters

who like to go after adult gobblers in the spring.

"Putting the shot where it needs to go can be plenty challenging," advises Ray Eye. "Turkeys have a habit of taking an extra step about the time the bowstring slips from your fingers. Even when they're standing still like a stone, you must hit them in the right place. I never shoot at a turkey with a bow if he's over twenty yards away. I prefer them at twenty feet! Also, when a bird stands sideways, keep your shots high and forward. My favorite shot is when the turkey faces away from me, because the target is so easy to see. Put an arrow through the upper part of the bird's back and you've struck home. A bird that's walking straight at you offers a good shot as well. If it's a gobbler, try to put an arrow right where the beard enters the body."

As to which type of point works best on turkeys, every bowhunter has his own favorite. Off and on for the past few decades, broadhead manufacturers have offered special heads for hunting turkeys only. Most are built so they will not pass all the way through the bird. Instead, spur-like blades (or forward-facing barbs) actually make certain the head and arrow will penetrate only half-way and remain in the turkey—no matter whether it runs, flies or thrashes about following the hit. Also available are star-shaped washer arrangements which can be fitted between a screw-in type broadhead and the insert of an arrow shaft. These devices will slow the arrow on impact and keep it from zipping right through a turkey.

My preference has always been to shoot the same three-bladed, razor-sharp insert-type broadheads I used on deer. My bow has been tuned to shoot these arrows with great accuracy. I'd much rather put a 1^3/$_8$- to 1^1/$_2$-inch-wide cutting width straight through where it needs to go, rather than try to shoot something with a wider cut but hits in a different way than the arrows I use for whitetails. I tend to favor 100 to 125 grain Muzzy or Thunderhead broadheads. Normally, I shoot a 65-pound pull compound bow. I've also hunted on several occa-sions with mechanical-type heads that shoot like a field point, then open up on impact. The WASP Jack-Hammer points are definitely my favorites. They open perfectly every time I use them, whether on deer or turkey. I can cut a huge 2-inch swath, and anything hit with one is guaranteed not to go far.

"There are many theories about what makes the best turkey hunting arrow," comments Ray Eye. "I shoot the same thing I use for deer—a big three- or four-bladed broadhead. Its cutting edge is wide, and I can usually put an arrow where I want it. I'm convinced that accuracy is the key. Of the dozens of gobblers I've shot through the heart, lung and liver regions, few have done more than thrash about for a few mo-ments after the shot."

I know many bowhunters who swear by the use of string trackers when hunt-ing wild turkey. These devices attach to the bow, much like a bowfishing reel, and are spooled with an extremely lightweight white or brightly colored line attached to the rear of the arrow. When the arrow leaves the bow, the line freespools from the tracker. Thus, should a wounded bird run or fly off, the line will help locate the downed bird. Some experienced bowhunters, on the other hand, scoff at the idea of using a string tracker on turkeys, claiming that it creates unnecessary drag on the shaft and could impede its flight. Others insist that when a turkey flies or runs off, there generally won't be enough line on the tracker to do the hunter any good.

When given a proper shot, I always try to shoot through the spinal column, which immediately puts an end to any attempted fly-away or run-off. Of more than a dozen turkeys I've taken with a bow, about one-third either ran or flew off after being hit. By paying close attention, I've recovered all but two turkeys I've hit with an arrow. One particular gobbler I shot while living in the Ozarks of Missouri was a classic example of what a center-shot gobbler will do when an arrow passes through his vitals but misses the backbone. I was on my way out from bowhunting for deer a few days before Christmas when I spotted several gobblers making their way through thick undergrowth about a hundred yards from where I had stopped to catch my breath. The two big birds were headed directly to where I stood leaning against an ancient old oak. When they passed behind the trunk of another oak about 75 yards away, I quickly slipped around to the other side of the tree and readied an arrow on my bow.

I tracked the turkeys' progress as they walked in the dry leaf cover. Carefully, I peeked around the tree. They were barely 25 yards away, coming on at a brisk pace. Using the trunk of the big oak for cover, I came to full draw and waited. Barely two or three minutes later, one of the birds stepped out from behind the trunk of another tree 15 yards away. My sight pin was dead center on his chest slightly above the beard. At the instant I released, I knew the bird had spotted me, but it was too late. The arrow drove home and zipped right through the gobbler and sent him rolling all the way down the steep ridge I had just climbed. I ran to the edge of the ridge and watched the bird thrash around for half a minute or so before rising to its feet and heading up the hollow at a relatively fast walk. I couldn't see the bottom of the hollow, but the sides of the ridge surrounding it were visible. I stood and watched for ten minutes, but the turkey was apparently not headed up the steep slope.

I eased back to the bottom of the ridge and made my way slowly along the rocky wash, working upward in the direction I'd last seen the turkey. Then, about two hundred yards up the hollow, there it lay, all sprawled out on the leaves. The arrow had hit solidly through the chest cavity, but a slight angle on the hit had caused the arrow to miss the spinal column altogether. By observing closely where the bird had gone following the hit, I was able to recover it. Had I run after the 22-pound tom, I may never have located it.

The one spring gobbler I did take with my bow was a classic hunt I'll never forget. It was also the first gobbler my son Adam had called in for ol' dad. We were hunting a large tract of private ground used for raising elk, red stag, fallow deer, sika deer and a few other exotic big game animals. The 1,800-acre ranch was also home to one of the largest Watusi cattle herds in the United States. The landowner wasn't too crazy about our hunting for turkeys with guns

Good concealment and effective camouflage are vital when shooting a wary wild turkey with a bow. Eric Miller is shown as he prepares to release an arrow.

The author relies on the same bow, arrows and broadheads whether he's after a big wild turkey gobbler or a large whitetail buck.

on his property, but when I asked if we could go after the numerous birds who lived there with a bow, he was quite agreeable.

My 14-year-old-son had been practicing quite a bit with a box call and had become quite good with it. So when he asked if he could call for me, how could I refuse. We made contact with a gobbler at daybreak but were unable to get the tom to work. Since I knew where this particular bird like to strut, we made our way slowly to a known strut zone. Using two strips of camo netting, we quickly erected two blinds—one for me and the other for Adam, who would be calling from 20 yards behind me.

About ten o'clock, I motioned for Adam to make a couple of calls. He stroked the paddle of the box call and the gobbler answered immediately from about 50 or 60 yards away. Barely a few minutes latter, we spotted his fanned tail headed up the side of a slight rise, working in our direction. Like a pro, Adam clucked and lightly purred on his call, causing the tom to spit and drum in response to those seductive sounds. As the gobbler eased behind the trunk of a big tree scarcely 10 yards away, I rose up on my knees and brought the bow to full draw. At the same instant, Adam clucked a few more times and the tom stepped out, his attention riveted in the direction of the call. I refined my sight hold at the butt of the wing and released. The bird flopped a couple of times and then lay still.

Like most turkey hunters who purposely go after these birds with a bow,

Ray Eye feels that the fall season provides bowhunters with their best chance for taking any kind of turkey with a bow. At that time of year, hens often group with other hens and their poults of the year. By scattering these flocks, an adept caller can easily call some of the young birds back in by imitating the sounds of an adult hen trying to reassemble her brood. Fall is also the time of year when you'll begin to notice groups made up of jakes only. When these juvenile gobbler become rowdier than the old hens can stomach, they're often banished from the flock of hens and other poults. In so doing, they can be extremely vulnerable to being called. Bachelor groups of adult gobblers in the fall also offer bowhunters a chance to hang their tags on trophy class birds. While calling pros like Ray Eye have developed techniques to get these birds to respond. I personally haven't had much luck in calling adult toms. Whenever I have my sights set on harvesting a big bird in October, November or December, I usually revert to "spot and stalk" tactics.

In general, fall turkeys can be quite patternable. Even big adult gobblers get into the habit of doing the same things--following the same route and feeding in the same places, especially during early winter when the weather begins to turn cold and snowy. By observing these patterns for a few days, a patient hunter can put up a blind and wait for some old gobblers. He can also glass for them, then try slipping ahead to intercept their movements. Dried or

Spotting and stalking a turkey can be extremely challenging. Watching a flock of birds through binoculars for a short period often provides a bowhunter with clues on when to slip ahead and wait in ambush.

frozen creek beds, heavy brush, standing corn, broken terrain and other natural or manmade places of cover should be utilized to their fullest. Never forget: you are hunting wild turkeys. Anything they feel is out of place, or any movement made by the hunter no matter how slight, can spook them. Still, the bowhunter who looks for a dandy gobbler with a well-placed arrow should seriously consider the spring seasons. Because of their exceptionally strong breeding instincts, the big adult gobblers are the most vulnerable. It's also the time when they respond best to calling.

As Ray Eye explains, "The spring seasons aren't usually as lengthy as in the fall, and they're for gobblers only. But they do have their advantages. For one thing, there's usually more foliage in the spring to help hunters get off a shot without being seen. Then watch these birds start strutting, gobbling and carrying on. If you think the hunt is exciting with a gun, you ought to try it with a bow!"

Any hunter who knows what he's doing can squeeze a lot of fun out of the spring season. With skill and some luck, he may even carry home one of the most coveted prizes in bowhunting. ∎

Chapter 7

Hunting Toms With a Muzzleloader

WITH ■ William "Tony" Knight, *Founder, Knight Rifles* ■
Tim Lenartz, *President, Lenartz Muzzleloading*

It's been said that the wild turkey represents the greatest

challenge a muzzleloading hunter can tackle. A wise old gobbler's uncanny ability to give a hunter the slip makes him as worthy a trophy as any big game animal. In fact, many experienced hunters, who often refer to this magnificent animal as America's "Big Game Bird," treat the wild turkey with the same respect given to a trophy class whitetail buck or bull elk. One thing is for certain, the muzzleloading hunter who underestimates the survival instincts of this big bird is destined to go home empty-handed. The wild turkey is no dummy, and it takes a hunter with above average woods savvy to be successful season after season, especially when hunting with a muzzleloading shotgun.

Success with a frontloader rifle in bringing down whitetails and other big game has encouraged a growing number of hunters to go after gobblers with a slow-to-load, often short-range frontloading smoothbore. Where it was once nearly impossible to get drawn for a turkey permit, hunters can now—thanks to exploding turkey populations—purchase tags across the counter. In many states the season limit is often two or three birds. To instill fresh challenges into taking one or more of those toms, many accomplished wild turkey hunters have turned to the muzzleloading shotgun.

The fact is, lure a gobbler close enough and it can be taken cleanly with almost any muzzleloading smoothbore. However, a big ol' wild turkey that's strutting down a ridge or across an open field straight toward you can look a lot closer than it is. Even at 30 or 40 yards, a wild turkey can seem far too large a target to miss. But keep in mind that a big gobbler topping 20 pounds can be a tough target to put down. The target is not the entire bird, but rather the head and neck. That translates into a kill zone measuring approximately two inches wide by 10 inches long. Put

Taking a wild turkey gobbler with a muzzleloading shotgun can be a challenging task.

enough pellets into that area and a turkey will be flapping his last even as the smoke thins. It only takes two or three pellets into the neck vertebrae or brain of a turkey to produce a clean kill. Most flintlock or percussion ignition shotguns from the past (and their modern copies) feature cylinder bore barrels that facilitate loading through the muzzle. These guns can be loaded to throw nice even patterns producing enough center density to ensure enough pellets will hit the head and neck of a 20-yard target.

To obtain patterns like that from a barrel with absolutely no choke generally requires loading the shotgun with almost equal volumes of powder and shot, along with the proper sequence of wads. Load one of these guns with a light powder charge and heavy shot load—or a heavy powder charge and a light shot load—and the patterns will lack the center density needed to put pellets in the kill zone with consistency. One of my favorite muzzleloading turkey shotguns in years past was a side-by-side percussion 10-gauge offered by Dixie Gun Works. According to its Italian manufacturer, the barrels featured a cylinder bore in the right barrel and a modified choke in the left barrel. The left barrel was at best a true improved cylinder, so for my hunting I loaded both barrels as if they were cylinder bore.

The big smoothbore performed well with 110 grains of FFg black powder behind a 1 5/8 ounce load of No. 4s, which is close to being equal in volume. To achieve the patterns I was looking for, however, called for a heavy .125" card wad to be inserted over the powder charge, followed by a 1/2-inch thick fiber cushion wad. Next, I loaded a shotcup (taken from a one-piece 10 gauge plastic wad unit) and pushed it down

the bore with a ramrod before pouring in the shot charge. Over the entire load I seated a thin (.030" thick) over-shot card wad. At 25 yards, the gun printed at least 70% patterns with each barrel, keeping 15 or so of the No. 4 pellets squarely in the kill zone. I took a half-dozen good gobblers with that Dixie 10-gauge. It's a good reproduction of a fine English percussion side-by-side (c. 1850) and is effective on turkeys. Several excellent frontloading shotguns

William "Tony" Knight, founder of Knight Rifles, poses with a super Iowa gobbler taken with a Knight MK-86 muzzleloading 12-bore with an extra full Hastings choke.

To down this impressive Eastern gobbler, Michelle Bartimus of Knight Rifles used her firm's new TK-2000 muzzleloading shotgun with a "jug choke" system. Michelle was at the time only the second woman to take a "Grand Slam" with a muzzleloader.

now on the market were designed especially for the muzzleloading turkey hunter. They throw nice tight patterns that rival the 30- and 40-yard performance of a modern 3-inch magnum breechloading shotgun.

The Knight MK-86 muzzleloading 12-bore (now unavailable) won immediate acceptance from turkey hunters who refused to accept mediocre performance from their guns. Like all Knight muzzleloaders, this one featured an efficient in-line percussion ignition system. Its 24-inch 12-gauge barrel came threaded at the muzzle to accept Remington-style REM-CHOKE screw-in choke tubes. To further support the manufacturer's claim that the MK-86 had indeed been designed to appeal to the turkey hunter, Knight shipped the MK-86 with a Hasting's .665" extra-full tube. Other features included Knight's double safety system, a receiver drilled and tapped for easy installation of scope bases or a peep sight, and a removable breech plug for easy cleaning and unloading.

The Knight MK-86 ranks among the finest muzzleloading turkey guns I've ever used. I especially liked its rifle-like handling and sighting, which made for more comfortable shooting of hefty hunting loads from the sitting position. It was also a lot easier to center a gobbler's head precisely in the dense pattern thrown by the extra-full screw-in choke. I used one of Knight's shotguns to harvest five good gobblers the first season I hunted with it, and I've taken many others since. That first spring I

relied on a Simmons 2x "Pro-Diamond" shotgun scope for exact placement, later switching over to a Williams peep-type receiver sight, both easily adjusted.

Because of the tight constriction of the Hasting's choke tube, it's impossible to load through the muzzle without first removing the choke tube. To prevent getting fine powder in the threads, I first pour in a measured charge of 110 grains of Pyrodex "Select." Once the powder is dumped through the choke tube and down the barrel, I remove the tube from the muzzle. Next, I push a "Turkey Ranger" one-piece plastic wad unit (available from Ballistic Products, Corcoran, MN) down the bore with a ramrod. Then a two-ounce load of No. 5 shot is dumped in and the entire load topped with a tight-fitting Knight over-shot wad to keep the pellets from rolling back out of the muzzle while the shotgun is carried with the muzzle pointed down. Once the Hasting's choke tube is threaded back in place, the MK-86 is ready to take a tom out to 40 or 45 yards.

My Knight MK-86 and its load could print 100% patterns at 30 yards, and with excellent center density. The way it was loaded, though, eliminated any "fast" follow-up shots. However, when time was taken to install a rear sight or mount optics on this gun, the tight-shooting Hasting's chock ensured that any gobbler strolling within 40 yards would soon be flapping its wings for the last time once the smoke cleared.

I remember well the first gobbler I ever took with the gun. Knight had just

The author displays an early season Illinois tom taken with a hefty load from a Lenartz "Turkey Taker" muzzleloading 12-gauge.

introduced the MK-86 and I'd been invited to hunt on Tony Knight's family farm in northern Missouri. That first day found me calling with fellow outdoor writer John Sloan, who also hunted with a Knight MK-86 shotgun. Right off the bat, I called in a huge gobbler, but it came in too fast and we had to let the tom walk. An hour later we were working some birds a half-mile away in a small clearing. When the toms decided to come in, they did so from John's extreme right. Unfortunately, he couldn't turn on three adult gobbler who had moved to within 20 yards before turning and heading back in the direction of a hen who was calling desperately to get

them back. Then suddenly we found the bird we were looking for: A very lonesome gobbler. We were walking a ridgetop at the time, and I would stop and call every quarter mile or so. The fourth time we stopped and called we were answered immediately by a deep gobble from the valley below. Two minutes later I repeated the call and was answered immediately. Quickly, John picked up his Knight MK-86 and rested it across his knee. A few seconds later, a big 24-pound gobbler came running in, and moments later John was collecting his first muzzleloader turkey at just over 30 yards.

Early the next morning a video cameraman named Gary Holmes and I drove to a farm about ten miles away in search of wild turkeys. Within a few hours we had listened to more than 20 different gobblers, none of which responded. Having gotten the cold shoulder from all those birds, we moved over to an adjacent ridge where we had heard some gobblers earlier. As we walked to the crest of the ridge, I called lightly and was cut short by a deep gobble barely a hundred yards away. We dropped down next to a small oak where I made a few purrs and clucks. Minutes later, two fine gobblers came strutting up the side of the ridge, heading right for us. The curvature of the hill prevented me from getting a shot, and both birds were barely five yards away before we could see more than the tips of their fanned tails. I had the head of the biggest gobbler in the diamond-shaped reticle of the Simmons 2x scope when the bird lifted its head to look for the source of the seductive hen calls. At that distance, I knew the pattern—barely 6" across— would literally decapitate the turkey, so I shifted the diamond reticle until the bottom point rested on the top of the tom's head. A split second after squeezing off the shot, the bottom inch of the pattern caught the gobbler directly on top of the head, sending the big 25-

Before adjusting the rear "peep" sight on a Knight MK-86 shotgun, the muzzleloader printed low.

Adjusting the aperture sight enables the MK-86 to print tight 30-yard patterns centered at the point of aim.

pound bird rolling down the hillside. Gary's camera caught it all, and when the tape was played later in slow motion, the impact of the shot looked like someone had hit the gobbler on top of its head with a 20-pound sledge hammer.

As well as the MK-86 performed on wild turkeys, many shooters disliked having to remove the choke tube every time the shotgun was loaded. For that and other reasons, the gun was dropped from the Knight line in 1999 and was later replaced by a new gun, called the TK-2000. Tony Knight, who designed the new model, claimed it was "capable of printing patterns as good as the screw-in choke of the earlier MK-86." The newer model reverts to an old system known as a "jug choke" and does not rely on any constrictions at the muzzle. Instead, the TK-2000 features an extension to the barrel wherein a short section is machined slightly larger than 12-gauge before returning to the original bore diameter. Shot traveling down the bore tends to push outward against the inside barrel wall. As the pellets enter the jug choke, they continue to move along the constraints of the bore, so when the bore returns to its original size (an inch or so from the muzzle) these pellets are redirected toward the center. The result is "good patterns."

Years ago, I equipped several, single-barreled smoothbores with jug chokes. One was a 32-inch barreled percussion 12-gauge that I'd built myself, and the other was an accurate 20-gauge flintlock fowler. The recessed jug-type chokes on these guns resulted in better patterns made possible by a straight cylinder-bored barrel, but they hardly matched the performance of a true choked bore. The light 20-gauge, which weighed barely six pounds, was a delight to carry in the woods. Even though the bore was small for turkey hunting, the gun performed well with hefty loads consisting of 90 grains of FFg black powder and 1¼ ounces of No. 5s. I loaded the gun with the same combination of wads I used when loading any cylinder bore muzzleloading shotgun; i.e., .125" thick over-powder card wad, one ½" thick fiber cushion wad, and one .030" thick over-shot card wad. So loaded, my little flintlock printed close to 70% patterns at 25 yards. I used that 20-bore shotgun on only one turkey hunt, dumping a fine 20-pound tom at about 20 yards.

The beauty of a jug-choked muzzleloading shotgun barrel is that the wads can be stuffed down, making it easier to load, which was exactly why Knight chose such a barrel. Although I've not had the opportunity to work with the TK-2000, my experience tells me that a jug-choked barrel simply won't produce the kind of patterns I look for from a serious turkey-hunting shotgun, whether modern or otherwise. I'll stick with a muzzleloading shotgun with a screw-in choke tube, much like the old Knight MK-86, which will always have a spot in my gun cabinet.

Fortunately, there's another similar in-line ignition frontloading shotgun on the market with a screw-in, extra-full .665" Hastings choke. It's the Lenartz "Turkey-Taker" (Lenartz Muzzleloading, Inc., Alto, MI). What makes this front-loading turkey gun so much nicer to hunt with is it's unique ignition system. "To prime this gun," explains company president Tim Lenartz, "the hunter sim-

According to Lenartz, the No. 209 primer produces easily 15 times the amount of fire possible from a No. 11 percussion cap, and more than four times as much fire as the hottest winged musket cap. Shotshell primers are also manufactured with a moisture-proof seal, making them much more

Speed load tubes make carrying pre-measured powder charges and shot loads easy and quick to use when fast reloads are called for.

ply flips the handle of the ignition or primer cover upward and drops a No. 209 shotshell primer into the opening. He then flips the handle downward to close the ignition system. To make the gun legally 'unloaded,' the hunter flips the handle upward, tips the gun sideways and the primer falls into his hand."

weather-resistant during a hunt in the spring turkey woods, which can be the wettest time of the year. Ignition with this system is practically guaranteed—and spontaneous. Even with the added fire from the No. 209 primer, I continue to snap a primer in the ignition system (on an empty shotgun) before loading the Lenartz Turkey-Taker. This burns out any oils or cleaning solvents left in the flash channel, which leads from the primer to the sources of powder at the rear of the barrel. Once the ignition system is cleared, I dump in a charge of powder, with the choke tube still threaded into the muzzle. This prevents any powder granules from remaining in the threads of the barrel. Just like loading the Knight MK-86, I remove the choke tube and continue loading with basically the same load; i.e., a 110 grain charge of Pyrodex "Select," a "Turkey Ranger" plastic wad (made by Ballistics Products), a two-ounce load of No. 5 shot, and a thin .030" over-shot card wad. At 30 yards, this frontloading smoothbore will, like the Knight MK-86, print right at 100% patterns.

Thompson/Center's "New Englander" 12-gauge single barrel shotgun with a screw-in full choke makes an extremely efficient muzzleloading turkey shotgun with traditional styling.

distance, this was truly a tight pattern. When the Lenartz shotgun arrived, the load tended to print a trifle low and to the left. It took basically three shots to get the center of the pattern hitting exactly where I wanted it. That's the beauty of having an adjustable sighting system on a shotgun designed for hunting wild turkeys. The extremely tight patterns thrown by chokes like the .665" Hasting's extra-full tube are deadly on wild turkeys. On the other hand, they're not very forgiving, either. A pattern that consistently hits high, low, left or right will waste a lot of pellets.

For those who prefer hunting with a muzzleloading shotgun, but who don't want to remove an extra-full screw-in choke tube every time they load the shotgun, a few frontloading smooth-

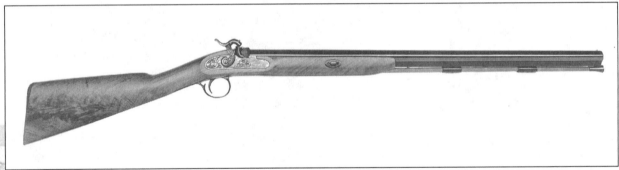

On my first hunt in western Illinois with the Lenartz Turkey-Taker, I managed to take a beautiful 24-pound, double-bearded tom at nearly 40 yards. The rifle sights attached to the barrel allowed me to hold squarely on the head. Even at 40 yards, it seemed as though 40 to 50 pellets had impacted the kill zone. In fact, when I cleaned the gobbler, not a single pellet appeared in the upper portion of the breast. At that

bores are available that come with standard full-choke screw-in tubes enabling certain wads and shotcups to be loaded right through the choke.

Thompson/Center Arms offers two frontloading smoothbores that are ideally suited for hunting the wild turkey: The modern System 1 in-line percussion model and the traditionally-styled New Englander side-hammer percussion model. Both guns feature screw-in chokes. The barrel on the 12-gauge System 1 is shipped from the factory with a standard "full" choke tube installed. The New Englander, on the other hand, comes with an "improved cylinder" tube screwed into the muzzle. Serious turkey hunters can, however, purchase a "full" tube, creating a shotgun that's well suited for both turkey hunting (with a full choke) and upland game (with the improved cylinder tube). With the full choke tube installed, either barrel can be loaded with a tight-patterning, one-piece plastic wad without first having to remove the tube. The Ballistics Products "Turkey Ranger" wad, which works so well in the Knight MK-86 and Lenartz "Turkey-Taker" shotguns, fits so tightly that it can't be pushed through the tube with a ramrod. On the other hand, the Thompson/Center 12-gauge barrels and full choke tube perform well with one of Ballistic Product's BP12 shotcups, which have been designed specifically for shooting steel shot waterfowl loads from a modern 3-inch magnum shotshell. When loaded into a Thompson/Center shotgun, the BP12 requires a single $1/2$-in thick (or two $1/4$-inch thick) felt "over-powder" wads to be seated between the shotcup and powder charge. Once the BP12 has been seated, pour in $1^5/8$ ounces of No. 6 shot, enough to fill the cup, and top the load with a thin card (or styrofoam) over-shot wad.

The design of the BP12—and possibly other wads designed for shooting steel shot loads in a modern shotgun—incorporates tiny ribs along the outside of the shotcup. In modern shotguns, these ribs reduce drag on the wad as it speeds toward the muzzle, while keeping the steel shot pellets away from the inside barrel walls. When loaded into a muzzleloader through a Thompson/Center full-choke tube, the walls of the shotcup are flexible enough so that it can be pushed through the choke constriction with relative ease. Like the "Turkey Ranger," the BP12 cup also comes without any slits whatsoever and must be cut (with four $1/2$-inch long slits) to ensure optimum performance. For several seasons, I hunted with a 12-gauge Thompson/Center System 1 in-line percussion shotgun topped with a Pentax Zero Power scope. With a 100 grain charge of Pyrodex "Select" and a 1 5/8-ounce load of No. 6 shot, the shotgun easily ran close to 90% of the pattern inside a 30-inch circle at 30 yards with excellent center density. The smaller No. 6 shot places more pellets to the ounce in a shot load than the larger No. 5 shot. Since I was shooting a lighter shot load, shot size proved decisive. (a 1 5/8-ounce load of No. 6 shot contains 366 pellets, a 2-ounch load of No. 5s contains 340 pellets). The combination of the shotgun and load consistently puts 35 pellets or more into the head and neck of a turkey target at 30 yards, a combination which has garnered several gobblers for me.

Wet, rainy weather can be a muzzleloading hunter's worst enemy, with April and May being two of the wettest months of the year. Because of their

This Wyoming Merriam's gobbler was taken by a hunter who relied on Cabela's 10-gauge muzzleloading turkey shotgun with screw-in chokes.

design, in which the ignition system is exposed to the weather, turkey hunters using muzzleloading guns are adversely affected by wet conditions. By taking a few precautions during loading, however, hunters can greatly increase the odds of firing their muzzleloaders despite the weather. Actually, most misfires with muzzleloaders are not due to the weather, but to the hunter who fails to clear the ignition system properly before loading his shotgun. Before pouring powder into the muzzle, the hunter must always take time to snap a few caps on the nipple, or to fire a primer through a primer ignition system. Either way, any traces of oil or cleaning solvents that were left in the nipple from the last cleaning will be blown out or burned. Before placing the cap on a nipple to clear the system, however, make sure the gun isn't loaded by dropping a ramrod down the bore. Assuming the ramrod is about the same length as the bore of the shotgun, it should sit nearly flush with the muzzle. When the rod exceeds the muzzle by two to three inches, that indicates the gun is loaded. If you're uncertain about it, take time to pull the load and start from scratch.

I like to blow oil out of the system by snapping a single cap on the nipple. Follow that by running a clean, dry patch down the bore, then back up and out of the muzzle. Then flip the patch over and push it down until it sits at the face of the breech plug. To rid the bore of any remaining oil, snap one or two more caps with the cleaning jag and

patch sitting at the face of the breech plug. This throws whatever's left in the ignition system onto a patch, not into the bore; once the ramrod has been pulled from the barrel, the burn spot on the patch should indicate what kind of fire has been created in the barrel. Bear in mind that Pyrodex and black powder are both very hygroscopic; i.e., they can literally pull moisture out of the air. Most powder flasks that are styled in the traditional way—indeed, most powder horns—are far from being airtight. Powder stored in these containers during wet weather can become damp and less effective. It's best to keep powder in a resealable factory can, measuring out what's needed for each shot and placing additional loads in moisture-proof, plastic "speed load tubes." I prefer two compartments of equal size with the powder charge at one end and the shot charge at the other, with both ends protected by weather-tight snap plastic caps. In addition to the load already in the gun, hunters should carry two or three of the speed load tubes with them as they head into the turkey woods, along with extra wads needed for additional loads.

When a wet day is forecast before heading into the turkey woods, it's a good idea to add some black powder lube between the over-powder and cushion wads that are used to load traditionally-styled muzzleloading shotguns. A small dab ensures a moisture-proof barrier that will prevent water from running down the bore and into the powder charge. Even when hunting

in bad weather with modern in-line shotguns loaded with one-piece plastic wads, it's a good idea to run a ¼-inch thick felt wad over the powder charge, then squirt a dab of the same lube onto the cupped back of the one-piece wad unit to form a moisture-proof barrier. A small rubber balloon or several strips of vinyl electrician's tape can be stretched across the muzzle to keep out moisture as well. Most weather-related misfires involving a percussion muzzleloader are more often caused by a wet percussion cap, not a damp powder charge. So, when hunting in really wet weather, be sure to carry percussion caps or a capper in a Ziplock plastic bag—and take time to replace the cap on the nipple several times during the course of the day.

Several years ago, I hunted most of the turkey season in Missouri with a light 20-gauge percussion muzzle-loading shotgun featuring a screw-in full choke. Spring came early that year—or at least the spring foliage did—making shots at turkeys limited to little more than 20 yards. At that distance, my little side-hammer 20-bore threw good tight patterns. Every morning that season seemed to begin with a near downpour before subsiding to a slow soaker. To make certain the priming compound inside the percussion cap was protected from the weather, I coated the cone of the nipple lightly with bowstring wax (mostly beeswax) and then pushed the percussion cap down on the tapered cone for an extremely tight fit. Next, I rubbed

that same wax around the bottom skirt of the cap for an additional moisture-proof seal. Each morning for ten days that gun was literally drenched—as was I. And yet I managed to fill my tags with fine, if water-logged, gobblers. My "weatherized" 20-gauge single-barrel muzzleloader never once failed to fire when I pulled the trigger.

Of all the muzzleloading turkey hunts I've experienced during nearly 30 years of turkey hunting, one stands out in my mind. During the 1993 turkey season in northern Missouri, I had spent most of my time guiding other hunters. It turned out to be one of my best seasons ever. And while I had managed to get out on opening morning and call in a good gobbler for both myself and my hunting partner, the second week of the season was gone before I knew it. As a result, I had to fill my second tag with only one day left. It so happened I was packing a big side-by-side, Italian-made 12-gauge shotgun with a screw-in choke imported by Cabela's. In the right barrel I installed a "full" tube, while in the left barrel was a "modified" tube. Both barrels were loaded with 100 grain charges of Pyrodex "Select" and 1¾ ounces of No. 5 shot. Even though the gun performed well using several one-piece plastic wads, I took a custom approach with the wads in an attempt to create the best patterns. Over the powder I loaded a single .125-inch heavy card wad, followed by a ½-inch thick fiber cushion wad. Next I loaded a shotcup that had been trimmed from a Remington "Power-Piston" plastic wad. Once

Tim Lenartz used one of his own "Turkey Taker" muzzleloading shotguns to bring down this big Illinois gobbler at close to 40 yards. The gun features a .665" Hastings "extra-full" screw-in choke.

the shot charges were dumped down the barrels, the loads were topped with a thin over-shot card wad. So loaded, the Cabela's double threw close to 90% patterns with the full tube and about 80% patterns with the modified tube.

Shortly after daybreak, I rolled a beautiful 24-pound Missouri gobbler with the right "modified" barrel. I took the bird directly to a nearby check station, checked the bird and immediately headed north to Iowa. I had drawn a late season tag there. In less than an hour after shooting my Missouri bird, I had filled it with a near identical bird in Iowa, this time with the left "full" barrel. I had scored a two-state double in less than two hours of hunting.

Muzzleloading for spring gobblers isn't for everyone, but it is a challenging way to hunt this elusive and wary game bird. If popping a gobbler with a 3-inch magnum pump or auto has lost some of its challenge for you, I suggest trying one of the excellent muzzleloading shotguns now available. It could put some of the excitement back into time spent in the spring turkey woods. ■

The short barrel of the Lenartz "Turkey Taker" makes this muzzleloading shotgun as easy to handle as most short-barreled, special purpose breechloading turkey shotguns.

Chapter 8

The Game Called "Scouting"

WITH ■ Jerry Martin, *Hunting Advisor, Bass Pro shops* ■ David Hale, *Co-founder, Knight & Hale Game Calls* ■ Harold Knight, *Founder, Co-founder, Knight & Hale Game Calls* ■ Mark Drury, *Founder, M.A.D. Calls*

I have an old friend in western Illinois who doesn't

place much importance in scouting before turkey season. Truth is, he doesn't have to. He lives smack dab in the middle of 500 acres of the most prime wild turkey habitat anywhere. On any given morning he can walk out on the porch of his home at daybreak in early April and hear no less than 25 to 30 different gobblers greeting the coming dawn. And those are just the birds he can hear from the house. On a good morning, the hunter on foot who walks to the backside of this little piece of turkey hunting heaven may hear upwards of 50 different gobblers.

Filling my friend's tag is simply a matter of walking up the hill a few hundred yards, setting out a decoy, and then, once the birds have flown down, stroke an old Lynch box call a few licks, sit back and wait. Actually, calling is unnecessary; at least four or five adult toms will head for the landowner's grassy clearing almost every morning anyway. Usually well before the sun rises above the horizon, a good gobbler can be found strutting back and forth around his decoy. My friend says it's even easy carrying a turkey back home because it's all downhill. "I don't know what all this fuss is about turkey hunting," he'll exclaim. But I know this old codger loves it as much as the rest of us; he wouldn't miss this spring ritual for anything. He carefully guards the quality of hunting enjoyed on his land, including provision for the birds throughout the year to ensure plenty of turkey and deer for him and select others to enjoy.

Unfortunately, most of us don't have it so good. Often, we're faced with hunting turkeys on large tracts of public hunting ground, such as National or State forests, or perhaps even large wildlife management units—anyplace

To hang a tag on such a fine bird on opening morning generally means putting in lots of scouting time before the season opens.

Expert caller and turkey hunter Will Primos uses an owl hooter to try locating a nearby gobbler.

where the birds have considerable seasonal movement, thanks to the availability of food sources. In the real world of turkey hunting, most of us need help, putting in lots of pre-season scouting in order to be where the birds are come opening morning. Many serious turkey hunters begin next year's spring turkey hunt by watching and following the birds through the other three seasons.

In late June, I like to ride around the areas where I hunt close to home and glass for hens and their broods early in

Fresh tracks in soft mud indicate that turkeys have traveled through the area. Big tracks like these indicate a gobbler was a recent visitor.

the morning, or about two hours before dark. Soybeans are often up 8 to 10-inches in height, with nice wide rows for the young poults to scurry along behind the mother hen. Spotting the young birds can be tough, because most aren't much taller than the beans they eat. Even so, when you see the dark form of a hen against a distant

edge of a field, it's a good bet that young birds are scooting along close behind her. With a good pair of 10-power binoculars, you can pick up the bobbing of their heads as they feed along the manicured rows or along the edge of the field.

Other good areas to watch for hens and their poults are in freshly mowed and bailed hay fields and pastures. Young birds simply can't fight their way through thick, tangled ground cover, and the mother hen knows this. She will frequent areas only where the young birds can move freely as they chase down an obliging grasshopper and feed on other small insects. For a month or so after the hatch, wild turkey poults can barely fly. The hen will purposely lead her brood to areas where she can teach them to feed, scratch, dust and learn other turkey traits with minimal threat from predators. That means getting out into the open.

What significance does watching hens and their poults have on the quality of hunting several months in advance? Not much when it come to "next spring." It's only when the hens make it through the summer with eight or nine poults that a hunter can look forward to hearing more gobblers a few years down the road as opposed to the usual two or three poults. Besides, there's no more enjoyable way to spend a summer evening than riding around the fields glassing turkeys and deer.

Fall is when turkeys become more visible. The observant turkey hunter will begin to notice three distinct groups of turkeys. Later, as fall heads into winter, three different groups are formed: adult hens and young brood hens, flocks of juvenile gobblers, and groups of nothing but adult gobblers. Sometimes all three groups eventually end up togeth-

turkeys. The most common group consists primarily of adult hens and their broods. When five, six, seven or more of these family groups band together, fall flocks of 30, 40, 50 or more are not uncommon. As the young gobblers become more unruly and hard to manage as summer draws to an end, the hens will often banish them from the family group. These exiled "jakes" will then band together to form flocks of juvenile gobblers. At the end of the spring mating season, the adult gobblers often form small groups comprised of four to six older birds. As fall progresses, it's not uncommon for several of these bachelor groups to join er, looking as if they were a single flock. If you were to watch these groups as they leave, however, you'll note that the hens often head off in one direction while the juvenile male birds travel in the opposite direction, and the adult gobblers go their own way. While feeding in a harvested corn or soybean field, these groups will usually keep some distance from each other. In areas where suitable roosting areas are far apart, it's not uncommon for these birds to roost close to each other, though they tend to avoid mixing. Some real battles can erupt when a jake has violated a space belonging to either the hens or the older gobblers. For that matter, jakes

From late fall through early spring, turkeys can be quite visible, doing much of their feeding in open exposed fields.

are nearly always fighting with one another, mostly because of their need to establish dominance. This unruliness eventually gets them banished from the hens and hen poults.

Those who hunt in the fall should concentrate on known feed areas. Like the white-tailed deer, the wild turkey relishes the white oak acorn. Each fall, while bowhunting deer, I carry an archery turkey tag. More than once, while waiting for deer, I've arrowed turkeys from my elevated tree stands. Some of the most productive spots are those where a good mast crop has covered the ground with white oak acorns. Over the years, I've noticed that deer favor certain white oak trees and will travel long distances to feed under them, often walking over ground

literally covered with acorns from other trees. I believe turkeys share that same partiality. So when you're hunting deer, there's a good chance you'll find wild turkeys feeding on acorns from the same trees. When hunting turkeys in late October or early November, my advice is, don't overlook a good stand of white oak trees.

When a late spring frost or long summer drought result in poor mast crops, wildlife will often concentrate around harvested crop fields, especially corn and soybeans. Like deer, turkeys will often establish certain points where they enter or exit these fields most often. Some years ago, I hunted the edge of a 20-acre soybean field in western Illinois for several evenings before I could bring down a big tom with my

Mark Drury often relies on a "silent"-type dog whistle to force gobbles from a tom turkey.

David Hale scouts his hunting areas with great care, looking for just the right gobbler.

bow. Each evening, between 300 and 400 turkeys would feed in the field for about an hour before heading to the roost. Most of them left the field right about where I had set up my tree stand for deer. I could have easily taken shots at hens or jakes, but I wanted one of those gobblers who always seemed to pass just out of range from my stand. When finally I got my shot—and missed!--all those adult gobblers never left the field at the same exit point again. Eventually, though, I arrowed a plump jake for the dinner table.

As fall draws into winter and mast crops are all but cleaned from the forest floor, turkeys of the woods become more and more "turkeys of the open field." In late December or early January throughout the Midwest, hundreds (if not thousands) of turkeys can be glassed almost any afternoon while cruising down back roads. Large flocks of birds are visible in snow-covered fields, scratching for remnants of corn and soybeans. This is a good time to take stock of the overall turkey population, but it doesn't mean those same birds you saw in the dead of winter will still be around come next spring. Several winters ago, I watched a winter flock of nearly 800 birds gather. This wasn't a single flock, but more like several dozen small flocks that happened to be drawn to the same field

where a great deal of grain had been left behind. Some mornings, I would drive to one edge of the field and watch as one group after another showed up and began feeding. Most

times, I could count 50 or more adult gobblers in the field at the same time. Best of all, that field was right in the middle of 400 acres I had leased for hunting. I knew it was going to be a dynamite spring season for me—but no better than any other I'd experienced on that same piece of property. Most mornings, I could hear five or six gobblers, about the same number as during seasons past. Interestingly, all those birds concentrated on my cornfield during the lean winter months didn't translate into a noticeably larger number of

Most turkey hunting experts warn against turkey calling before the season opens (it's illegal in many states).

gobblers come spring. As winter warmed into spring and fresh green growth began sprouting everywhere, that huge collection of birds slowly diminished as they headed back to their home ranges.

David Hale and Harold Knight, who were introduced earlier in this book, have built much of their reputations and business around the sport of turkey hunting. They agree that too often hunters see scouting only as an immediate pre-hunt undertaking. But, like the author, these two highly respected turkey hunters view scouting as a year-long endeavor. They are constantly compiling and upgrading data on resident turkey population trends, new hunting areas, landowner contacts, and other bits of information that might contribute to a successful spring or fall turkey season. As David Hale explains, "One way I scout is during deer season. I'm in the field a lot in the fall, and I always keep a lookout for turkeys and how large the broods are. Also, when I find a flock of fall birds, I'm basically scouting for two years down the road. That's how long it takes for jakes to turn into gobbling adults.

"Say I'm deer hunting," he continues, "and I see three or four old hens with 25 poults in a cornfield. That tells me this area enjoyed good reproduction for this age category, and that 18 months later there should be plenty of two-year-old gobblers around to hunt. Now sure, these particular turkeys may move a long way during that time. But the point is that turkeys are in the area, and the hatch has been good. So it'll pay to come back here and scout some more later on."

Harold Knight adds, "Another good time to do some 'long range' scouting is during spring hunting season. If you locate a big flock of jakes, that's likely to be a good spot the next year. You can bet I'll go back there a morning or two the following spring before the season starts to listen for gobbling. This is the kind of thing you need to remember, and I recommend writing it down in a note pad; (i.e.) your thoughts about landowner contacts, names and phone numbers, what you observed about deer and turkeys, things like that. Over the years that'll become a valuable little notebook."

Once you've pinpointed those areas where turkeys thrive and you've received permission to hunt on a farm or two, it's time to settle down to some serious pre-season scouting. A month or so before the mating or breeding seasons begin, large winter flocks will start breaking up into smaller groups. All winter long, five or six adult gobblers may have coexisted in peace, but as the spring mating rituals grow closer, the dominant gobblers will begin to exercise that dominance. It's not uncommon for the "boss" bird to tolerate the company of a subordinate tom, but always it will maintain that air of dominance. The closer it gets to breeding time, though, the less company he'll accept. Meanwhile, small groups of two-year-old gobblers who are roosting together will become extremely vocal

HUNTING AMERICA'S WILD TURKEYS

Mark Drury, an experienced turkey hunter with hundreds of gobblers to his credit, often begins his search for a huntable tom close to a constant water source.

THE GAME CALLED "SCOUTING"

at daybreak, making it easy for turkey hunter scouts to locate good hunting areas. Another good way to locate gobblers in the spring is simply to get out and listen in the areas where you plan to hunt. To maximize the opportunities for identifying these gobbler areas, many experts, including five-time world champion turkey caller Mark Drury, recommend scouting from a high point where you can see and hear everything around you. "Be out there before daylight…and listen," he urges. "Get those birds to gobble. Use owl hoots, crow or hawk calls, or even coyote yelps. Any of these can shock a turkey into gobbling. I definitely don't recommend calling to them before the season opens, though."

Mark Drury concentrates his scouting around water sources, which act as magnets for wild turkeys. They're excellent places to begin searching for signs that reveal where turkeys have been in the area, such as scratching for food, droppings and tracks. Few successful turkey hunters dispute the fact that the best turkey sign of all is the barrel-chested gobble of an old gobbler. But, as Mark Drury points out, lots of other "sign" are available as clues for the hunter about where turkeys spend much of their day, whether that sign was left by a hen or a gobbler.

Jerry Martin, a hunting advisor for Bass Pro Shops (Springfield, MO) and one of the best turkey hunters this writer knows, maintains that, "Tracks can tell you a lot about the turkeys that left them. When you come across a fresh track in soft dirt or mud that measures four inches or longer in length, you can pretty well bet that it was left by an adult gobbler. The tracks of a hen are considerably smaller, usually measuring around two-and-a-half to three inches in length. And because of a hen's lighter weight, her tracks won't usually push down as far as those of a gobbler."

Jerry goes on to point out, "Droppings left by both gobblers and hens are different and readily identify the sex of the bird leaving it. Gobbler droppings can measure two or more inches in length and are shaped something like a "J" or fish hook, while hen droppings tend to be a slightly rounded pile, and not quite as large." And David Hale adds: "When I find droppings, I usually check them with a stick to tell how fresh they are. They dry out after a day, so if they're soft you know it hasn't been long since the turkeys were there."

Jerry Martin looks for well-used areas where turkeys take dust baths for relief from the bites of mites, lice or other skin parasites. These places tend to be located along old dirt, timber or field roads and along the edge of grassy clearings or fields. Another great place to locate a dusting area, he advises, is in a shortly cropped pasture where the birds flop around in the microscopic dust, flapping their wings and preening themselves with their beaks. Dusting areas are also great places to locate breast feathers, which can identify the bird's sex. "The breast feather from an adult wild turkey gobbler," he explains,

HUNTING AMERICA'S WILD TURKEYS

"is generally very iridescent, often a striking combination of copper, green and purplish hues, with a distinct black tip. On the other hand, the breast feather from an adult wild turkey hen is dull in comparison, usually a dark blackish-brown tipped with a lighter brown or buff color."

Some serious gobbler hunters concentrate on locating established "strut zones" where the big birds often go after courting receptive hens. Both hens and gobblers know where these zones are, and they become natural meeting areas. One way to distinguish an area that's being used as a strut zone is to look for parallel drag marks in the dust or dirt caused by the wing tips of a strutting gobbler. Such marks look as though someone had purposely made them with the tip of a stick.

Where there's a large population of turkeys, all the sign above can be found easily by anyone with an eye for detail. Probably the easiest sign to find and interpret are the scratchings caused by turkeys with their powerful legs and sharp-toed feet as they scratch away the leafy forest ground cover in search of acorns or insects. A knowledgeable turkey hunter can look at fresh scratching and know exactly in which direction a turkey is headed. As they move along, turkeys naturally kick debris along with the leaves. So when looking at fresh

scratchings, note on which side the debris is found. Where there's no debris on one side, the birds were probably moving in that direction.

David Hale makes a good point, too: "Scratching indicates that turkeys have been feeding there. Unless these scratchings were made after a recent rain, it can be hard to determine how old they are. Same deal with dusting. Dusting bowls tell you that turkeys are using an area, but that's about all. I consider them to be secondary sign. Many

The sign most hunters look for is the sound of a deep, lusty gobbler. These five jakes, when gobbling together, can sound like one or two big birds.

hunters have the same problem—they hunt where gobblers have been, not where they're going. While all these other sign are okay, the object of scouting is to listen for gobbles, and that's what I focus on."

I tend to agree with David. I spend a lot of time in the woods, not necessarily scouting for turkey sign, but simply to be in the woods. I make mental notes of everything I see, and often I'll carry a small note pad to record things that

Scratchings are the most common sign found by hunters in search of turkey.

HUNTING AMERICA'S WILD TURKEYS

may help me be more successful as a hunter—be it deer or turkeys. When I come across a lot of turkey sign, some of which were made by gobblers, I make note of it. Later, before turkey season comes around, I'll be back in the area, listening for the tattletale roll of thunder that tells me a huntable gobbler is on top of the ridge.

Many turkey hunters carry topographical maps or aerial photos of properties where they plan to hunt, indicating exactly where they've heard gobblers. Most of my time, though, is spent hunting on property I've hunted before, in some cases on the same farms year after year. I don't need a map or aerial photo to tell me where to begin hunting for a gobbler. One exception I often make occurs when I'm headed into a huge new tract of ground—especially if it's in a national or state forest, or a wildlife management areas covering thousands of acres. Then a good topo map helps me identify areas that are most likely to hold turkeys. I note the high points that are closest to water, such as creeks, rivers or lakes. Then, according to the topography of the land and the proximity of access, I'll mark the direction that seems most approachable. More than once I've marked up maps indicating what I thought were the most promising areas and proceeded to hunt the area successfully without ever having been on the property.

During the late 1980s, I usually headed to northern Missouri for the turkey season opener. But one year I couldn't leave until later that opening week. Since I wasn't about to miss the first two or three mornings of the season, I scouted a sizable piece of the Mark Twain National Forest located only a few miles from my home. After three mornings of pre-season "listening," I located the bird I'd targeted. The gobbler in question roosted each evening at the head of a deep hollow cut into the side of a towering Ozarks ridge. Each morning, from a gravel road nearly a half-mile away, I listened to that big tom gobble his fool head off at every sound in the woods, from the hoot of an owl to the rumble of a nearby school bus.

The stage was set. Well before day break on opening morning, after pulling my pickup a few hundred yards from the gravel road, I slowly made my way up the backside of the ridge, topping out right behind where the hollow shallowed out into the ridge. Figuring the bird must be roosting a hundred or so yards below, I found myself a comfortable oak, slipped on my mask and gloves, got my calls ready, and settled back for dawn to arrive. Right on cue, that tom began to gobble nonstop from its roost. I had decided to wait until it flew down before calling, when suddenly a hen began calling 300 yards or so off to my right. A few minutes later more hen yelps sounded, only this time I immediately recognized the calls as those of another hunter, not a real hen.

Disgusted, I sat quietly for a few minutes before deciding to get into the

game. I began with a fly down cackle, followed by a series of soft yelps. The tom gobbled right back, whereupon the other hunter cut loose with a barrage of cackles, yelps and cuts. I popped right back, causing that gobbler to go ballistic. When a second gobbler began calling a mile down the ridge, I picked up my gear, slipped back from the top of

started calling with a long series of soft clucks and "feeding" yelps.

At first nothing happened, so I kept up the clucks and soft yelps, throwing in a purr now and then. I was about to increase the volume when, to my surprise, a beautiful bronze gobbler strutted up the ridge and headed straight toward me. In the distance, I could hear

Dusting areas are often visited daily by wild turkeys during dry weather.

the hollow, and hot-footed in that direction, where it was less crowded. An hour later, the tom I now pursued gobbled once more, and that was it. I had pinpointed his approximate position in a saddle along the top of a long point that jutted off the main ridge. About 30 minutes after first hearing the bird, I eased to within a few hundred yards of the gobbler, sat up in some open timber right along the ridge top, and

the loud-mouthed tom answering to every sound the other hunter was making. The only sound my bird made was that of an occasional footstep in the dry leaves. He dropped immediately after a perfect 20-yard shot with a magnum load of No. 6s. And so ended my first week of Missouri turkey hunting. As I packed the 20-pounder back to the truck, I could still hear the other gobbler responding to calls. By the

HUNTING AMERICA'S WILD TURKEYS

time I reached the pickup, the gobbling had quit. I told a friend about that noisy turkey and he decided to go after it. He told me several days later that he had spent an entire morning chasing the bird without success. He had, however, encountered three other hunters who were after the same loud-mouthed bird. I don't think anyone ever killed that turkey.

"I'll tell you the kind of turkey I like to hunt," David Hale once told me. "It's not one that gobbles 50 or 60 times two or three days before the season. He's probably going to do one of two things. He's going to attract a lot of hunters—and I don't want to get caught up in a crowd—or he's going to wear himself out and go silent for a few days. He just can't keep up that intensity for too many days in a row. I like one that gobbles a couple of times off the roost, then maybe four or five times when he hits the ground."

David Hale comments further that some of the best hunting often takes place where the turkey density may not be as high as in well-known hot spots. Many of these areas are on the periphery where turkeys seek to expand their range. While there may not be as many turkeys as you might find in more established areas, neither is there much, if any, hunting pressure. Hale feels that if a hunter can locate a gobbler in a fringe area, he stands a much greater chance of working the bird without interference from other hunters.

When "scouting" becomes little more than listening for gobbles, there really isn't much difference between "scouting" and "locating." I'll often

The dark tip of a breast feather is a sure sign that it came from a gobbler.

listen to the same gobbler for four or five mornings in a row, hoping that the bird will keep gobbling as it leaves the roost area. If it can be established that most mornings the tom will move away from its roost in the same direction, I'll wait until I'm sure the bird has left the immediate area. I'll then slip in and look over the terrain, trying to determine the best spot to set up for a particular bird. Which is the best way to get to where I want to be without alerting the roosted turkeys?

Years ago someone told me, "It's always easier to call a gobbler in the direction he already wants to go!" There's not a truer statement in turkey

hunting. Too often we look for the easiest access to a gobbler. Just because it's easy to reach a certain spot from one direction doesn't mean it's the best direction—especially if you've heard this bird enough to know that his travel plans are usually in the opposite direction. Good scouting also means knowing how to be where a gobbler want to go.

Scouting likely areas for turkeys is an important part of a successful spring

The roundish shape of these turkey droppings indicate they were left by a hen. The droppings of a gobbler are generally shaped like an elongated "J."

turkey season, but it's possible to actually "over scout" an area. I'm a firm believer in getting into the woods as much as possible. It helps a hunter to develop keen woodsmanship, which can produce almost as much instinct as clear-headed thinking and reasoning. If you know the land where you hunt intimately, and you know the way the birds are likely to go before they ever head in that direction, you'll find that

you're beginning to make more "right moves" without having to sit down and plot a battle strategy. You're learning to react to the situation at hand. You've learned how to play the gobbler's game, not the other way around.

Too often hunters educate the birds they're after well before the season opens. After being holed up for the winter, it's good to get out into the early spring woods and hear once again the gobbles of a mature wild turkey.

Too often this is more than a novice turkey hunter can resist. He simply has to call back to a gobble. When the bird responds, the urge to see if he can actually call the bird in is irresistible. Even though the season may still be two or three weeks away, there's a feeling of achievement for such inexperienced turkey hunters.

Unfortunately, getting a bird in close enough for a shot before the season begins encourages many inexperienced "scouters" to try again with a different tom. What they don't realize is that they are actually *educating* these birds. Maybe "educating" is the wrong word. Turkeys aren't all that smart, but they are sharp, which is the result of conditioning. Call to a mature gobbler enough times and it doesn't take long for him to realize there's no use responding, because there's never been a hen there when he did respond. Instead, the tom will stand in one spot and gobble—or worse yet, gobble as he walks away in the opposite direction in pursuit of a hen.

Worse still is when an inexperienced hunter calls a gobbler in close and is spotted. Never forget that wild turkeys have remarkable vision and can pick up the slightest movements. There's a reason why these birds have to be so wary. Since hatching, there's been a predator out there 24 hours a day trying to eat him, including hawks, owls, coyotes, foxes, house cats and humans. Even when a hunter is perfectly still, there's a good chance the gobbler will spot something out of place, and for the rest of that spring he may never again work your calls close enough for a clean shot. As one veteran hunter from North Carolina told me, "You sneak into the woods...and you sneak back out!"

When scouting, try not to join your buddies. At most, go with one other hunter, someone who takes scouting as seriously as you. Avoid walking across open areas where you're sure to be spotted by turkeys standing close by in the woods. Save the loud chatter until you're back in the truck. If you must try to "see" the gobbler of your dreams, do so from long distance, preferably through a pair of binoculars. Bust a bird off its roost a few times, or spook the turkeys traveling along their normal travel routes once too often, and they'll quickly change their patterns. At that point, all of your "scouting" may have become a waste of time. ∎

Chapter 9

Hunting The Early Seasons

WITH ■ Mark Drury, *Founder, M.A.D. Calls* ■ Harold Knight, *Co-founder, Knight & Hale Game Calls*
■ David Hale, *Co-founder, Knight & Hale game calls* ■ Stever Stoltz, *World Champion Turkey Caller*

Producers of hunting videos, such as Mark Drury, Harold

Knight and David Hale, are envied by turkey hunters who must squeeze only a week or so from their work schedules in order to get in a little turkey hunting. Whereas these film producers get the action-filled footage they need by hunting turkeys in five or six states each spring. To do so, they generally start somewhere in the far south and follow the seasons northward. It's not uncommon for them to begin hunting as early as mid-March and finish up their seasons in early June.

Some of the toughest hunting experiences they encounter each year occur when faced with hunting an early season. That term—"early season"—can have two different meanings. It can mean simply that the season has an "early" start date. In many states—Iowa and Illinois, for example—the Department of Natural Resources schedules three or four separate seasons. Hunters must apply for one or two, thus spreading out the pressure

while allowing a greater number of hunters an opportunity to hunt wild turkeys. It's not uncommon for the earliest season to begin around the first week of April, which means (in the upper Midwest) that snow may still be on the ground.

The term "early" can also have an entirely different meaning; i.e., the timing of the season is actually no different than its usual mid-spring schedule, but the seasonal weather patterns may be "late." As a result, a season may commence with weather usually associated with that of a month or so earlier. In a "worst case" scenario, a hunter may have applied for an "early" season tag, only to be faced with hunting in extremely cold weather.

One spring I headed south to Tennessee to begin my spring season in early April. I also had an Iowa Second Season tag, which opened around April 15, and planned to be there for that hunt. I proceeded to enjoy a successful

Hunting brothers Mark (left) and Terry Drury have the enviable job of hunting turkeys in several states each spring. Some of the toughest hunting, they insist, takes place during the "early" seasons.

four-day hunt, with temperatures reaching the 60s by late morning. The foliage on the trees was about half-filled, making it easier to move without being spotted by sharp-eyed gobblers. In short, it was a very pleasant, typical spring turkey hunt. As I headed north through Kentucky and southern Illinois on my way to Iowa, though, the foliage was noticeably less full. By the time I crossed the Mississippi at Hannibal, Missouri, and continued on toward south-central Iowa, the foliage had diminished to little more than a few

The early spring woods is a great place to be after a long cold winter. Lack of foliage can make for tough hunting, though.

buds on the maple trees. About 30 miles from the Iowa border, drifts of snow began showing up in the fields and road ditches; and as I crossed the line and drove some 20 miles farther north, nearly 30 inches of snow covered the ground. There I experienced one of the worst, most non-productive turkey

hunts of my life, even though the area was loaded with big toms.

Weather can indeed play a major role when hunting in an early season. In the South, it can rain every day, while in the North all that precipitation can come down in the form of snow. A little snow, of course, doesn't always mean that the hunting is going to be difficult. I can remember one northern Missouri opener when a light snow cover had an entirely different effect on the gobblers. Missouri's spring turkey season always opens on a Monday, and the six or seven others who shared the same camp with me had all made our way to an area 20 miles northwest of Kirksville, Missouri, two days earlier. This allowed us time to listen for birds on Sunday morning, and to do a little walking in the woods scouting for sign later in the day. Actually, scouting is nothing more than a ritual in this part of the country. Every tract of timber in north-central Missouri holds large populations of turkeys, making it a great place to be just before daybreak on opening morning. The day started out warm, and by noon the temperature was seasonal, topping out at about 60 degrees. Then some dark clouds slowly moved in and it began to drizzle and grow colder. By dark, the temperature had slid to the lower 40s. By morning, about four inches of snow lay on the ground and the turkeys were gobbling

their heads off. There must have been at least 50 different gobblers that morning—some far off, others fairly close. By 7:30 that morning, I had a fine 24-pounder on the ground. In fact, all but one of our group tagged his first bird of the season that morning. Turkey hunters dream about warm spring mornings, when everything seems perfect. But if you wait to hunt those rare mornings only, you'll end up missing a good part of the season; or, in the case of a short five- or six-day early season, you could miss out entirely. It's sometimes necessary to brave a little bad weather and make the most out of the situation.

"There are some positives about hunting in bad weather," David Hale advises. "For one thing, bad weather makes turkeys want to move faster as a group. If you can get a turkey to gobble on a rainy or windy day, that bird's a good bet to work—sometimes in a hurry! A gobbler's not likely to stand around strutting in the wind, so there's a chance he might walk right on in. If I call on a windy morning and get an answer, I know a turkey's close by or I couldn't have heard him. I know he's likely to come in fast, so I set up right there."

David adds, "Another thing about bad weather is that it keeps other hunters at home. That's when I like to try areas that are avoided when the weather is good. All the competition is home

Early open woods allow hunters to spot turkeys much farther away, but by the same token every movement the hunter makes is seen by the tom more easily. This hunter would have been better concealed with a camouflaged blind.

Well-known turkey hunter Harold Knight says that calling
a gobbler away from the hens requires great patience.

HUNTING AMERICA'S WILD TURKEYS

in bed, which means the turkeys won't be bothered. So I go hunting, regardless of the conditions."

The father north and west one travels during the first week of a long spring season, the better the chances for a spring snow storm. Rarely will I let a few inches of snow keep me from hunting. But when things get really bad, and there's a chance of being snowbound for several days, and you know you're not going to be able to get out and hunt, there's nothing wrong with using good judgment and getting out while the "gettin's good!" I recall one northern Nebraska turkey hunt in particular when nearly two feet of snow blanketed the area in a few hours. I was hunting at the time with Bill Miller, who was then editor of North American Hunter magazine. We were working a bird on the first morning of our hunt when snowflakes as big as snowballs flew into our faces. We tried working the bird for another 45 minutes without luck, then headed back to the truck. Less than an hour after the first snowflake had fallen, the ground was covered with a white blanket. By early afternoon, it was nearly impossible to drive through the snow. We decided to load up and head for home before the area was crippled by more than two feet of snow. Ten days later, I was back hunting the same area in picture-perfect spring weather. All in all, it's been my experience that a light snow actually affects a turkey's spring mating ritual less than do several days of soaking cold rain. The only thing worse is when that rain is accompanied by howling winds. I hate the wind—and I don't think the turkeys are all that crazy about it, either.

The weather is only one factor that can make an early season tough on turkey hunters. As discussed, lack of foliage can make it difficult to move in and get set up on a gobbler without being spotted. Once the low brush and sapling leaves reach half-maturity, a hunter can often move amazingly close to a gobbler and set up without much fear of being spotted. When these same branches are as barren in early April as they were in early February, though, getting close can be tough. In some woods a hunter can see clearly for several hundred yards, but a turkey can see even farther.

When there's little or no foliage, roosted birds can be even tougher to set up for. From their elevated roosts, wild turkeys can see for long distances; so if a hunter is intent on setting up within 100 or more yards, he may have to arrive at the area well before the first hint of daylight. If a hunter relies on locating a particular bird by inducing him to gobble on the roost, it's probably already too late to get any closer. By the time most gobblers have begun sounding off from a tree, it's almost impossible to get any closer. By that time it's already getting a little light— at least light enough for a turkey to spot even the slightest movement within a few hundred yards where no leaves exist to help camouflage a hunter's approach.

When approaching a roosted turkey, Harold Knight recommends playing the terrain. Trying to determine exactly where a turkey will fly down is something of a guessing game. After years of experience, Harold has learned how to read the situation at hand, and how to judge where a bird is roosting in relationship to other terrain features. Knowing these things often helps him set up in the right spot. "In hill country,"

a little knob or spot that's slightly higher or more open than the surrounding area. Whichever, I think a turkey knows where he's going before he flies down. He already has his spot picked out. Usually, he's going to fly down to the easiest spot he can get to, the path of least resistance. So you make your guess where a turkey will fly down, then set up and hope for the best."

Harold explains, "a gobbler will usually roost on the side of a hill or down in a hollow. If he's roosted on a hillside, he'll usually fly into the hills, so it's best to be on the same level or a little above him. If he's in a hollow, I'll get in that hollow with him. If he's in bottomlands or swamp country, he may fly down to

Good pre-season scouting pays big dividends when the woods are extremely open, especially when hunting roosted gobblers. It's a good idea to get out at daybreak a week or two before the season opener. From the gobbling on the roost, you can then determine exactly those areas that the birds use most frequently. Turkeys tend to favor certain areas, and while they're not likely to roost in the same tree each night, they often stay in the same general area. As Harold Knight pointed out, they seem to have a predetermined travel route once they leave their roost at daybreak.

Instead of trying to slip in as close as possible when setting up on a bird that's still in the tree, I try instead to guess which way the gobbler will go once he flies down. If you know that nine times out of 10, he'll head down a ridge, then strut along an old logging road, or wherever, then why chance busting him off his roost? A better approach is to move in before daylight and set up 200 or 300 yards away, in the direction the gobbler usually travels. This strategy reduces a hunter's chances of being spotted—and puts him right in between where the turkey spent the night and where he's headed come daybreak.

While camouflage is always a good idea when hunting turkeys, it becomes even more important when hunting the open woods or the edges of a field in the early season. This is especially true when hunting with an inexperienced turkey hunter. An old gobbler working the sounds of a good call can spot the turn of a hunter's head, a flicker of hand movement, or maybe even the shine of an unmasked face or ungloved hands long before the bird has been spotted by a hunter. While a few veteran turkey hunters may scoff at the idea of packing along a small portable blind—even if it's

nothing more than a camouflaged, curtain-like arrangement—a blind of some kind can help mask those small, telltale movements that can give a hunter away in wide open woods. When taking young, inexperienced turkey hunters into the woods, I always carry a 30- to 36-inch high blind made of camouflage netting with fiberglass poles. It weighs nothing and can be set up in a minute or two, providing the concealment required to lure a wary old bird close enough for a shot.

When setting up for a gobbler during the early seasons, a hunter should learn to use the terrain to his advantage. For instance, it's important to stay off the top of open ridges. If there's a bird at (or near) the bottom of a ridge, cross over and keep that ridge between you and the turkey until you've eased back up above him and set up. Rely also on creeks, draws, hollows or simply the curvature of a hill to hide your approach. Be as sneaky as humanly possible. And never saunter out across an open field or pasture as if it were a walk in the park. As we've learned, a wild turkey depends on its keen eyesight for survival. It can spot a human form walking across an open area at unbelievable distances.

Another problem common to early season hunts arises when the birds are still flocked together. Every experienced turkey hunter will tell you that it's more difficult to hunt a tom who's with other birds than it is to hunt a lone gobbler. The greater the number of birds in a group or flock, the more difficult it is to

bring a gobbler into shotgun range. Mark Drury says this about early season hunting: "Finding a lone gobbler, setting up on him and harvesting the bird can prove nearly impossible. In fact, a hunter is much more likely to encounter a flock of turkeys in early spring rather than a single. Anyone who has hunted turkeys knows the difficulty involved in hunting multiple birds. A lone gobbler and one who's surrounded by others are two completely different animals."

Mark has chased birds all over the country during every stage of the season, and he has learned that when a hunter sets his sights on a gobbler who's with a flock, the hunter's tactics must change. Once a caller has gotten the old hen in a flock all fired up, it's time to forget about calling to the gobbler. Rather, it's time to call to the most dominant hen in the flock. If she begins yelping and cutting aggressively, the hunter should call back to her with equal aggressiveness, challenging her. Unfortunately in these situations, the gobbler(s) often brings up the rear. Before the tom has gotten anywhere near shotgun range, the caller may be literally covered with hens and jakes. Great camouflage, a good calling position and nerves of steel are essential when trying to avoid being spotted by a turkey who may be only five yards away. In such situations, the hunter must anticipate far in advance exactly where the gobbler will move into range. When surrounded by a flock of birds, it's rare when a last-minute adjustment can be made without being spotted.

David Hale says that even when you can't see the gobbler, there are clues when he's with hens, claiming "One of the biggest clues that a gobbler is with hens is when he answers your calling, then two or three minutes later he's going the other way. His hens don't want to share him with competitors, so they lead him away."

Hale adds, "Another clue is when a gobbling turkey moves in some random direction very slowly. Maybe he's headed down a hollow or along the side of a ridge for no obvious purpose. What he's doing is following his hens, but he's encouraging you to join his harem. When he's not moving directly to or away from you, chances are he's already got female company."

There's a third clue, David points out, that indicates a gobbler is with hens: "When a hen starts calling back to the hunter, it's a good situation to be in. She'll likely come looking for you, pulling the gobbler along with her. The problem is, the hen will arrive ahead of the gobbler. If she spots you, she and the gobbler will both spook. When I know a hen is coming, I slide down against my tree as low as possible and put my head behind me knees, hoping she'll go by. If she does, the gobbler will come right on."

Harold Knight adds: "One good indication that a gobbler is with hens is if he gobbles a lot on the roost, then shuts up when he flies down. Trying to call a gobbler away from hens is, in my opinion, one of the toughest challenges a hunter faces. This is one situation

When the woods are open, a good calling position with plenty of concealment for the hunter is extremely important.

where I try a lot of loud, aggressive calling, trying to get the gobbler to split away from the flock. It's hard to get him to do this, though, and there's always the chance that an old boss hen will take the gobbler away from the competition. If that happens—and I can tell where they're going—I'll make a big circle and set up in front of 'em. Then I'll wait without calling and try to ambush the gobbler as he walks by. There's one other strategy that I try sometimes. If I

Early spring mornings can be on the chilly side, so don't put those insulated hunting clothes away just yet.

Steve Stoltz, another world champion caller from Missouri told me, "One of the most common excuses that a turkey hunter can make for an unsuccessful spring morning is that the darn gobblers had hens with them. Well, hens will be a factor almost anytime during the spring mating season, so you simply have to adjust your hunting tactics accordingly. At no other time is it more important to know the lay of the land in your hunting area. When a gob-

get on a gobbler with hens, I'll run in and scatter those turkeys, separating the tom from the hens. If I'm successful, I guarantee that turkey will be gobbling again in an hour or less. He'll be lonesome then, and I'll have him all to myself. He'll be a lot more vulnerable."

bler gets off the roost and gets with hens, he's following her on her daily routine. Keep in mind, a gobbler is always willing to take in an extra hen. This desire, along with a lot of patience on the hunter's part, can be the downfall of any gobbler."

I agree with Steve that there's much more to scouting an area than simply listening for gobblers on the roost. Not only does he spend a great deal of time looking for sign advising him where the birds regularly visit certain parts of his hunting area, Steve is also a firm believer in seeing the birds he hunts. He will spend many hours glassing feed areas and travel routes to establish definite patterns of movement. That kind of woodsmanship is what separates the successful early spring turkey hunter from the less proficient hunters who fail to succeed during tough times.

In those rare instances when Steve Stoltz is unsuccessful at working a gobbler off its roost, one of his favorite tactics is to invest an hour or so to glass established travel routes and feed areas. Even when he spots birds in such areas, he will often watch them for some time in an attempt to pinpoint exactly where the gobblers are headed. Steve will then circle around and get ahead of the birds. Once that's been accomplished he'll often glass again to see if they remain on course.

Steve is a firm believer in two things: that it's a darn sight easier to call turkeys in the direction they already want to go, and it's a good idea to use decoys, especially during early spring hunts. Satisfied that his setup location is near the route already established by the turkeys, he keeps well out of sight while setting up several decoys. Before ever seeing the turkeys, he makes a few calls, using something like a "spot and stalk" or "stalk and set up" tactic. As a result, Steve has put his tag on many a fine early season wild turkey gobbler.

Years ago, during my first turkey hunt in Nebraska, it was colder than usual for early spring, putting a serious damper on working birds off of the roost. Spring was definitely arriving late that year, and so I bundled up in layers of warm clothing before heading out each morning. After three hard mornings of hunting, not a single gobbler had worked my calls. Virtually every bird I spotted was surrounded by a flock of 15 to 20 hens. Each evening I glassed a

Outdoor writer Phil Bourjaily (left) and the author double-teamed this gobbler until it came close enough for Phil to take his first muzzle-loader turkey.

flock as it worked along the far side of a large alfalfa field. On the fourth morning the wind was blowing hard, so I slept in, spending the day hunting another farm, looking for flocks I could slip ahead of and find a good ambush point. The tactic nearly worked, but each time the turkeys kept barely out of shotgun range as they worked past. Several hours before I'd seen those turkeys in the alfalfa field each day, I had headed for an irrigation pivot. I knew if the birds followed the same route, they'd be working past me from right to left, so I placed several hen decoys about 25 yards off to my extreme left. I didn't want to chance spooking the turkeys by placing the decoys where they could see them even at a great distance. The pivot I used would also serve as a cover, keeping the decoys partially hidden until the turkeys stood directly in front of my position. At that point, I might already have the shot I was looking for. There was also a chance that the sudden appearance of two more hens might, out of curiosity, bring the birds even closer.

As I sat with my back to one of the irrigation pivot tires, I could see down the hay field for more than 300 yards. Right on cue, a flock of Merriam's-Eastern hybrid-cross turkeys fed into the field and began working in my direction. It took nearly an hour for them to reach my position, and if they stayed on course I knew I'd be faced with at least a 40-yard shot. Just as I hoped, the birds spotted the two decoys and turned quickly toward me. I dumped the big gobbler who was bringing up the tailend of the flock at only 18 yards.

Early in the season, decoys can sometimes be worth their weight in gold. More than once I've used them to lure a gobbler in close—or at least close enough for a better shot. Decoys are great when the foliage is thin. It gives the gobbler something to look at as he works his way ever closer. If there's a down side to using decoys during the early seasons, it's that some hunters become far too reliant on them. In so doing, they take a chance on being spotted. This is especially true when hunting roosted birds. Inexperienced hunters often try to set up too close to the bird. The extra movements the hunter makes as he slips out to place the decoy increase his chances of being spotted through the thin leaf cover.

When the woods are extremely open, it's not uncommon for a seasoned gobbler to work to the point where you can actually see him, whereupon the turkey will simply stop and strut. He may gobble each time you call, and occasionally he'll come out of strut and stretch his neck as he looks and listens for the hen. When he can see all the way down into a valley, or maybe 100 yards along a ridge, or out across a reasonably open hardwood flat, he knows the source of those hen calls. He also knows that if there's a hen that close, he should be able to see her. When he fails to do so, or when a hen fails to approach him, the gobbler will soon lose interest and walk away.

HUNTING AMERICA'S WILD TURKEYS

The movement of the paddle in this box call can be easily spotted by a wary gobbler. The more open the woods, the quicker a turkey will hone in on a mere flicker of movement.

HUNTING THE EARLY SEASONS

That explains why two hunters working together stand a better chance of harvesting a gobbler. One becomes the caller, the other the shooter. Outdoor writer Phil Bourjaily and I once double-teamed a northern Missouri gobbler, drawing him in close enough for Phil to harvest his first muzzleloader tom. We had a set up on a small grass field at daybreak, hoping to lure one of more than a dozen gobblers I knew would be roosted several hundred yards from the opening. Frost covered the ground and

roost. None sailed into the open field; instead, they stuck to the wooded points from where they could look down at the decoys I had placed 20 yards out in the open. Each gobbler, so eager for those hens to come to him, refused to leave their higher advantage points. Only one of the birds was actually close enough for us to see. He would strut right up to where the point dropped sharply, then gobble, turn and strut back out of sight. He was trying to lure those two "hens" up to his posi-

there wasn't a hint of a leaf on any of the trees. For late April, the woods were wide open.

My first owl hoots were greeted by half a dozen big birds who continued gobbling to each other for another 15 minutes before flying down from their

tion. The third time he strutted away from the edge and out of sight, I motioned for Phil to follow me. We eased down into a shallow creek, then moved around the point and up a small hollow. Less than ten minutes later, we had eased our way almost to the top of the point. That's where Phil took a position next to a big oak less than 20 yards from where we figured the gobbler would appear.

I called and the gobbler answered back less than 100 yards away. A few minutes later, he gobbled again, but this time he was only 50 yards away. I began crawling back down the leafy hollow, scratching and purring as I went. Phil sat ready with his modern in-line percussion 12-gauge shotgun, and a few minutes later the tom eased up to take a peek at the hen below. Phil's 20-yard shot instantly put an end to the bird's reluctant antics.

Two hunters can definitely be effective on birds who are quick to move within 50 or 75 yards of calling. On the other hand, according to David Hale, "If one member of the pair is a novice hunter, then there is some handicap involved. Constantly teaching a beginner can eat up valuable time. But if both people are good hunters and there's no jealousy involved about who's going to pull the trigger, team hunting can be the deadliest way to kill a turkey. Now, if I sound negative about taking novice hunters along, I don't mean to be. Sharing the thrill of turkey hunting with a beginner is one of my great pleasures. I get a kick out of watching other people experience the things I've enjoyed all these years."

David and Harold Knight both agree that hunting with an experienced, seasoned turkey hunter is the best way for first-time hunters to learn how to be successful on turkeys. Anyone who decides to hunt with a novice, though, must realize the handicap that's been imposed on him. The beginner doesn't know when to move, when to get his gun up, what the "spit and drum" sounds like, where a gobbler is likely to show up, or most anything that an experienced turkey hunter recognizes instantly and reacts to almost without thinking. Patience is very important for both the experienced and inexperienced turkey hunter if such a hunt is to be rewarding for both.

When the buddy system works well, and with both hunters calling, it sounds to a nearby flock like more birds are in the area. This is especially true when one caller takes a position 20 to 30 yards ahead of the second caller and both men cluck, purr, and scratch leaves. Those sounds will put a flock at ease, often to the point where they walk right in to join the feeding spree. "If both callers get aggressive with their dominant hen calls," Steve Stolz advises, "it can really intimidate the dominant hen in a flock that's reluctant to move closer. It can draw her and the others right in."

It's true that the early season turkey hunter often gets "first shot" at the birds in his area. Unless a hunter has been calling to the birds before the season opens, they shouldn't be call-shy. But it doesn't mean the birds are push-overs, either. A lot of factors determine how well gobblers will work. Consistently successful early season hunters are those who have learned to rely on tactics that at first may seem unorthodox. ∎

Chapter 10

The ABC's Of Hunting In The Spring Mating Season

WITH ■ Eddie Salter, *World Champion Turkey Caller* ■ Chris Kirby, *World Champion Turkey Caller* ■ Brad Harris, *Public Relations Director, Outland Sports/Lohman Calls* ■ Mark Drury, *Founder, M.A.D. Calls/World Champion Caller* ■ Harold Knight, *Co-founder, Knight & Hale Game Calls* ■ David Hale, *Co-founder, Knight & Hale Game Calls*

When it comes to turkey hunting, knowledge and experience

are one and the same. Hunting down a wary old tom frequently becomes a game of wits. The more a hunter does his homework, the better he'll know the turkey's terrain and the better his chances of hanging a tag on a tom. That doesn't mean turkey hunting is like Zen, where the hunter becomes "One With The Bird!" On the other hand, the more a hunter knows about a turkey's habits—especially its daily movements—the more likely he'll get a shot at that bird.

Even the most experienced turkey hunters sometimes draw blanks and go home empty-handed, especially when they're focused on taking one particular gobbler. This happened to me once during the Missouri season, when I failed to take a single shot, much less bring down a turkey. After I'd scouted my hunt area several weeks ahead of the season, I glassed a huge old bird

feeding along the fence line of a neighbor's pasture. Through my 10-power binoculars I could tell easily that I was looking at a really good gobbler. I didn't know how good it was, though, until the bird joined two other adult gobblers. The larger one was easily a third larger than the other two, and it dawned on me that I was looking at an honest-to-gosh 30-pound gobbler. I also realized that I would probably spend the entire season chasing that bird.

I saw it twice more before season opened while working the same area. Since I last spotted him in the same pasture only half an hour before dark one evening, I figured the bird must be roosting nearby. And so I began the next morning by hunting the backside of the wooded pasture. I sat up within 100 yards of five or six gobbling birds and could have easily filled my first tag on opening day, what with three fine

The author displays his biggest gobbler, a 28½-pound Iowa tom taken at the height of the spring mating season.

Turkey hunting expert Harold Knight claims there's no better time to harvest a good gobbler than at the peak of the mating period.

20- to 22-pound toms strutting within 20 yards of where I sat. At that time, the largest bird I had ever taken weighed in at a few ounces more than 26½ pounds. Only the thought of getting a shot at an honest 30-pound bird kept my finger off the trigger.

Two hours later, I was working another tom with a deep-throated gobble. This bird was tougher to lure in close enough for a shot, and his deep gobble made me think I was looking at the huge gobbler I had spotted three times before season. When I spotted the tips of his fanned tail working up the backside of a small incline 40 yards away, and with my shotgun resting on my left knee, I was ready for the shot. A moment later, a beautiful 25-pound class gobbler topped the rise within easy range of my old 3-inch magnum Remington 870 pump. Letting that bird walk was one of the hardest things I ever did. The gobbler eventually grew tired of looking for the hen (which never materialized) and slowly walked on down the hill. Soon after I heard "my" gobbler on the adjacent ridge. His gobble sounded unlike any I had ever heard. It sounded as if Paul Bunyon had dropped a 30-pound rock inside an empty 55-gallon steel drum, lifted it over his head and shook it back and forth—or so I like to remember.

In Missouri, hunting hours end at 1 p.m., forcing me to end the day without ever getting the bird to work. I hunted hard for that gobbler for the rest of the week, calling in eight other mature adult toms whom I could have taken easily, but never once did I lay eyes on "my" bird. I did hear him gobble now and then, but never more than once or twice at a time. On the fourth day of the second week, I came as close as I ever got to taking this bird. It was late in the morning, and I was walking back across the wooded pasture when I spotted a movement through the trees. When I took a closer look through the binoculars, I discovered that "my" bird was strutting in a small, flat-bottomed depression several hundred yards away. I didn't see a hen or any other gobblers, so I decided to move to within 100 yards before calling him in close enough for a shot. Everything went as planned—except for the shot. Using a small creek ditch for cover, I moved quickly to within 80 or 90 yards of the bird. As I crawled up to the trunk of a big oak, I could spot the tom moving around in the depression below. My plan was to wait until his head was blocked by his tail before moving. The instant he began to turn, I would freeze. It took ten minutes to crawl five or six yards to the tree, but I managed to do it without spooking the bird.

The first sweet, seductive tones from my box call were cut short by the bird's unbelievably deep gobble. A few minutes later, "my" huge tom began to move slowly in my direction. A few downed limbs directly in front of me provided good cover, so I could work the call without fear of being spotted. That big old tom never once gobbled again, but he would spit and drum every time I clucked or purred on the

Since the biological order is for the hen to go to the gobbler, the hunter may find it necessary to get comfortable and prepare for a long wait.

Decoys, such as this Feather Flex hen, are used to lure a
reluctant tom within effective shotgun range.

173

call. It was a beautiful sight to watch that magnificent gobbler work ever closer. But when he got to within 50 yards, he refused to budge an inch closer. For the next hour, that bird strutted back and forth only a few yards from where I felt comfortable taking a shot. And that's how the morning ended. When 1 p.m. rolled around, I sat there without making a sound for 15 minutes. The gobbler eventually dropped out of strut and slowly moved on across the pasture. I heard the bird several more times that week, and even though I entered the area from every possible direction, I never did get him to work again. As the season drew to an end the following Sunday, I summed up my two weeks. In all, I had called in 21 adult gobblers to within 20 yards, including the big 25-pound bird (the one I almost regretted not shooting). However, if I had filled my tags early at the beginning of each week, I wouldn't have spent so much time in the turkey woods. Even though I did not get "my" bird—or any bird, for that matter—it had been one heck of a season.

Most veteran turkey hunters can tell you a similar story about becoming obsessed with taking a particular gobbler. Usually, their stories end much like mine, with the bird emerging the victor. These are the tough encounters, however, that can make a fair turkey hunter a good one—but only if he chooses to learn from the experience. Even during the peak of the breeding season, turkey hunting can be either extremely rewarding or equally frustrating. In the follow-

ing pages, we've asked some of the country's most respected turkey hunters to share their experiences, advice and how-to tips, all of which can minimize frustrations and make your time in the turkey woods during the peak of the breeding season much more rewarding.

The first bit of advice most successful turkey hunting experts share is to forget about hunting one particular bird and—*hunt where there are multiple gobblers*. It only stands to reason that hunting where there are five or more adult gobblers will greatly increase your chances of taking a bird than if you were to concentrate on only two or three gobblers. Turkey hunting can be a numbers game: find lots of turkeys and you will usually find good hunting. Let's assume you've found plenty of huntable gobblers. It's time now to find the "right" gobbler, one who will gobble and respond to your calls. Harold Knight (whom you've already met) is one of many experts with a real knack for finding the "right" bird.

"Hopefully, you've located several gobbling turkeys through pre-season scouting," he instructs. "You've heard 'em, you know where they are. But the problem is, one day a turkey may gobble a lot, then the next day he won't gobble much at all, or he may go totally silent. Some days he's more excited than others."

Harold adds: "So what you have to do is be prepared to move from one place to the next in search of a turkey that's vocal on a particular day. If I know

where there are ten gobblers, I'll start a morning hunt knowing that maybe half of them will gobble, and half won't. So I advocate moving from one place to the next in search of a turkey that's sounding off. Early in the morning, I like to listen from someplace where I can hear a long way—a powerline on a ridgetop, up a hollow or valley, or any place that opens to a broad area."

David Hale points out, "One mistake hunters make is listening from a noisy place. They'll stop their truck and get out and walk off in the gravel or weeds or leaves. Then they'll shuffle around and make noise they're probably not even aware of, but it'll come right at the time that a far off turkey gobbles, and they won't hear him."

"When I stop," David continues, "the first thing I do is walk down the road about 40 yards to get away from the sound of the truck engine as it cools down. If it's a back road and there's not much traffic, I'll stay on the pavement or the hard part of the road, because it's quieter. Or I might climb up on a stump, if one's handy. That can be an ultra-quiet place to listen."

"I guarantee that the first thing David does when he gets out to listen is to take off his cap. He can't hear a turkey with his cap on," Harold Knight (David Hale's partner at Knight & Hale Game Calls) jokes. "But all kidding aside, he's probably the best and most serious listener I know. When daylight's breaking and he's up on a ridge, he's got his

The hands-free use of a mouth diaphragm allows a hunter to get set for a shot once a boisterous gobbler has approached his calling position.

The small saplings in front of this hunter may make it difficult for the hunter to move the muzzle of his shotgun around to the left in the event a bird approaches from that direction.

HUNTING AMERICA'S WILD TURKEYS

radar on for turkeys. He's tuned into 'em. He's not thinking about business or sipping coffee or whatever. He's concentrating on listening for a gobble, and he'll hear turkeys most hunters will miss."

When the bird you're after isn't gobbling on its roost, you must be ready to make things happen, to force a gobble or two out of silent birds. The best method probably is to imitate the hoot of an owl. With a little practice at forcing the sounds up from the diaphragm, most hunters can learn to make these hoots sound realistic enough to make a tom gobble. The basic rhythm of an owl's hoot, remember, is something like, "Who cooks for you? Who cooks for you all?" If you can't make the sound real enough, owl hooters are available from most of the major turkey call manufacturers. Once the birds are off their roost and on the ground, a few blasts on a crow call can often trigger a gobble out of a bird. Other effective calls include the howl of a coyote and, more recently, the peacock call. Don't laugh, they work. For some reason the sharp, high-pitched yelping of a coyote or the screeching call of a peacock can cause even the most reluctant gobbler to sound off. I even reverted once to using an elk bugle. Its shrill sound made many a gobbler reveal its location. The moral of this story is: *When things get tough, get innovative.*

"If you decide to blow an owl or crow call," Harold Knight advises, "there are a couple of things to remember. I blow both of these calls, short and loud. If you drag your calls out, a turkey might answer, but you'll never hear him because your own noise covers up the gobbling. When I'm by myself and I'm blowing the owl hooter, I give one quick, loud "Whooo"—what I call the "squall"—and then cut if off abruptly. After listening hard, I'll blow the crow call three quick loud notes. You've got to be aggressive with these locator calls and put some feeling into them."

World champion caller Chris Kirby agrees: "A crow call is great to use when you're trying to get a turkey fired up in mid-afternoon. The biggest mistake hunters make is to call as if you're calling in crows. You're not calling in crows; you're just trying to get a turkey to gobble. Three quick bursts are all that's needed. You just want to get that bird to hammer back one time. Once that happens, you can move in and go to work on him."

As Chris Kirby points out, "A box call is a tremendous locator call. It carries a lot farther than a mouth call, or any other type. Quaker Boy's 'Boat Paddle' in particular has a nice high-pitched sound. You don't want to do a whole bunch of calling—just some quick sounds to get that turkey to answer. Keep it short and keep it quick. Don't draw out these calls too long. You can't hear that turkey gobbling if you're still working the call.

Once you've located a bird that wants to gobble, the next step is to set up wherever the bird can be lured within shotgun range. If the gobbler is far off, you must determine how to cut the distance without being spotted as

you move along an open ridge, across an open pasture, or around farm fields. Knowing the terrain is important. Steep slopes, deep hollows, creek beds and even thick foliage can provide enough cover. How close should you get to the bird before setting up? That can depend on how much cover there is between you and the bird, obstacles such as a woven wire fence which could prevent the tom from coming on to you, or maybe if there's a chance of the gobbler running into real hens while on his way to your calls. If I have the right cover, I'll try to move as close as I possibly can. Late in the season when low bushes are nearly fully leafed out, I have set up within 75 yards of a gobbling bird. However, most times 150 yards can be pushing it.

When setting up on a roosted bird at daybreak, the cautious hunter can often slip within 100 yards of the roost tree. One rainy Missouri morning after moving to within 150 yards of a loud tom on the roost, I set up a decoy on an old logging road, settled in next to a huge oak, and at first good light made a few light calls with a diaphragm call. To my amazement, a tom gobbled directly above me. As I slowly looked up, I was surprised to see two good gobblers roosted not more than 30 feet above me. A few minutes later, the gobblers I had set up for specifically came easing in, whereupon the two birds above dropped to the ground 25 yards away and went into strut. Why they never spotted me, I'll never know.

Years ago, a veteran turkey hunter told me never to call a turkey unless I was standing right next to the tree I intended to set up on. That's pretty good advice. When moving through the turkey woods slowly in mid-to-late morning and trying to locate a gobbler with a turkey call, don't be surprised if a bird answers back practically in your face. If you're standing out in the open, or you're far from a suitable tree to set up on, a nearby bird will certainly spot your movement as you run to the closest set up. But if you're already standing next to a tree that looks suitable, you can settle down slowly and get the gun up into the ready position.

When I have enough time to select a perfect calling position, most times I'll try to place the curvature of the hill, a bend in an old logging road, or maybe a small stand of thick foliage between me and the oncoming gobbler. I don't want to watch that bird approach from a long distance, because the longer I can see him, the greater the chances the tom will spot something that gives me away. The ideal position for calling and shooting is when the gobbler steps into sight within shooting range. In your zest for concealment, though, don't put obstacles between you and the bird that might cause him to hang up. And when hunting field turkeys, keep in mind that birds who prefer wide open spaces can prove to be some of the toughest ones to hunt. They can see for incredibly long distances. What's more, a wary old bird has a knack for keeping a great distance between himself and edge cover where danger may lurk.

**Mark Drury carries a good Missouri gobbler that he
duped into range earlier by good calling.**

179

Mark Drury, one of the country's more successful turkey hunters, often uses several calls simultaneously to fire up nearby toms. He's shown here with both a mouth diaphragm and a box call in an attempt to sound like more than one hen.

When approaching a bird that has roosted near the edge of a field or open pasture, avoid walking in the open. Stick to the edge of the timber when closing to within 100 to 150 yards of the roost tree. Set up so you can cover both the edge of the field and the timber itself. An open field or pasture may offer the turkey easier walking; but older, more experienced gobblers will often skirt the edge, staying just inside the timber. Once they see a hen, or a flock of hens, in a field, they'll generally move out into the open. That's when packing a few lightweight, collapsible hen decoys can prove worth the effort. Don't get too bold, though, when setting out a decoy in pre-dawn light. Crawl on your belly as far as you dare, move in slowly, stake out the decoy, then crawl back.

In some cases where your scouting has pinpointed a field where turkeys tend to congregate in mid-to-late morning, another great opportunity arises for putting decoys to work for you. But if you know the birds will be in a particular field at, say, 10:30 in the morning, don't wait until 10:15 to get there. Be set up and in position a full hour earlier than the gobblers are expected, with decoy (or decoys) placed within shotgun range. When hunting late morning field edges, it's a good idea to set out three, four or five decoys, simulating a small flock of birds. One way to tick off an old boss gobbler, by the way, is to use one of those full-strut tom decoys.

A common scenario during the peak of the spring breeding season is for the dominant gobbler to stick with the hens through most of the day—at least until the hens have headed for their nesting areas. Unfortunately, the season too often draws to an end before the dominant boss bird finds himself without a female companion. Most of the adult gobblers harvested by hunters are in reality "satellite" toms, i.e., they may still weigh in at 20 to 25 pounds, but most are not considered the dominant breeding toms of that particular area. Since these birds have been chased away repeatedly from the hens by the dominant gobbler, they're often so lonely they'll come running to the calls of a lone hen. Not surprisingly, these are the most huntable birds.

If your sights are set on taking the "Big Daddy" of an area, you've got your work cut out for you. One way is to locate a field, pasture or other open area where the boss tom is apt to strut and show off for his harem of hens. If you can locate such an area, get there ahead of the flock and set out a couple of hen decoys and a strutting gobbler decoy. The sight of another tom strutting in his own area is enough to drive a boss tom berserk, especially when you've thrown in a few realistic gobbles.

"Today's decoys have sure come a long way," says Mark Drury, "particularly in the last ten to fifteen years. I can remember when I first tried to hunt with a decoy. I never liked those early hard plastic decoys because they were always loud, bulky, and generally a pain in the neck to carry into the turkey woods. However, with today's fold-up

and collapsible models available, there's no reason not to carry at least one hen decoy in the rear pouch of your hunting vest."

"Why are decoys such an important part of almost any hunting set up?" asks Mark Drury. "Because turkeys are so dependent on their eyesight. When they come into a call, they know there should be a hen there somewhere. It's amazing how they can tell exactly where the calling source came from! It's always nice to have

When setting up decoys, Mark Drury likes to keep his within 10 to 15 yards of the calling position. That way, if a gobbler hangs up 25 yards on the other side of the decoy, he's still not out of shotgun range. Mark commonly places his decoys off to one side or the other of his calling position, or the direction from which he expects a gobbler to appear. The decoy will then do a better job of drawing the attention away from him; and in some instances it will actu-

a visual aid. Turkeys switch from hearing to eyesight when approaching a hunter's calling position. First, they hear the call, but when they arrive at the calling location, they want to see the source of the call. That's why a decoy can be such a good tool for a hunter who wants to bring a gobbler within effective range."

ally draw the bird on past the hunter's position, making it easier for him to make last-second changes in aim with fewer chances of being spotted.

Hunting field turkeys is a great time to hunt with a partner, if for no other reason than to help each other carry in a flock of collapsible decoys. If that ol' boss bird strolls in with four or five hens, looks down the field and spots another gobbler with seven or eight hens, it's a good bet he'll challenge the intruder and claim his ladies. Whether in the open or in the woods, decoys provide a visual for oncoming gobblers. Often they're sufficient to lure the tom a little closer. The sight of another bird—be it a hen, jake or gobbler decoy—can divert a tom's attention from the hunter's calling position. In addition, small hand or head movements can easily spook a bird. For first-time turkey hunters, using a decoy is a smart move.

The peak of any breeding season varies considerably from North to South. In the Midwest, where I do most of my turkey hunting, the season usually falls somewhere around the second half of April into early May. In the South—Florida, Georgia, Alabama and Texas, for example—the season can peak as early as mid-March. The actual dates change from year to year by as much as two or more weeks, depending on the weather. I've seen gobblers in Illinois with as many as a dozen hens on the last day of the season! Hunting a gobbler who's with hens can be a challenging task, even during the peak of the breeding season.

Toxey Haas (founder and C.E.O. of Haas Outdoors, maker of Mossy Oak Camouflage) agrees that "the number one turkey hunting tip I could share is to practice plain ol' patience. You hear a lot about how to locate turkeys, how to call aggressively, how to scout, and how to set up. A lot of important factors are involved in being a successful turkey hunter. But the honest truth is that it takes patience, whether it's sticking with it when the weather is bad, or to stay

seated once a turkey has stopped gobbling. Instead of getting up and leaving after 10 or 15 minutes, try staying 30 minutes or an hour."

There's no such thing as an easy gobbler. Sure, hunt turkeys long enough and you'll run into a tom who will practically run you over before the sounds of your first call have echoed throughout the hardwoods. But for every adult wild turkey gobbler who runs right in, you're sure to match wits with dozens of others eager to test your turkey hunting skills and patience. Those are the birds you'll remember the most.

Often the more ground covered, the better when locating a tom. In the hope of hearing a responding gobble, the author is shown calling to a ridge top from a back road.

During the peak of the turkey season, world champion turkey caller Eddie Salter (Hunter Specialties Pro-Staff member) likes to cover lots of ground while locating gobblers, a style of hunting often referred to as "runnin' and gunnin'." Packing only the bare essentials, Eddie swiftly covers ridgetops, field edges, old roadways, clear cuts, and any other terrain feature that allows him to cover an area with enough

Hands cupped to the ears can help a hunter hear those far-off gobbles.

aggressive calling to squeeze a gobble out of a nearby tom. This is especially effective during mid-morning to midday, once the hens begin to leave the gobblers and head back to their nests. It's a time when gobblers can be the most vulnerable. "What I like to do is some serious cutting," explains Salter, "then come back right after the cuts with one or two real sharp yelps.

Sometimes when I come off that cut into a yelp a turkey will cut me off with a gobble. It gets him really fired up."

Too often, hunters try to work a bird that's already with a hen or hens. Now and then, some aggressive calling may break that gobbler away from those hens—but not often. A gobbler who has come to your calling may not be the dominant gobbler, but instead a satellite tom who's been waiting for one of those hens to break away from the boss. To him, your calls can sound especially sweet. But should one of the gobblers who's been with the hens gobble back to your calls but refuses to leave them, don't get frustrated and head for home. Some of the best turkey hunting takes place after 10 a.m., once those hens have begun to head for their nesting areas.

Outdoor writer Gary Clancy is one of the finest turkey hunters I've ever worked with. We were hunting on a farm in northern Missouri a few years ago. On opening morning, I took a long wooded ridge while Gary headed for an adjacent ridge. I managed to elicit a few responsive gobbles from roosted birds, but the real action took place on the ridge Gary was hunting. He never did shoot, but he must have had a dozen mature gobblers hammering back at every call he made. When I returned to camp for a cup of coffee at about 9:30 that morning, however, Clancy already had a fine big tom hang-

When calling on the move, and to avoid being caught in the open, a set-up spot should be established before calling. The hunter shown can drop next to the large tree in the event a tom gobbles right back.

ing from a nail on the front porch. He hadn't shot the bird on the ridge, but down the road in a neighboring pasture. I quickly sipped my coffee without much ado, then drove back to the ridge where he'd been hunting earlier. I walked down an old logging road, stopping every 100 yards or so to make loud cuts on my Rohm Brothers box call. Half a mile down the ridge I heard a gobbler just over the crest of the ridge. I settled down next to a big oak and called a few more times. Nothing. A few minutes later, I called again. Still nothing. Frustrated, I cut on the call loudly, and followed up with about three or four yelps. Finally, I put the call down and waited…and waited…and waited.

About 30 minutes later, a flash of bluish-white color caught my eye. I glanced in that direction and watched as two 25-pound toms came strolling down the road. After they'd disappeared behind a big oak, I eased the muzzle of my shotgun around so that when they stepped out the bead would be right on the first bird. Slowly the tom closed the distance from 50 to 40 yards, then to 30 yards. I rolled him with a 3-inch magnum load of No. 6 shot. When I arrived back in camp around 11:30 a.m., I immediately walked up to Gary Clancy and thanked him for "warming up" those birds for me.

To be a consistently successful turkey hunter means learning to size up a particular situation in a hurry and adapt to every hunting situation. This includes knowing whether to call softly or loudly, conservatively or aggressively, or not to call at all.

David Hale agrees: "I'm not a real aggressive caller. Once I set up on a bird, I don't do a lot of calling. Remember, the louder and faster you call, the more you indicate to the gobbler that you're a hen who's willing to come to him. But when you don't show up, he might get the notion there's a fly in the ointment. So once I get a gobbler to answer my call, I may let him gobble four or five times until he gets impatient—instead of me getting impatient. Then I'll give him maybe one or two little yelps to keep the turkey gobbling. Some callers get hung up on several note sequences with a cluck or a fast cut behind it. But when a hen doesn't show up, all you're doing is making him stand there and strut. What I do by calling softly is as natural as making a long, loud call. If the turkey responds to me, it means he's recognized me as a hen. In most cases, he'll come faster to conservative calling than he will to aggressive calling."

David Hale is the first to admit that often a hunter will lose a gobbler by not being aggressive enough. Calls that are overly aggressive, he feels, can frighten away a timid tom. His conservative approach provides an opportunity to see if the bird will respond to softer, more conservative calling. If that fails, David can always turn up the volume and rhythm.

"Certainly aggressive calling works sometimes," he acknowledges, "but when a hunter calls aggressively all the time, he's going to lose a lot of birds he might have killed had he been more

conservative. A conservative caller can play both sides, but an aggressive caller plays only one side. I believe the biggest mistake many callers make is calling too much. They like to hear themselves call, and they like to make the turkey gobble. I only want my turkey to gobble now and then, not incessantly. When working a turkey, a hunter's job is to get him to break strut and start walking. I think it's easier to do this by being conservative rather than aggressive."

Harold Knight tends to agree: "Lots of people who use a mouth diaphragm don't realize they call so much, because it's so easy and convenient to use it. They get caught up in the excitement of a turkey gobbling at every sound, so they pour it on. This is often the wrong thing to do. I like to fire up a gobbler from a distance. Pretend it's dawn and I'm up a hollow where a turkey is gobbling on his own. I may answer with some cuts and cackles to get him excited and convince him that some hens are flying off the roost. At that point, I tone down my calls real low. I want that gobbler to think those hens are on the ground and going about their business."

The peak of the breeding period is a good time for harvesting a wild turkey. Twelve-year-old Zack Opel took this Illinois gobbler during his first hunting season.

Harold Knight is right about one thing: today's calls are the best we've ever seen (and heard), including the simple push-button yelper (from Knight & Hale Game Calls), which can be operated by one finger. Each push on the button creates a realistic sounding yelp, making it easy to call to a gobbler. Another call design that's sure to revolutionize the turkey call industry is Lohman's "Pump Action Yelper" (Outland Sports). This call incorporates a diaphragm call that fits inside a hand-operated, pump-action chamber. The hunter simply pumps a slightly larger outer sleeve that fits over a body with a smaller diameter. The air compressed by this action does the rest. This call does produce extremely realistic yelps, cuts and clucks. As for ease of operation, I taught my neighbor's five-year-old boy to use the call with enough proficiency to produce great sounding yelps in only five minutes. It even features a dial adjustment that allows a hunter to change the pitch and tone of the calls quickly and easily. This new turkey call can also be operated with one hand by placing the base of the outer sleeve against a leg or the ground. Turkey calling doesn't get any easier than that! If you've always liked the sounds produced by a mouth diaphragm call, but you couldn't keep from choking on them, here's a call capable of producing those same sounds.

Probably the number one question asked by inexperienced turkey hunters is this: How often and how loud should I call? That question can't be answered without first knowing the weather conditions, the terrain, the thickness of the foliage, what stage the breeding season is in, and how much hunting pressure there is in the area, among several other factors. So when it comes to turkey hunting, knowledge and experience become one and the same. A good turkey hunter must learn to adapt to every hunting situation, and that includes when to call and when not to call. When it comes to calling, Mark Drury agrees: "Calling frequency and volume should decrease the closer the gobbler gets."

Now, that's *"sound"* advice. ∎

Chapter 11

Harvesting The Late Season Gobbler

WITH ■ Jerry Martin, *Hunting Advisor* ■ Harold Knight, *Co-founder, Knight & Hale Game Calls* ■ Ray Eye, *World Champion Caller* ■ Gary Clancy, *Outdoor Writer*

In the dim light of dawn, my 17-foot aluminum fishing

boat rocked back and forth on the submerged log. I knew the old tree trunk was there; I had simply misjudged how hard to hit it in order to slide over the log. With the boat now perfectly balanced on the log, I shut down the outboard motor. Then my son Adam and I quickly moved to the bow, transferring enough weight to lift the stern and shift the balance of the boat forward. The slick hull slid forward off the log as I idled our way up the small stream. During a normal spring, I would be forced to stop nearly a mile down stream; but a much wetter spring than usual had filled every river and creek tributary, so that I was able to motor my way slowly into hunting country I had never seen before—at least, not from the water.

Nearing an area I suspected was a roosting location, I cut the engine and moved to the bow of the boat. Using the electric trolling motor, I eased our boat quietly up the swollen stream for another quarter of a mile. My first hoot was greeted by at least a half-dozen toms located several hundred yards up the side of a gentle Missouri ridge. Making as little sound as possible, we eased the nose of the boat onto the bank and anchored it to a big maple tree. A few minutes later, we were moving our way slowly through the hardwoods at the base of the ridge. I hooted once more and a single bird gobbled back. This one was much lower—about 100 yards off to our left—so we moved a few yards in that direction to a small grassy opening. As Adam set up, I eased out to the edge of the clearing and staked out a single hen decoy. Then we sat and listened to the sounds of daybreak.

By the time we heard the gobbler fly down from its roost, we had discovered at least ten other gobblers sounding off from the ridge at our back. I called to them lightly, and I swear every one of

them gobbled back. At that moment, the bird we had set up on gobbled, and we knew that this bird was probably the best of the lot. His gobble was deeper and more distinguishable than any of the other birds. Best of all, each time he gobbled, the tom moved closer. Adam was ready, steadying our old Remington 3-inch magnum Model 870 pump on his knee. As we watched, two fanned tails made their way through the thick creek-

bottom underbrush, eventually popping out at the opposite side of the opening. In my mind, I was preparing myself for a lot of coaxing in an effort to get the turkeys within shotgun range.

It was the last weekend of the Missouri season and these birds had been hunted hard. We were hunting on public land administered by the U.S. Army

Corps of Engineers and maintained as a wildlife management area by the Missouri Department of Conservation. Each morning, as I drove past a parking area more than a mile back, I had observed four or five hunters' vehicles sitting there. I obviously wasn't the only one who knew about this tremendous concentration of turkeys. I also knew that a small creek bordered the backside of this area. During a normal year, hunters could enter the wildlife management tract from that side and wade through water that was normally a foot or so deep. But this spring, there were easily four or five feet of water cutting off the back entrance to the area.

Earlier, Adam and I had launched our boat in pitch darkness at a public ramp ten miles away, then made our way up a rain-swollen river to the mouth of the creek. Having traversed the submerged log, we now had the whole backside of the public hunting area all to ourselves. We were about to discover just how well the tactic worked.

As the two big toms strutted into the grassy clearing, they immediately spotted our decoy. Instantly, both birds dropped out of strut and came at us at a dead run, then stopped barely ten yards from the decoy only 25 yards from the muzzle of Adam's shotgun. I whispered to Adam to take either bird. The words were barely out of my mouth when his shotgun roared and the 25-pound gobbler rolled. It had taken us longer to launch the boat, load our gear, make the ten-mile run and ease up the creek than it did to set up and call in those two magnificent toms.

Using a boat to "come in through the back door" is a tactic I learned from Jerry Martin, a good friend and hunting advisor for Bass Pro Shops. During the late 1980s, he and I worked together to produce several turkey hunting videos, one of which (Big Game Bird II) proved to me just how effective the "back door" approach can be. Three mornings in a row, we had used Jerry's bass boat to work the shoreline of Missouri's sprawling Truman Reservoir. All along the nearly 1,000 miles of shoreline lies a buffer of land owned by the U.S. Army Corps of Engineers. In most places, this strip of land is barely a quarter-mile wide, but in other spots it can be close to a mile across. Best of all, the vast majority of this land was home to a dense turkey population.

The region also attracts thousands of turkey hunters, most of whom park their vehicles in numerous parking areas provided along public roadways encircling the huge Truman Reservoir. Before the birds are subjected to around-the-clock pressure from hunters for the early part of the season, a good caller with the right set-up will usually find the turkeys fairly responsive. But call to an old gobbler each morning in the same general direction and it doesn't take long before he catches on and begins working in the opposite direction.

"Coming into these areas by boat kind of throws these gobblers a curve," Jerry Martin comments. "Practically all of the hunting pressure has come at them from one side of the area. The hunter who goes to the trouble of launching a boat and making a 20-minute run to the backside generally

Foliage is often so heavy toward the end of a spring season that concealment is no longer a problem—but seeing a gobbler only 20 yards away can be.

stands a much greater chance of success on these gobblers...especially late in the season."

Another advantage of using a boat to hunt the corridor of public land which surrounds Truman Reservoir, and just about any other Corps of Engineers lake for that matter, is the ease in covering lots of ground...or water. Like the landlocked hunter, Jerry Martin relies on owl hoots to squeeze a gobble out of a tom at the first hint of light. Then he'll move in, tie up his boat and make his set-up.

the last few days of the season. A lot of fishermen were on the river, snagging for giant paddlefish. Because of the noise they made, it was almost impossible to hear a turkey gobble. So Jerry would nose his boat into shore and I'd climb the steep bank and call with a box call. It was a tactic that worked. During the final weekend of one season, we managed to take a pair of fine 23-pound gobblers.

When a bird is close to the shore, hunters coming in by boat must take

extra precautions to avoid being spotted. Unless the turkey is far up a ridge, or well back of the water's edge, setting up within a few yards of the shore may be necessary. Once a call has been made with a box call, you've already sent out an invitation to that tom, so getting set up quickly becomes important. When you've got to gather up your gear and tie up the boat in a hurry, being well organized is extremely important.

Later in the morning, Jerry likes to slowly cruise the shoreline, stopping his outboard every quarter to a half mile and calling with a sharp-toned box call. Often, a responding gobble can be heard from quite a distance, especially if the bird is close to the water.

One spring, he and I hunted the Osage River in central Missouri during

"I remember one hunt," recalls Jerry with a laugh, "when a buddy and I were so anxious to get set up on a nearby bird that I must have forgotten to tie up the boat. I threw a couple of wraps around a tree trunk, but I never actually tied it off. We got the bird okay, but when we walked back to the landing my boat was a hundred yards off shore! I had to strip off my clothes and swim out to the boat. That was the coldest water I've ever skinny-dipped in!"

During the late season hunt, especially where the turkeys have been hunted aggressively, covering lots of ground is often the key to locating a gobbler. In areas where spring seasons extend three or four weeks beyond the peak breeding period, the hens often stay with their nest for longer periods of time, causing gobblers to become lonesome. Where a large number of turkeys is involved—especially those that have experienced light to moderate hunting pressure—getting a tom to respond to your calls late in the season can be relatively easy. But birds that have felt heavy hunting pressure are often reluctant to respond to the point where they are "call-shy." Such situations often require an approach much different from what was employed at the beginning of the season.

Gary Clancy, a noted outdoor writer and turkey hunting authority from Minnesota has developed a personal late-season tactic that works well for him. To locate a gobbler, particularly late in the morning, he must first cover a lot of ground. He hikes the ridge tops, cutting hard on either a box or mouth diaphragm call. But once he has located a bird, his calls become quite conservative. "Some hunters try to outcall every other hunter in the woods," warns Clancy. "When faced with shy toms, such an approach virtually guarantees failure. Gobblers that have been hunted aggressively learn that loud calling signifies danger."

To improve the odds of bagging a call-shy gobbler, a hunter must often change his calling pattern. Too often, hunters get hung up on one or two repetitive calls and use them endlessly. It's like throwing up a red flag to any gobbler who's been pursued hard all season long. Indeed, one of the best tactics is simply to put your calls away.

According to Harold Knight, "One of a gobbler's main vulnerabilities is that he's a creature of habit. He's got things that he's going to do every day. He may walk the same route looking for hens. He may strut in the same strut zones. He may feed in the same fields. He may

Heavy late season foliage allowed this hunter to slip around with less chance of being detected by a gobbler.

During the late season, turkey hunters must be ready to use a variety of calls in order to find a tone the bird likes—or hasn't already heard dozens of times that season.

HUNTING AMERICA'S WILD TURKEYS

roost in the same area. Recognizing this and patterning a gobbler can be extremely important. A hunter can reach a gobbler's destination before the bird does, because he can predict what the bird's going to do when he gets there. Repetitious behavior is a major vulnerability."

The best time to pattern a gobbler is at the tail-end of the season, when gobbling activity naturally begins to wind down and hard-pressured gobblers tend to ignore calls. In those instances, hunting becomes more a practice of waiting rather than pursuing. If and when a hunter calls during the late season, Gary Clancy advises, it's best to do so sparingly. Instead of trying to fire an old gobbler up with loud, seductive and inviting yelps of promised love, it's best to stick with subtle clucks and purrs—the same sounds associated with contented hens as they feed. Raking some nearby leaves with your hand can add to the realism.

One of the biggest mistakes hunters make when going after closed-mouthed gobblers is to go right at the bird using the easiest, most direct path. Unfortunately, this is probably the same approach taken by other hunters who tried working this bird. A much wiser approach would be to study the area (if it's new to you) or call on previous knowledge of the terrain. Instead of beating a direct path toward the source of that hard-earned, late morning gobble, try an alternate approach, one that hasn't yet been used by anyone else.

This could mean dropping down off a ridge top and circling the area where the bird last gobbled. This might mean having to cover a mile in order to travel a few hundred yards on the side opposite where the turkey was heard earlier. No one ever said turkey hunting was easy!

While switching things around and trying to throw a wise old tom off guard, think about the type of call being used. If you know that other hunters who've pursued this same tom before relied heavily on a diaphragm mouth call, try a box or slate call. Breaking the pattern could be the key to breaking

A gobble tube, such as this one from Quaker Boy, can help to get a wary old gobbler in close enough for a shot. Caution should be used when making "gobble" type calls.

the bird loose and getting him into your sights. One tactic used by veteran turkey hunters in pursuit of a call-shy, late season gobbler who's on the roost is to forget about calls altogether. One old-timer I know likes to slip within a hundred yards or so of a roosted tom, place a decoy ten or so yards off to his left, then pull out a turkey wing. Just before fly-down time, he'll rake the wing slowly across the trunk of a near-

down from the roost. At that point, he will lay the wing down and ready his shotgun. This trick has fooled many a gobbler—without one single yelp, cackle, cut, cluck or purr.

Just as a gobbler may be reluctant to come in to calling, he can be equally reluctant to gobble. After being pushed hard all season long, don't expect a tom to roll off a deep-throated gobble with each step, as it often does early in

Realtree camouflage designer Bill Jordan took a fine late season Georgia tom by using a very conservative call.

by sapling several times. The barely audible popping of the wing tips creates a sound like a hen switching positions on a limb, preparing to fly down. A minute or two later, this woods-smart turkey chaser again flaps the wing against the sapling or the ground, simulating the sound of a hen or two flying

the season. At best, we can only hope to squeeze a "shock gobble" out of a tom as a way to get a fix on his location. Once the toms are on the ground, a few loud blasts on a crow call—or a few notes with a coyote yelper—will do the trick. But don't expect much more than that. If you can get the bird to work (maybe gobble four or five times as he approaches you), consider these gobbles as bonuses.

It's extremely important to stay alert when going after a late-season tom, because he'll probably come in silent. Try picking up the bird's soft clucks, or even a few slow-paced, barely audible yelps (yes, gobblers also make these sounds). Once you've picked up these and other sounds—such as footsteps in dry, crunchy leaves—it's time to get your shotgun ready once the wary bird has arrived at a point where he can actually see your calling location. Big 20-pound-plus gobblers have a habit of appearing when and where you least expect them. There are times, though, when call-shy birds will often respond to a call but refuse to move in close enough for a shot.

When setting up on a gobbler that is moving within 70 yards or so of your calling position, it's sometimes a good idea to double-team such reluctant gobblers. To begin, place your hunter (or shooter) and then move back 40 or 50 yards before calling. If the bird responds and follows his normal pattern, the hunter could be in good position to get off a shot. If the turkey hangs up short of shotgun range, though, the caller should crawl back

another 20 or 30 yards and call the gobbler again in hopes of closing the gap. Remember, the caller isn't the one who is taking the shot, so it's important that he set up at a point where he has enough freedom to move, as opposed

to where he can actually see the bird. In the latter case, the turkey will pick up on any move he makes and thus add to its education.

World champion caller Ray Eye grew up hunting turkeys in the sprawling Mark Twain National Forest of southern Missouri, an area that offers excellent public hunting. Over the years, Ray has learned how to cope with heavy hunting pressure. "It's important that you know how to deal with other hunters in the area," he instructs. "When a hunter spooks a bird that you're working, screaming at the guy isn't going to help. I've taken several spooked birds by waiting 15 to 30 minutes, then call-

A hunter tries to locate a cooperative late season gobbler by calling while trolling along a small stream.

ing softly like a nervous hen that was spooked but is still interested."

Ray goes on to say that when birds have been spooked repeatedly for days on end, a hunter must show a great deal of patience and change his style of calling. "Blind" calling, he finds, is fairly effective during the late season, or when he moves from one calling position to another. Ray tends to move shorter distances while staying in each spot for a longer period. He's a strong believer in using soft calls which, to a gobbler, sound like a nervous hen. Ray will often scratch in the leaves with his hands to add a sense of realism. Perhaps the gobbler might think Ray is a real hen and not just another hunter. "Where there's lots of pressure from other hunters," Ray explains, "you can expect less gobbling. Keep in mind also that gobbling can bring in the competition (other hunters). Don't encourage it. I seldom use locating calls on crowded hunting areas."

One sure sign that the season is winding down is the sight of adult gobblers grouping together. When I drive past a field or open pasture in early May and see several adult gobblers grouped together, I know the breeding season is over, or close to it. A week or two earlier, those same birds were literally beating the heck out of each other. Now they seem to be enjoying each other's company. An effective call at this time of the season is the gobble. If you happen to hunt regularly on heavily hunted public land, you may not want to consider using a gobble. Not only

will the call attract other gobblers, it will attract other hunters as well. A sudden gobble, a quick flicker of movement, a hasty shot, could result in another turkey hunting accident. Even when hunting on private land, the gobble call should be used sparingly. If you know about others who are hunting the same piece of property, try to arrange ahead of time for the areas in which each group will operate. And should your morning hunt bring you close to where others are hunting, use the gobble with great discretion. No turkey is worth getting shot over.

If a gobbler thinks there's a hot hen still in the area, there's a good chance he'll come running to dispatch the loud-mouthed tom who dares to intrude on his territory. On the other hand, should his breeding instinct have subsided for the season, he might start looking for the camaraderie of fellow gobblers. Either way, using a good gobble tube, such as the rubber "shaker type" call (Quaker Boy Calls), can lure a tom close enough for a shot when all other calls have failed.

Outdoor writer Gary Clancy says, "If calling proves to be unproductive, despite your best efforts, put away your calls and rely strictly on knowledge, hunch and patience." He recommends sitting along the edge of a field, a woods road, along the top of a ridge line, or within shotgun range of any known or suspected turkey travel route, then wait. If any birds who show up are out of range, don't attempt calling. Clancy rationalizes that if the birds didn't

When attempting to locate a late season tom, Will Primos uses a tactic known as "runnin' and gunnin'."
He stays on the move, stopping and calling every several hundred yards until a bird answers.

respond to earlier calling, why would your calls work now? Instead of calling, he recommends rustling some leaves lightly to simulate the sound of other turkeys feeding. Gary is also a firm believer in decoys. He will often set one out along a travel route and do absolutely no calling whatsoever. He has found that toms who are otherwise reluctant will come all the way in once they spot a decoy.

Author Toby Bridges spent many mornings patterning this big northern Missouri gobbler before putting a plan together.

Clancy likes to recall the story of a super bird he took in northern Missouri with a muzzleloading shotgun. He had nicknamed the gobbler "Old Tight Lips" following a close encounter one dark, overcast morning. Clancy had been calling to another gobbler down in a wooded hollow when he noticed "Old Tight Lips" standing in an alfalfa

field. The bird just stood there and never made a sound. Soon the gobbler was joined by four hens but continued to ignore Clancy's calling. The hunter eventually slipped back away from the field and left. A few mornings later, he returned to the same field, only this time he moved closer to the edge of the field, where he staked out a hen decoy. The only tree in the area was a scraggly wild plumb tree 25 yards away.

Minutes after settling down for a long wait, Clancy was surprised to see the big gobbler standing directly in front of the decoy. "Old Tight Lips" never made a peep, but he did begin to strut for the motionless hen—that is, until his wing tip brushed against the decoy's tail. The lightweight decoy spun around on its aluminum stake, exciting and surprising the gobbler. As he turned his attention to the decoy, Clancy inched the butt of the muzzleloading shotgun to his shoulder, took aim and, with a twitch of his finger, sent forth flame and shot from the frontloader. A good portion of the two-ounce load of No. 5s put "Old Tight Lips" down for the count. The 26$\frac{1}{2}$-pound tom sported an 11$\frac{1}{2}$-inch beard and hooked 1$\frac{5}{8}$-inch spurs.

When calling and waiting in ambush fail, Clancy advises turkey hunters to "put the sneak on them!" He points out

World champion callers Mark Drury (left) and Steve Stoltz worked together to lure this reluctant tom into shotgun range.

that while a turkey's eyes and hearing are extremely acute, hunters should take advantage of heavy foliage and terrain features—a ridge, point, creek bed, or what have you. Hunters would then have a good chance of slipping within shotgun range of an unsuspecting gobbler. Under no circumstance should they try calling. I took his advice once and shot a good-sized northern Missouri gobbler in that same alfalfa field where Clancy had harvested "Old Tight Lips" a few days earlier. For two mornings in a row I had glassed a large gobbler strutting near the edge of the field about 100 yards from the spot where Clancy had muzzleloaded his tight-lipped gobbler. The tom usually showed up at roughly the same spot

around 10 o'clock each morning. On the third morning, I eased up a small wooded draw to within 30 yards of the spot, sat down next to a huge oak and waited. Right on cue, the gobbler showed up around 9:40 a.m., but he was about 50 yards farther down the ridge. I called lightly to get his attention, whereupon the big bird exploded into full strut. I called to him again a little louder, and he continued to strut. I waited five minutes, then purred and clucked lightly on my mouth diaphragm call. The turkey came out of strut, gobbled briefly, then resumed his full strut, moving back and forth in short four- or five-yard rushes. After ten minutes or so, I called again and the turkey continued his strut. Another ten minutes went

Harold Knight contends that during the late season hunters would be wise to keep calling to a minimum. After two to four weeks of hunting, many birds have been called too often by overly zealous hunters.

by and that old gobbler had moved not an inch closer. It was time to pursue a more aggressive strategy.

Thigh-high native grasses grew all along the edge of the alfalfa field, and so I decided to crawl slowly through the tall grass and close the distance between us to 40 yards. I knew the .665-inch extra-full choke tube of my Remington 3-inch 870 pump would keep 20 to 30 pellets in the head and neck at that distance, provided I could get that close. When the tom turned his fanned tail toward me, I made my move. Like John Wayne in a World War II movie, I held the shotgun with both hands and inched my way through the grass, hugging the ground as closely as I could. About 15 yards from the point I wanted to reach, I decided to take a peek, just in case I needed to correct my route. I lifted my head far enough to peer through the sparse upper grass. That old turkey was gone!

Then, a few yards to my right, I heard something and slowly turned my head. There, only four or five yards away, was the gobbler, sneaking through the tall grass in the same direction I'd been calling from. The bird spotted me at the same instant, but he had no idea what I was. He only knew I wasn't the hen he was looking for. And so there we were, looking

eyeball-to-eyeball. The gobbler turned and ran back into the open field, perhaps seriously contemplating an airborne maneuver. That's when my two-ounce load of No. 6 copper-plated shot impacted the back of his head.

As we've seen, not all turkey hunts end up the way you predict. Some are quite different. During late season hunts, once the birds have been pressured hard, hunters feel the need to be a little creative. Don't be afraid to try something different, because that's what it often takes to end the season with your tag on a good bird. ■

Jerry Martin, a senior hunting advisor, often uses a gobbler yelp to get the attention of call-shy, late season gobblers.

Chapter 12

Rainy Day Gobblers

WITH ■ Harold Knight, *Co-founder, Knight & Hale Game Calls* ■ Mark Drury, *President, M.A.D. Calls* ■ Steve Stoltz, *World Champion Caller* ■ Steve Burnett, *World Champion Caller*

A light drizzle made it even more difficult to navigate the rain-swollen river in the dark. Through the night torrential rains had brought the Osage River to the top of its banks, and whole trees floated past as I slowly headed upstream in my 16-foot aluminum boat. My 14-year-old son, Adam, worked the spotlight as I carefully maneuvered around the debris that filled the river. Thirty minutes after leaving the boat ramp, our craft finally nosed its way up a small creek.

Earlier that week, I had taken a beautiful 23-pound gobbler close to the place where we tied up the boat. At the same time, a hunting partner had put his tag on an almost identical twin. We'd been hunting a 30 or 40-acre tract that had burned off late the previous fall, or perhaps during the winter. The blaze had consumed the heavy ground leaf cover and had burned most of the thick underbrush choking much of the surrounding hardwoods. Nearly a dozen birds had gobbled at daybreak that morning, and when the two came waltz-ing into my calling only minutes after flying down from the roost, my partner and I collected an easy double and were on our way back down the river. The now grassy burn seemed like a logical spot for my son, Adam, to fill his tag during the first weekend of the Missouri spring season.

The remains of a long-abandoned gravel roadway made the walking easy. Minutes after leaving the boat, Adam and I were standing at the edge of the burn. Daybreak arrived slowly as low hanging clouds filled the air with a fine mist. We settled in next to a huge old oak and quietly waited. Finally, a bird gobbled less than 200 yards from where we sat, soon followed by two more across a grassy stretch of timber. As the dim light grew stronger, several more birds began to gobble—and that's when we knew we were in for a successful hunt.

Several dark forms sailed from near the top of a big tree about 100 yards

This old abandoned roadway offers a "damp-free" strut zone
for an old gobbler following a night of hard rains.

RAINY DAY GOBBLERS

Following a night of rain or during a slow daytime rain, turkeys will often head for an area where short grass abounds. The author intercepted this Iowa gobbler with a Thompson/Center muzzleloading shotgun.

away and landed in the short grass. A few minutes later, I filled the damp morning air with light, barely audible hen yelps. More than a half-dozen gobblers hammered back with deep, hearty gobbles. Adam eased up his shotgun —a 3-inch magnum pump 12 gauge— and rested it on his knee. He didn't have long to wait. Only minutes later, three big adult gobblers were strutting back and forth barely out of shotgun range. They all gobbled to every yelp, purr and cluck I made with a triple reed diaphragm call in the roof of my mouth, but none would step an inch closer.

Suddenly, a fourth and even bigger bird slowly worked his way in on Adam's right. I continued to cluck and purr lightly with the call, enticing the strutting bird ever closer. Finally, the turkey was in range, but still too far to the right. Sensing that Adam was fighting the urge to swing his shotgun on the turkey and take a shot, I whispered instructions to him: keep the gun pointed straight ahead. Inch by inch, the old tom moved away to our left, eventually disappearing behind a big oak about 20 yards distant. With that, Adam eased the muzzle slightly to his right. Seconds later, the bird stepped clear. I putted lightly on the call and up came his head. At that instant, the shotgun roared and the big bird went flopping across the wet ground. In a flash, Adam laid the shotgun down and ran out to claim his prize. As I walked up to him, he was all smiles, his foot solidly planted on the head and neck of a beautiful 25-pound trophy gobbler.

We were hunting a huge public hunting area that practically rings western Missouri's sprawling Harry Truman Reservoir. On the first weekend of the Missouri spring turkey season, the area usually experiences some heavy hunting pressure. On that particular morning, the wet weather had caused most hunters to pull the covers back over their heads and sleep in. Nearly all of the distant shots we heard were well after mid-morning. Meanwhile, once a hazy sun had poked through the cloud cover, we shot photos of Adam and his trophy gobbler. For this young hunter, the reward of the morning had definitely been worth braving a little wet weather.

How many times have you allowed rain to rob you of a day's hunt? There's no denying that spring turkey hunting is a lot more enjoyable when the weather is ideal, including mornings that break cool and crisp without a cloud in the sky before warming into the 50s or 60s by mid-day. But in the real world of springtime gobbler chasing, experienced turkey hunters realize that such days can be few and far between. March, April and May are traditionally wet months; in fact, a week to 10-day rainy period can pretty much eat up an entire two-week season in many states. Under such circumstances, a turkey hunter who consistently fills his tags year after year must learn to cope with hunting in the rain. There are no surefire tactics or techniques for hunting turkeys during bad weather, but with more than 25 years of turkey hunting to draw on, I've

come up with several common denominators that have contributed heavily to my success in less-than-perfect weather.

Mark Drury, who spends eight to ten weeks each spring chasing wild turkeys all across the country, comments, "If I'm hunting down south and there's a shooting box next to a nice green field, I may spend most of a rainy morning sitting out of the weather, but most of the time I don't hunt during a drenching downpour. If it's only misting or raining lightly, though, I'll stay out there. For one thing,

A week of rainy weather enabled the author to motor his boat up swollen side streams to areas where he had never hunted before. The reward was a large gobbler.

tor among these successful hunts was the hardheaded persistence that got me out of bed and into the turkey woods. One things is for certain: if a turkey hunter elects to roll over and go back to sleep once he hears rain pecking against the window pane, he's cutting his season short. For one thing, there's always the chance the weather will clear up after daybreak. When the sun suddenly pops out after a night-long rain, gobblers often explode into a mating rampage. The hunter who is

most of the other hunters have either headed for home or didn't even bother to climb out of bed."

Through the years, I've tagged a number of excellent gobblers on mornings when the weather was so foul that even die-hard turkey hunters wouldn't have left home. The only common fac-

still in bed can miss some of the best turkey hunting of the year—perhaps of his life!

A couple of years back, while hunting the late spring season in southern Iowa, I came close to missing one of the greatest hunts of my life. The rattle of the alarm clock woke me well before

dawn that day, and the distant flashes of lightning and the rumble of thunder promised an approaching storm. I turned off the alarm and settled down for another forty winks. But the season was coming to a close—there were only two days of hunting left—so I reluctantly got out of bed and made the 30-minute drive in the rain to one of my favorite hunting areas.

I was about to park my pickup close to a pasture gate when a torrential downpour made me regret the decision. When it comes to weather that bad, even I'm no glutton for punishment. So I kicked back the seat of my truck, closed my eyes and fell asleep to the rhythm of the storm. I woke up about an hour later just as daybreak arrived. The rain had all but stopped,

and the twinkling light of stars to the southwest meant that the sun would likely shine through before the morning was over. I quickly slipped on my camouflaged hunting vest and slid my in-line percussion muzzleloading 12 gauge shotgun from its case. I was in the act of pressing a No. 11 percussion cap onto the nipple when a turkey greeted the coming day with several deep throaty gobbles.

It was early May, with most trees and bushes close to fully leafed, providing plenty of cover for moving in and setting up on the gobbler. I elected to set up at the edge of a small grassy clearing surrounded by mature oaks. The turkey was still on his roost as I set my decoy some 20 yards away and settled back against the trunk of an ancient

In windy weather everything tends to move slightly, making it easier for hunters to make small movements without being spotted.

white oak. A few minutes later, I heard the big bird fly down less than 100 yards away. After a few light yelps, the gobbler came toward me at nearly a dead run, rolling off gobble after gobble as he made his way through the open timber.

Suddenly, a huge dark form loomed at the far edge of the clearing. It was without doubt the biggest gobbler I had ever seen. At the sight of my decoy, the bird went into full strut, moving quickly toward his newfound lady love, As I tracked the gobbler's every move with the bead of my front-loading smoothbore, the turkey stopped a few yards short of the decoy and stretched his neck for a better look. The trigger came back and my target momentarily disappeared as the shotgun roared. Once the smoke had cleared, the sound of wing tips beating feebly against the ground assured me that the gobbler must be lying close by. As I walked over to where he lay, my first impression was that of a Boeing 747 with feathers! The old bird was definitely a trophy, tipping the scales at slightly more than 28 pounds and sporting a full 12-inch beard and 1½" spurs. It was definitely worth getting out of bed for!

Despite this successful outcome, I've discovered that extremely damp days can have a completely different effect on turkeys. Most wild turkey hunters I've known can easily recall days when all the persistence and determination in the world failed to get a rainy-day gobbler to answer a call. Those are the days when we all wished we had pulled the covers back up over our heads. Just as frustrating can be those soggy mornings when a gobbler answers almost every call imaginable but refuses to fly down from its roost. In really wet weather, turkeys are often reluctant to fly down. Following an all-night rain, the birds are already soaked to the skin. An old gobbler is more likely to sit on his lofty perch rather than face getting even wetter in tall grass or thick undergrowth.

Steve Stoltz, world champion caller and veteran turkey hunter, shares this tip: "When hunting turkeys in foul weather, you must realize that the birds are still out there. Hunt as if the weather wasn't even a factor. You may have to call a little louder, though, to overcome the sound of rain or wind. You may have to cover more area, too. Turkeys like to head for the open during a steady rain."

Some gobblers who inhabit a pasture or closely manicured section of timber often offer hunters a rare opportunity. A finicky old tom is more likely to drop down onto a carpet of short, closely grazed grass or the floor of an open stand of hardwoods than a place where the ground foliage is thick and heavy. How many times have you driven the back roads through turkey country on a rainy day and witnessed birds standing on the road? Old logging roads, clear cuts, abandoned country roads and long private drives are all excellent places to look for gobblers during wet weather. Even if you can't

HUNTING AMERICA'S WILD TURKEYS

Acrylic-faced friction calls, such as this Primos "Power Crystal,"
are affected less by damp weather than are true slate calls.

find a bird roosted near such areas at daybreak, there's a good chance that, should it rain before the day is over, some turkeys will be found in these same spots.

The burned area where Adam took his big 25-pounder was such a place. Its lush green grass provided not only a food source for the turkeys, but its

Damp weather can also cause gobblers to be pretty quiet at times. It's not uncommon for a gobbler to sound off like there's no tomorrow while he's still in the tree, but then work in silence while on the ground. To call in a silent bird across an open pasture, a burned area, or any open space where there's no cover takes a lot of patience. If there's

carpet of short grass brought on by a late, wet spring gave gobblers a place to strut without making damp feathers still wetter. That same area produced five more birds for Adam, myself and several others during the second week of the season. Almost all were taken along the fringe area, where the burned and unburned stretches of timber came together.

a good chance a gobbler may still be in the area after he has flown down, stick with it—even if it means sitting still for several hours. Also, when calling to silent birds in wet weather, try to avoid calling too much. Most turkey hunting experts agree that you shouldn't call excessively to a gobbler while it's still on the roost. Some will argue, however, that the rules change during wet weath-

HUNTING AMERICA'S WILD TURKEYS

er. If I can get a roosted gobbler to gobble back when it's raining, I'll start throwing some loud cutting while he's still on the limb. There's a good chance that, sooner or later, he'll pitch off his limb and come sailing right in. By calling too conservatively at such times, there's always the chance that a gobbler will lose interest, stop calling, and remain in the tree.

If a rainy day gobbler refuses to answer sounds made with a diaphragm call, hit him with a couple of yelps from a box call. For some reason, a reluctant tom will quite often respond to the higher, sharper tones of a box call while ignoring the flatter tones of, say, a latex rubber mouth call. When using a box call as a locator call, though, don't be surprised if a turkey gobbles back practically in your face, even if you've stopped and called every 50 yards or so. When the weatherman predicts a stretch of rainy weather, it pays to spend a little extra time to roost a gobbler or two. If it rains through the night, you may find it necessary to slip in closer than normal during good weather. Fortunately, the floor of a rain-soaked forest can be as quiet to walk on as deep pile carpeting. Assuming you know exactly where the turkey roosted the evening before, you can slip in under the darkness of heavy cloud cover and set up practically under a roosted gobbler. Even so, I like to keep 60 or 70 yards distance, enough to give a bird room to fly down. Setting up this close to a roosted bird requires extra precaution, however, even when it's pitch black. Never waltz right in with a lighted flashlight to find your way. Instead, feel your way in, especially during the last several hundred yards. The last thing you want to do is stumble through thick undergrowth or trip over dead limbs and branches. A loud pop or crack underfoot is all it takes to alert a turkey that something's not quite right down below. Give yourself an extra 15 minutes or so to ease in as quietly as possible.

When hunting a wide open area, where a roosted gobbler can easily see your set-up, a decoy can make a big difference. The sight of a hen on the ground at first light is more than even the most reluctant tom can resist. But getting the decoy in position without being spotted can mean getting into the woods a full 30 minutes before the first hint of day. If you can make out the silhouette of a roost tree, there's a good chance the gobbler will spot your movements on the ground. When setting a decoy in the dark, it's best to crawl out to set the decoy, then crawl back—very slowly—to your set-up.

I'd much rather hunt during a light or moderate rain shower than when the wind is whistling through the tree tops. At least I can still hear a gobble when it's raining, provided it's not a toad strangler. But on windy days I've actually watched birds gobble less than 100 yards from where I sat and never heard a sound other than the wind. Conversely, it's equally hard for the turkeys to hear your calls. As world champion caller Steve Burnett comments, "When

it's windy, turkeys like to go into open areas where they can see a long way. That's because they can't depend on their hearing. Pastures and clear cuts can be a hunter's best advantage when it's windy or raining."

At times, windy conditions can prove advantageous for a turkey hunter. I can get away with a lot more movement when the wind is moving leafy branches around. The birds have a difficult time telling the difference between the shift of a shotgun muzzle and the movement of branches swaying back and forth in a strong wind. For one reason or another, possibly because they feel more secure with other turkeys around, gobblers often work quicker and easier when the weather's on the breezy side. As Harold Knight says, "One good strategy for windy days is to drive from one bottom or hollow to the next, then stop and call up each one—loudly! You cannot call too loudly on a windy day. The louder your calls, the more likely you'll get a turkey to gobble through a hard wind."

One of the most miserable turkey hunts I've ever experienced took place in northern Nebraska. The ranch was located right on the Niobrara River, about 40 miles south of the South Dakota state line—a beautiful mix of river bottom hay fields, oak-covered flats and ridges topped by ponderosa pine. The place was absolutely loaded with Merriam turkeys. I hunted the first two days of the season with one of the state game commissioners, calling in a good bird for him and myself. Having purchased a second tag, I headed out on the third morning of the hunt on my own. More than two dozen gobblers greeted the coming day with nearly nonstop gobbling. I had moved to within a few hundred yards of the birds and had several of them slowly working in my direction when the first snowflake landed right between my eyes. The toms kept on gobbling for another ten minutes or so, then all went quiet.

The snow continued to come down harder and harder, so after a while I headed back to my truck. By the time I made the half-hour walk, the ground was covered with five inches of the white stuff. By noon, nearly a foot of snow covered the ground. When it let up, I decided to try an afternoon hunt and returned to the ranch. Within 15 minutes after leaving my truck, I heard a bird gobbling even as the snow storm returned. This time, the tom kept answering my calls, and I finally spotted the strutting bird less than 20 yards away. Snowflakes as large as a half-dollar made it difficult to sight in on the bird, but my aim was good—and so was the 21-pound Merriam gobbler.

It was a good thing that I packed along some cold-weather clothing that day. As Harold Knight recommends, "Always pack for the worst possible conditions you can imagine. If you're planning a five-day hunt down south in late March or early April, I guarantee it'll rain at least two of those days, and maybe more. At home, you might decide not to go hunting on those rainy days; but on a trip, where time is short, you'll probably hunt in anything but a

A hunter prepares for a wet day in the turkey woods by slipping on a set of lightweight, breathable rain gear.

hard downpour. So it's important to go prepared for such conditions."

Quite a few clothing manufacturers now offer excellent lightweight rain gear containing such waterproofing materials as Gore-Tex and DuPont Hytrel. A complete set can be easily stuffed into a small daypack or in the game bag of a turkey vest. When dry, these rain suits generally weigh less than a pound, offering excellent protection from even the strongest deluge. An excellent example of this type of foul weather protection is the light Mossy Oak camouflage rainsuit that goes everywhere with me. If there's even a hint of rain in the air, I won't head for the turkey woods without one of these outfits neatly stuffed into the game bag of my turkey vest. I may not be able to hunt when it's raining cats and dogs, but weathering out a sudden storm can put you in store for some great hunting once the rain stops.

Friction calls, such as the wooden box call or the slate call, also require protection from wet weather. Once the paddle—or even the chalk on the paddle—of a box call or the surface of a slate call become the least bit damp, the friction is lost, and so are the tones that produce the calls. I always carry my box and slate calls in quart-sized Ziplock bags, which have proven effective in keeping out dampness. I also carry a Plexiglas "slate-type" call and an acrylic striker to use when it's raining. Within reason, a little rain doesn't greatly effect these calls.

At best, the window for spring turkey hunting is narrow, often made even more so by a short season or restricted "morning only" shooting hours. So don't be forced out of the woods by a little inclement weather. Go prepared, and you can still enjoy many productive turkey hunts. ■

Chapter 13

Hunting Turkeys In The Fall

WITH ■ Ray Eye, *World Champion Turkey Caller* ■ Gary Clancy, *Outdoor Writer*

Wild turkey populations have reached an all-time high,

causing every state but Alaska (which is too far north for wild turkeys to live) to legalize hunting them. In addition to allowing turkey hunting in the spring throughout the U.S. (including Hawaii), all but a few states now permit hunting these big birds during the fall as well. But even with more than two million turkey hunters now in North America, less than half actually take advantage of the opportunity to hunt turkeys during the fall seasons. Many die-hards claim that hunting turkeys in the fall is dull by comparison to spring hunting, when the gobblers are extremely vocal and can be more easily called. To them, harvesting hens and young poults is less appealing. Without the gobbling activity, fall turkey hunting simply isn't exciting enough.

World champion turkey caller and noted wild turkey hunting expert Ray Eye disagrees. Maybe the real reason a lot of people don't get too fired up about fall hunting, he insists, is because they simply don't understand it very

well. This extremely knowledgeable turkey hunter, who has gone after turkeys from coast to coast, spring and fall, notes that fall turkey hunting means hunting for *real* turkeys. During the fall seasons, turkeys act normal, as they do during 300 or more days of the year. Ray notes that only during the spring mating seasons are a turkey's actions and behavior something other than normal. Too often, he points out, hunters who've been weaned on the sport during spring seasons step into the fall woods, make a few seductive hen yelps, and wonder why there's no answering gobbles. With little or no understanding about how to hunt during the fall seasons, they conclude that it's a second-rate season. Nothing could be farther from the truth.

"The key to having fun in the fall," Ray Eye insists, "is understanding the turkeys and what they're doing. This is often a time when flocks range from two to two dozen or more. Understanding and knowing how to take advantage

Taking a good gobbler in the fall generally means spending time locating and patterning a particular bird or small flock of adult gobblers.

of their gregarious nature is the first step to successful hunting."

Fall flocks are often made up of a single hen with her poults, especially early in the fall. Later, especially during early winter, many of the smaller single family groups ban together. Then it isn't uncommon to encounter flocks of 50 or more birds, including a half-dozen or more mature hens. Flocks numbering into the hundreds have been spotted on occasion. One recorded winter flock in northern Missouri during the late 1980s numbered an estimated 5,000 turkeys, drawn there mostly for an abundant food source during an especially harsh winter.

"Still caught between adolescence and adulthood," Ray Eye continues, "groups of jakes often band together and wander in the woods. They can number anywhere from a pair to a dozen or more shortbeards in one bunch. Barren hens—those who didn't raise a brood—will often band together in a similar manner."

Adult gobblers also tend to band together in the fall. Numerous times, though, I've seen single adult toms seemingly content to spend the fall months alone. But even most of these recluses seek the companionship of other toms as fall turns into winter. Bowhunting on Thanksgiving morning has long been a tradition for me. While the family starts putting together the afternoon or evening meals, I invariably head for a favorite bow stand to get in a little deer hunting. One Thanksgiving morning in northern Missouri stands out

in my memory. The weather had been unusually mild for late November. A cold front was pushing into the area, though, and by Saturday the oak forest would be coated with a white blanket. But on that Thanksgiving morning I was greeted by only a light drizzle and temperatures in the lower 50s.

Everything was on the move. At first good light, I watched as more than 30 turkey sailed down from their roost on a ridge overlooking a small river valley, landing in a harvested soybean field 300 or so yards to my left. Through the binoculars it was hard to distinguish beards on any of the birds; but from their size I figured most had to be adult gobblers. As I was trying to get a better look, a movement caught my attention. A big doe with several yearling fawns

Hens are nearly always legal game during the fall turkey seasons, thereby increasing the opportunities to harvest some good eating. The hen shown sports a five-inch beard.

eased along the travel corridor where I had placed my stand 20 feet up a big burr oak. I'd already taken a buck earlier with my bow and was looking to tag a doe for some great eating. Now, as the deer passed within 20 yards of the stand, a well-placed arrow brought it down cleanly after only a 40-yard run.

I thought about getting down from the stand when it dawned on me that the sound of turkeys—lots of them—had suddenly grown louder. I turned

eyes. As the last bird in the line was passing beneath me, I knew it was now or never. As the nock of the arrow came back to my anchor point, my sights were dead center on the last bird's back. I released and the arrow found its mark, taking out the tom's spine. A few wild thrashes and it was over. Moments later, the skies opened up and I packed out my gobbler and retrieved my doe in a cold pouring rain. Back home, everyone assumed I'd been

Fall turkeys commonly band together to form large flocks, much like these Rio Grande turkeys in south Texas.

slowly to my left and was surprised to witness a line of gobblers—38 in all—walking directly toward my stand. They were all adult birds, and every one of them passed directly beneath my stand.

I stood motionless, afraid to draw the compound bow to full draw for fear of being spotted by all those sharp

rained out, until they took a look at the back of my pickup.

The group of 38 longbeards still represent the largest flock of adult eastern gobblers I've personally encountered. Most bachelor gobbler groups number between five and six to perhaps a dozen or so big birds. When it comes to the

When locating fall turkeys, a good set of binoculars can prove invaluable;
the bigger the country, the more boot leather they'll save.

HUNTING TURKEYS IN THE FALL

makeup of fall turkey flocks, though, there are no absolutes. Hens and hen poults generally make up the majority of the flocks encountered by fall turkey hunters, with bands of juvenile gobblers being the next most common flock. Bachelor groups of adult gobblers are the least encountered.

"Almost any combination is possible," says Ray Eye, "I've seen longbeards with hens and poults. You're liable to see a jake with anything that will tolerate it. Late in the fall, it's not

harvesting these turkeys. They taste mighty fine. Bear in mind, too, that if a state game department felt that fall hunting was jeopardizing its turkey populations, the season would become more limited, or even curtailed.

Scouting for fall birds is essential for success. For the most part, there's not a lot of gobbling to tell a hunter where to hunt—which isn't to say that fall gobblers don't gobble. I well remember those October and November mornings when I was tempted to head back home and check my calendar to make sure I hadn't been asleep for six months. There are certain times in the fall when gobblers go ballistic, but those mornings are the exception and not the rule. In the same light, fall gobblers seldom gobble when called to. To locate good, huntable populations of fall birds usually means spending lots of time in the woods looking for the telltale signs of a wild turkey.

The most recognizable sign is that of *scratching*. Given a heavy, white oak acorn crop, you can bet that most turkeys will stick to the woods until most of that crop has disappeared from the forest floor. When necessary, these birds can move a lot of leaf cover searching for acorns. During dry periods, it sometimes takes a

uncommon to see turkeys of all ages and both sexes in one huge flock."

Because hens, hen poults and juvenile gobblers tend to be the most abundant turkeys in the fall, they understandably make up the majority of birds harvested by hunters at this time of year. There's absolutely nothing wrong with

trained eye to discern fresh scratchings from old ones. But if all the scratching along a wooded ridge looks as if it's been rained on—and it hasn't rained a drop in a week—you'd best look elsewhere for turkeys.

Acorns aren't the only things turkeys scratch for. In wooded areas where the ground is covered with leaves, the birds will rake away the leaves in search of insects and tender green shoots. In heavy pine woods, they'll scratch back dead pine needles looking for pine seeds. Along creek banks they can be seen scratching away at bare dirt surfaces searching for worms, grubs and insects. And in crop fields, turkeys will scratch through whatever cover is left behind looking for remnant kernels of corn or soybeans. Whenever turkey

travel they leave behind other sign, such as droppings, tracks and feathers. Check the earlier chapter on "Scouting" to see whether the sign you've uncovered came from a gobbler or hen, an adult or a young bird.

One of my favorite places to look for fresh sign is along a small creek. Turkeys like to walk up and down the bottoms of sandy creek beds, leaving behind tracks that instantly tell you if turkeys are in the area. During an exceptionally dry period, small water holes remaining in a creek become even more of a draw. Large fall flocks become quite visible and are relatively easy to pattern. For weeks on end, these birds will follow the exact same travel route from their roosting area to the feeding areas where they spend most of their days.

Many fall gobblers are taken by patient hunters who spend long hours waiting along known turkey travel routes.

Where a travel route crosses or includes large open areas, a good pair of binoculars is useful for watching birds from a distance. This helps to avoid spooking the birds, perhaps causing them to change their travel pattern. It also cuts down on the footwork considerably.

Fall birds are known for being relatively noisy while still on the roost and also when they first hit the ground. Keep in mind that most of the birds who make up fall flocks are the young-of-the-year poults. They really aren't that much different from our own children, squabbling over almost every-

Smart ol' gobblers who fail to respond to spring calls are often taken in the fall by hunters who've spotted them through binoculars. This tom with full two-inch spurs was taken by the author.

thing. It's likely the vocal establishment of the pecking order that causes a gobbler to sound off. A deep gobble or two lets the youngsters know who rules the roost, so to speak.

Even when a flock is on the ground and feeding, there is always some communication among the birds. It may not be the loud yelping or gobbling heard most often in the spring, but rather soft purrs, clucks and yelps. In fact, when the birds are busy scratching away for acorns, they make a lot more noise with their feet than with their mouths. When scouting for turkeys, always listen intently before charging over a ridge top. If the birds are feeding, you can usually hear them 100 to 150 yards away.

Ray Eye comments: "In the spring you usually call from one sex to the other, but in fall you often call from bird to like bird, (i.e.) poult to poult or old tom to old tom. One exception is calling like a hen to regroup a scattered brood. All types of birds can be called in the fall if you simply speak their language. As in the spring, some of your best prospects are birds on the roost. If you've done your homework you may already know the general location of a roosted flock."

If you haven't pinpointed the exact location of a roost before the hunt, Ray Eye recommends getting on a high piece of ground before daybreak and listening carefully for turkey talk as the sun slowly rises. Most people, he adds, are amazed at the amount of yelping, purring and other conversation that takes place at a fall roost. If you don't hear anything from your first position, try a few "kee-kee" runs. There aren't many hens in the woods who can resist the pleading calls of a lost poult, especially when it's on the roost.

Ray Eye likes to approach a fall roost the same as when he's working a spring roost; that is, get as close to the birds as possible and set up wherever the turkeys are most likely to land. "If you listen well," he advises, "you should be able to tell which bird is doing the most calling. You should then call directly to that bird, remembering to call from bird to like bird."

This experienced fall turkey hunter recommends imitating whatever calls the most vocal turkey is making, but to do so with more intensity. If the turkey yelps loudly, yelp loudly back at it. The same applies whether the turkey cuts or yelps. The excitement of all this calling can get other birds calling as well. When that happens, you're in for lots of fun!

One of the more commonly used tactics for hunting fall turkeys is to first locate a flock, then scatter it. The key to success here is to really *scatter* the birds, not merely run them off. It's important that the turkeys fly or run off in different, opposite directions. Younger birds and hens can't stand to be away from each other for very long, so if you do manage to bust up a flock, be sure to set up somewhere in between the scattered birds. Calling a turkey in for a shot after that should not be difficult.

To get a good scattering, Ray Eye says, you really have to surprise the birds. For the sake of safety, he recommends laying your shotgun down. When the time is right, jump up and rush at the flock, clapping your hands or barking like a dog. The closer you can get to the center of the flock, the better your chances of making a good scatter. A prime spot to set up is at or near the scatter point.

"I usually don't start calling until the turkeys try to regroup," Ray advises. "Sometimes scattered birds will start calling to regroup within a few minutes—but sometime they don't call for an hour. Once you get a bird to call, you can not only imitate it, you can make the sound even more pleading. When working young birds, you can do well with the kee-kee. You can often get results simply by whistling the sound. Or if you want to use hen yelps, try a long, lingering call of twenty to thirty yelps."

Outdoor writer Gary Clancy chimes in: "Hunting fall turkey with a dog is rare, but it's nothing new. A good turkey dog is expected to hunt for the scent trail of a flock, follow that scent to a flock, and then dash among the birds at full speed while barking excitedly. Since some birds always choose to run instead of fly, an experienced turkey dog will return to the scatter site and trail each individual runner until it flushes. After every bird has been routed, the dog returns to its master and

A decoy alone can lure fall turkeys in close enough for a shot. The hen in the middle is the decoy.

sits quietly. At that point, the hunter calls to the scattered birds. Some turkey dogs are even trained to lie inside camouflaged sacks so they don't spook returning turkeys."

Whether scattered by dog or by hunter, Clancy continues: "Once the flock has been scattered, set up near the dispersal site, wait five or ten minutes, then begin calling. Yelps and kee-kees are the best calls in the fall. Because the flock has a strong bond then, the birds will quickly try to re-

group. It's not unusual to hear birds calling to each other from all directions once a flock has been broken."

Both Ray Eye and Gary Clancy agree that one of the most successful scatters the fall hunter can make is to spook a flock of birds off the roost late in the evening, the later the better. Under the cover of darkness, the hunter can get close before rushing in and scaring the

birds off in every direction. If your mind is set on taking an adult gobbler, and you know where a bachelor group of toms is roosting, this can be an effective tactic. After spending the night perched alone on a limb, even an adult gobbler will be anxious to rejoin his running mates. A few long, drawn out gobbler yelps at first light in the morning are especially deadly.

Ray Eye feels that too much emphasis has been placed on busting up fall flocks before calling to them. He simply doesn't see much sense in running in and scattering a flock of birds you've walked miles to find. Most flocks, he feels, can be called to within shotgun range in the first place. As he explains: "Try to set up where your calls can be heard simultaneously in several good areas. Get comfortable and let the woods settle down before you start calling. Start off with soft, short calls in case there's a flock just beyond a ridge. As time progresses, make your calls more aggressive."

A master of the fall woods, Ray further warns that the sexy mating yelps used so widely during spring seasons probably won't do hunters much good in the fall. If you're hunting a state where it's legal to take any bird that comes in, and you're not too choosy, then stick with a lot of kee-kee whistles until an old hen responds. Duplicate her calls, adding just a little to each one.

Many fall turkeys are taken by bowhunters who are interested mainly in white-tails. Even when positioned 20 feet off the ground, camouflage is still important, for any movement can be quickly spotted by the wary birds.

HUNTING TURKEYS IN THE FALL

Eye prefers calling with a little rasp, such as a mouth diaphragm with a split reed, a good slate call, or a box call to duplicate the calls of mature birds.

Ray also feels that fall hunters don't spend enough time calling to adult gobblers. More than one "expert" has written that fall gobblers don't respond well to calls. That, according to Eye, is

nonsense. "It's a good thing gobblers can't read!" he exclaims. "There are no real secrets to calling fall gobblers. The basics are the same as calling young birds or hens. Call gobbler to gobbler

and try to break into the existing pecking order as the new kid on the block."

The calls made by gobblers, he points out, are commonly more drawn out and deeper than those made by a hen. For Ray, a good slate call is tough to beat when it comes to producing gobbler yelps, purrs, putts and cuts. For hunters who prefer a mouth diaphragm call, he recommends using one with a split reed to produce the deep, raspy tones of an adult gobbler.

"Hunting specifically for a mature gobbler in fall is tough," he continues. "Because there are few gobblers in any turkey population. Just finding one in fall can be difficult. Find a gobbler band, however, and you can rush and scatter it just as you would a flock of hens and juveniles. But because gobblers are not as flock-oriented as hens and young turkeys, they are not as eager to regroup. It may take hours—or even days—before gobblers reconvene. Only hunters with extreme patience consistently take fall gobblers."

Gary Clancy, an experienced and highly regarded outdoor writer, advises hunters to be prepared for a long wait when trying to call in a gobbler who's been scattered from a bachelor flock. He recommends waiting at least half an hour after busting up a flock before calling—and even then calling with only one or two coarse gobbler clucks or yelps. After that, a hunter shouldn't call any more than once every half-hour. Since it's nearly impossible to sit stone-still for hours at a time, a good portable blind or camouflaged netting stretched between several trees or saplings is a good idea. Very often a fall gobbler will slip in without making a sound, so fall hunters must be alert.

"Unless you hear a turkey walking in dry leaves," Clancy advises, "your first indication that he has arrived is when you actually see him, or when he calls at close range. The turkey knows he should be able to see the gobbler he has heard, so when he doesn't, he clucks or yelps, as if to say, 'I'm here—now where are you!' Odds are excellent the gobbler will be in range when he clucks, so try not to jump in surprise."

"I seldom intentionally scatter a bachelor flock of fall gobblers," says Ray Eye. "I've had pretty poor success getting them to regroup—in the near future, anyway!" Working adult fall gobblers off the roost, or while moving and calling through the autumn woods is Ray's idea of real *turkey hunting*. It's nothing, he insists, to call fall gobblers. Get a bird to respond, then imitate his calls, but with more intensity in order to get the tom fired up. Eye strongly believes that the most important ingredients for success fall turkey hunters must possess are confidence and patience. You don't have to be a pro caller. He's shared these same recommendations with many hunters who previously had doubted fall gobblers could be called.

Ray Eye's last bit of advice is simple: Never pass up the opportunity to work any bird that will answer a call, even if you're holding out for an adult tom. He has found that it's not uncommon to run into a mixed flock with a longbeard or two in its midst. He has also found that hens and poults can help a hunter make a gobbler flock respond. More than once he has called to a hen and her brood and their excited calls in turn have caught the attention of a nearby gobbler flock, which came running in to see what the commotion was all about.

"Even if it takes you some time to call in a fall gobbler, stick with it," Ray advises. "Sooner or later, you'll be sitting in some frosty woods in full color with your heart in your throat as you watch a flock of excited gobblers shoving each other back and forth as they approach."

Fall turkey hunting can be extremely difficult, or it can be very easy. It depends in large part on where the hunter has set his sights: whether to harvest a big adult gobbler or be satisfied with a young bird or hen. Fortunately, in many states fall hunters can harvest two or more birds, providing an opportunity to choose both the tender-eating and the trophy gobbler. Oddly enough, even though fall seasons generally allow the harvest of poults and hens, the average success rate of fall turkey hunters across the U.S. is only about .5 percent higher than the average spring success rate (34 percent in fall vs. 33.5 percent in spring). When all is said and done, it's not a platter full of tasty jake or hen fillets that draws the serious turkey hunter into the autumn woods; it's the lure of hanging a tag on a big gobbler. ∎

Chapter 14

Outfitting For Success

WITH ■ Ray Eye, *World Champion Turkey Caller* ■ Toxey Haas, *C.E.O., Hass Outdoors/Mossy Oak Camouflage* ■ Jim Crumley, *TreBark Camouflage*

In previous chapters, we've covered in great detail some of the guns, loads, archery equipment, muzzleloading shotguns, and calls preferred by some of our most successful turkey hunters. The gear items they've chosen have become their favorites for good reason: *the stuff works.* In this chapter we take a good look at the various camouflage patterns and the thought that went into them. Also featured are footwear, specialized turkey hunting vests, seats, blinds, decoys, gun rests, and any other goodies designed to make turkey hunting more pleasurable and successful.

CAMOUFLAGED CLOTHING

I well remember the camouflage clothing I wore on my very first turkey hunt back in 1972. My old friend Willis Corbett, who at the time was head of Winchester's recreational shooting program, had arranged for me to turkey hunt with Missouri turkey biologist John Lewis, while on assignment to cover the Intercollegiate Trap & Skeet Tournament for *Gun World Magazine*. I was fresh out of the Marine Corps and had several complete sets of the old Vietnam "Tiger Stripe" camouflage outfits. I'd had my share of wearing those duds, however, and purchased instead a brand new set of camouflage specifically for this occasion. As it turned out, the only items I bought were a light jacket, pants and a cap covered with the standard blotch or spot camouflage dating from World War II, which were about all we had to choose from back then. The first of what is now often referred to as "designer camo" hit the market in the early 1970s. Called "TreBark," this pattern was created by Jim Crumley. Instead of a random pattern of various brown and green splotches on a neutral colored background, similar to the World War II pattern I wore on my first turkey hunt, Crumley's new design attempted instead to duplicate the scaled pattern of tree bark (hence its name).

Jim Crumley, who is primarily an archer when hunting whitetails, also spends a great deal of time chasing turkeys each spring. "For a close range hunting sport like turkey hunting," he advises, "ridding yourself of a distinct human outline and blending into your background is very important. Camouflage patterns should closely match the surrounding terrain and foliage. Mixing different camo patterns from top to bottom is one way to do that; but in the final analysis the best camo is simply *to stay still* and learn how to move slowly once you've spotted an old gobbler."

I recall one successful turkey hunt when mixing camouflage patterns worked just fine, even though the combination of various camouflage patterns I wore that day was purely unintentional. The alarm rattled me out of bed that morning at 4 a.m., and I could hear the sounds of sleet hitting the window pane. I almost rolled over and went back to sleep; but it was opening morning of the Missouri turkey season, and I *knew* the exact tree a gobbler had roosted the evening before. So I climbed out of bed and, in an effort to avoid waking my family, got dressed in the dark, trying to identify my camouflage garments by feel alone.

Tiny ice balls bounced off the windshield of my pickup as I headed for a pasture several miles away. It was still dark when I pulled into the gate opening, parked the truck and made my way across the grass-covered ground. The evening before, I had noticed a fine gobbler roosting in a tree as I was picking morel mushrooms. If he hadn't moved to another tree during the night (which they

will often do), I felt confident I could get the tom in close enough for a shot. Overcast skies held back daybreak until finally I heard the tom gobble at the hoot of a real owl in the valley below. I had set up within 80 yards of the tree, with a decoy placed 20 yards in front of me. For the next 15 minutes, the turkey gobbled at every sound in the woods without leaving the tree. Going against my better judgment, I decided to call. Three or four soft hen yelps were met by a double, then a triple gobble. The next thing I knew, the tom sailed down from the limb and landed within 15 yards of my decoy. The front bead of my Remington 870 was fast on his head, and when the gobbler moved another ten years toward the decoy, I eased back on the trigger. A split second later, my first week of hunting the Missouri season was over.

By the time I returned home, the light was still dim and the kids were just getting out of bed and dressing for school. My son Adam had taken several photos of me with the big bird before I

The author harvested his first wild turkey gobbler back in 1971, before the days of "designer" camouflage patterns, he wore a camouflage pattern dating from World War II.

headed for work (I was at the time public relations manager for Bass Pro Shops). Prior to reaching the office, I dropped the film off and later, after picking up the shots, showed them to the head clothing buyer for Bass Pro Shops. The first words out of his mouth were, "You would think that someone who worked for an outdoor outfitter like Bass Pro Shops would wear a full set of the same camouflage!" It dawned on me then that the things I was wearing—hat, jacket, shirt and pants—were of completely different camo patterns.

Jim Crumley, who revolutionized the camouflaged clothing market with the introduction of his TreBark pattern during the mid 1970s, wears a more recent version of the pattern, known as "Superflauge."

Ray Eye, one of the best known turkey hunters in the U.S., insists that, "After calls and guns, good camouflage can be a turkey hunter's most important equipment. Hunting turkeys is a game

of getting an alert bird with razor sharp eyes into close range. Good camouflage can make that much easier to accomplish." Ray admits that his taste in camouflage has changed over the years. As a teenager just learning to call turkeys, he was quite content to wear an old ratty camouflage jacket, a somewhat matching hat, and a pair of faded overalls. Turkey hunting in Missouri was still in it's infancy during the 1960s, and while better quality camouflage was available even then, Ray Eye lacked the money to buy it. To him, making money meant having a job, and getting a job meant there would be less time for calling turkeys. So he was happy to wear what he had—and learn how to be successful with it.

"I made do with what I had," he recalls, "using good calling positions and the ability to hold stone still for whatever length of time it took to get a gobbler up close. The approach worked for me then, and it works for me now."

While Ray Eye admits that the best strategy of all is simply sitting still, he still feels that, with the great selection of camouflage clothing currently available, there's no reason in the world for a turkey hunter to head for the woods less than totally prepared. As for which pattern works the best, he recommends one that matches the terrain and foliage in which the hunter plans to work. For example, the darker bark, leaf and branch camouflage patterns that work so well in eastern and southern forests often don't blend on the open prairies of the West.

Among the more popular camouflage patterns today are Bill Jordan's "Realtree" and Toxey Haas' "Mossy Oak." Actually, several different variations of these two patterns are available, making it possible for hunters to match the habitats in which they plan to hunt. Several patterns are quite distinct, featuring actual bark patterns, branches and leaves printed in great detail, while others include more subtle areas of varying natural shades and colors made to resemble the patches of light and shadows covering the forest floor.

During the late 1980s, Toxey Haas, a Mississippi whitetail and turkey hunter, set out to design his "Mossy Oak" camouflage. He settled on a simple bark-type pattern in three distinct shades: olive drab green, a fairly dark gray, and black. The earliest Mossy Oak camouflage was known as "Bottomland." The first time I actually saw this pattern, outdoor writer Wade Bourne wore it on a turkey hunt we made together in the southern Ozarks of Missouri. I had dropped Wade off at a huge open pasture bordering several thousands acres of National Forest, assuring him I'd return around 11:00 that morning. I also dropped off outdoor writer Jim Zumbo, an outdoor writer and friend, at another location, while Tom McIntyre, another writer, stayed with me.

When we returned later to pick up Wade, we spotted a figure walking across the open pasture several hundred yards away. At first, I didn't recognize who it was. Wade had been wear-

ing camouflage when I let him off, but the man who now walked toward us wore only olive drab military fatigues. When the hunter got to within 60 yards of the truck, I could see that it was indeed Wade, and that he was wearing camouflage.

A few years after Toxey Haas' Bottomland hit the market, he went back to the drawing board and came up with a solution that gave his pattern more definition, adding as well bold branches and light tan splotches. The result was a distinct camouflage pattern which effectively broke up a hunter's outline while still blending in with the natural surroundings. This pattern, which became known as Mossy Oak's "Treestand,"

One of the most successful camouflage patterns ever introduced were the variations of Bill Jordan's Realtree Camouflage. Here Bill wears one of his Realtree X-Tra patterns.

played a significant role in establishing the company as a leader in the camouflage industry.

Since those early patterns, Mossy Oak has introduced several other top-selling camouflage patterns, including my own favorite, the "Break Up" pattern. Instead of a pattern with high definition, Break Up is a combination of softly outlined leaves, branches and bark with darker and lighter splotches shaded in. Having taken a good look at other hunters wearing this pattern, I've noticed that when settled in next to the base of a big tree they become almost

invisible. This is especially noticeable where branches of several small saplings are located directly in front and to the side of the hunter. Thus, nature's foliage tends to give "Break Up" something of a 3-D effect.

Another good camouflage pattern, known as "A.S.A.T.," has failed to win the acceptance it deserves. Instead of

trying to duplicate bark, branches or leaves, this pattern features a random overlay of bold, elliptical black and brown slashes printed on a light khaki or tan material. The resulting camouflage almost takes on a three-dimensional effect. In my opinion, it does a much better job of breaking up a hunter's outline than many of the more popular patterns. Unfortunately, when buying camouflage hunters are too often drawn to those patterns that are more aesthetically appealing. Keep in mind that effective camouflage is difficult to accomplish. Each pattern must be bold enough to break up the outline of the hunter, while at the same time it must have the capability of blending in with the natural surroundings without attracting the attention of a gobbler's sharp eye.

When researching a new camouflage pattern, scrutinize the pattern carefully. Try to visualize how it will look in the habitat where you normally hunt turkeys. Will the pattern fulfill these criteria? Is it bold enough to break your outline? Will it blend with the natural surrounding? I've hunted spring turkeys in just about every weather imaginable, from bone-chilling, knee-deep snow storms to steamy, mosquito-filled woods with nearly full foliage. In Chapter 12 ("Rainy Day Gobblers"), we covered some tactics that keep on producing turkeys even when the weather is less than perfect. We also touched on the need to wear clothing that allow a hunter to be comfortable in all types of adverse weather, whether rain or snow.

This is what Ray Eye has to say about good turkey hunting wear: "Good old cotton and cotton blends are tough to beat. I usually advise staying away from most of the synthetic fabrics. They'll keep you dry, but when you move they often sound like a handful of newspapers being crumpled. It's a good idea to select a jacket that's a little large, so you can move around in comfort. It also enables you to dress for the weather. When it's freezing, there's room for a couple of sweatshirts, and when it's hot and muggy, you can get by with only a long-sleeved T-shirt. As for style, I like a coat that hangs below my waist. And it absolutely *must* have plenty of big pockets in which to carry a wide range of calls, shells and other paraphernalia."

Ray looks for the same qualities when selecting a pair of camouflaged pants—something with lots of big pockets and loose enough to prevent binding. A pair I've used for several seasons now have become all-time favorites of mine. I refer to the "Weatherbeater" pants made by WestArk Pro Outdoors (Independence, MO) using super-soft and comfortable Saddle-Cloth. This multi-layered material incorporates a thin layer of duPont Teflon to ward off the dampness of a light shower. The pants feature a special waterproof lining that extends from the knee down, plus the seat of the pants. This product ensures against getting wet when walking through tall, dew-laden grass or when you must drop down by the nearest tree to begin calling. Zippered cargo

pockets contain calls, gloves, head nets, shells and so forth.

Turkey hunting vests designed especially for this purpose have won widespread popularity. They feature plenty of large, roomy pockets for carrying calls, shells, insect repellent, lunch, or what have you, plus a big game bag for

packing out a 20-pound (or more) gobbler. There's also a padded, waterproof seat to make those long waits more comfortable and drier. A well-designed vest makes things easier for turkey hunters who want everything ready to go. Just slip the vest on, slide the shotgun out of the case, and head for the woods.

The camouflaged face mask and gloves worn by this hopeful bowhunter augment a full camouflage job.

My vest in particular features two large, zippered front pockets with several smaller internal compartments for keeping calls, shells and other items separate. In addition, a smaller breast pocket has room enough for four or five small plastic diaphragm call cases. And while this vest does feature a big, roomy game bag, I usually carry a set

A quality pair of binoculars can save a turkey hunter a lot of needless walking.

of light rain gear there. As for a seat, I like something a little more comfortable than the simple closed cell foam pads that come with almost all turkey hunting vests. One of the best I've rested in comfortably is the Chapman Lo-Boy Lite Turkey Hunting Chair made by

Chapman Chair Company (Selma, AL). This compact 15"x17" tubular aluminum frame features heavy duty nylon webbing for the seat. Its front legs stand about eight inches tall and the back legs measure only five inches. When the seat is placed with the short legs toward the trunk of the tree, it automatically places the hunter's knees at the perfect height for holding a shotgun while slow-moving toms take their sweet time covering those last 20 or 30 yards. The seat weighs a mere $1\frac{1}{2}$ pounds and comes with a long leather shoulder strap for easy packing. It'll keep your seat off the damp ground, too, and is comfortable enough to sit on for hours if necessary.

Camouflage head nets come in a wide range of styles. Comfort and visibility are usually the two major factors that influence one's decision. Some head nets are nothing more than a fine, meshed nylon net bag that slips completely over the head, cap and all. About 20 years ago, I was headed south for the opener of the Arkansas turkey season when I realized I had left my head net sitting on my desk at home. As soon as I got off the interstate, I stopped at a Wal-Mart and bought a new head net. They had only one style—the full slip over mesh type—but it was better than no net at all. The next morning, I left camp well before daybreak and by first light had a Quachita Mountain gobbler answering every owl hoot I made. After slipping to within a hundred yards of the bird, I slipped the net over my cap and placed a diaphragm call in the roof of my mouth. As soon as I heard the bird fly down, I called lightly and the tom gobbled right back from only 50 yards away. The gun was ready and my eyes searched for the turkey in the dim light. Suddenly, out of the corner of my right eye, there he was, in full strut. I waited patiently for the bird to move, but nothing happened. Slowly—and I do mean slowly—I turned my head in the bird's direction. Nothing. The next time he gobbled, it was almost directly in front of me. Slowly, I turned my head and sighted down the barrel of my three-inch magnum pump. I could now see the tips of the bird's tail as he headed straight toward me. Before his head and neck came into view, something caught my eye. It was that strutting bird again. "Too bad," I said to myself. A few second later, a beautiful bronze-colored gobbler stepped from the thin underbrush and I dropped him with one well-placed 17-yard shot. The bird on my right, however, never even flinched. Sensing something wasn't right, I turned quickly in that direction. Nothing. I yanked off my head net and threw it on the ground. Then, as I reached down to pick it up, I noticed for the first time that the camouflaged pattern of the head net consisted of strutting turkeys. The bird I'd been watching peripherally was merely a splotch on my head net!

I now tend to favor the "half-mask" design, or one with large eye openings that can't hamper my vision. Occasionally, I'll use some camo face makeup, except I don't like the mess when it's time to clean it off. I want to see an oncoming gobbler before he pinpoints the exact origin of my calls, and I don't want anything right in front of my eyes. The quicker I can spot a gobbler, the more time and opportunity I have to get ready for a shot. This is especially important when calling with a box or slate call requiring the use of both hands.

Gloves are a personal matter, too. Most of the time, I use a pair of light-weight brown jersey gloves with the finger tips cut off. Because I use a lot of friction calls, direct contact of my finger tips with the paddle of a box call or

Knee-high rubber boots worn for an early season Iowa hunt allowed the author to traverse several small creeks in order to reach into the old bird's hang-out.

the striker of a slate-type call allows me to actually "feel" the tone of the call. Likewise, I want as little material between my trigger finger and the shotgun trigger as possible.

Even when camouflaged from head to toe, there's no guarantee you won't be spotted. I've hunted with many hunters who truly felt they were invisible to turkeys simply because they were fully decked out in camouflage from head to toe. I recall one incident in particular concerning a video cameraman who wanted desperately to get a muzzle-loading kill on tape. We were in southern Iowa, in an area absolutely loaded with turkeys. That morning, we heard more than 40 birds gobble, but none of them wanted to work. After hunting on another nearby farm without success, we went back to the area where we'd heard all those birds earlier. My first call was cut short by a gobble about a hundred yards away. I dropped down next to a huge oak, but to my surprise the cameraman simply sat down on the floor of the open woods. There wasn't time to correct the situation, and sure enough, about a minute later, a gobbler stepped into my sight 70 yards away. I managed to coax the bird to within 50 yards but, not liking what he saw, the tom turned and walked nonchalantly back up the slope and out of sight.

When I asked the cameraman why he had sat down in the open like that, he said it was okay because he was camouflaged! I tried to explain that, so far as the turkey was concerned, my companion probably stood out like a two-ton boulder that suddenly fell in the bird's backyard where it walked every day. "Always remember," warns Ray Eye, "that good camouflage is an aid, not a cure-all. No matter how you're dressed, there's no substitute for holding still."

It's nice when you can walk several hundred yards into a woodlot behind your own house on opening morning of the season, sit down and call a bird

into the gun. In the real world, each bird represents many miles of terrain covered on foot—and I wouldn't have it any other way. To me, the true joy of turkey hunting is learning how to move on the birds, to get around them, to call from a different direction, to head them off, or identify where they are headed and to be there waiting for them when they arrive. It's those tough birds we remember the most.

It's impossible to prescribe a pair of boots that are ideal for every turkey hunting terrain, simply because such a thing doesn't exist. A hunter who's headed for the mountains or some other rough and rocky country will more than likely want a pair of high-topped leather (or a leather- nylon combination) boots with a good non-slip outer sole. Faced with a long walk to and from the hunting area, the boots should be lightweight. Conversely, a turkey hunter who enters a southern swamp before daybreak will doubtless have a lot of wet walking to do. He or she will be better equipped wearing a pair of knee-high, all-rubber boots.

The boot I prefer is made of leather and stands eight or nine inches tall with little, if any, insulation. Good ankle support is a must. I also prefer an outer sole that offers good traction but doesn't fill up with mud the first time I cross the edge of a wet field or skirt along the bank of a small creek. Most important is that the boot be built with a waterproof membrane, such as Gore-Tex. Even when hunting high on a ridge, I've had to walk through tall, wet grass at some time during the season. In that event, with wet feet you have a tough walk ahead of you—and it's going to be a long morning.

Have you ever sat with your back against a tree, your shotgun resting across your knee, and waited for what seems an eternity for a gobbler to poke his head through the thick foliage of late spring and slowly move into range? It's amazing how much an eight-pound shotgun can weigh while you wait for a shot that can make or break a successful season. I've never been a fan of the big 10-gauge automatics for turkey hunting. For one reason, they're too dammed heavy! Shotguns like the old Ithaca Mag-10 or the current version of that same gun (Remington's SP-10) do offer a lot of punch. Indeed, they may be the "bee's knees" when taking shots at ducks and geese from a duck blind. But weighing some 11 pounds, they're a real pain to pack all day in the turkey woods. For many hunters, moreover, they're next to impossible to hold in the aiming position for more than a minute or two, even when resting across a knee.

During the early 1990s, I guided a hunter who insisted on taking his bird with a 10-gauge autoloader, for which he'd spent close to a thousand dollars specifically for turkey hunting. I'll admit

that gun threw tremendous patterns out to 50 yards, but I never would've packed it a mile to shoot a turkey. Right off the bat that first morning, I called in two fine gobblers who strutted right up to within 25 yards of where we sat. The birds had taken their time covering the last 20 yards, and my fellow hunter had been holding his shotgun on target for more than five minutes before I whispered "Shoot!" At the roar of the shotgun, the leafy ground cover seven or eight feet in front of the birds literally exploded, causing both birds to leap

No turkey hunter should be without one or more of these lightweight collapsible decoys.

into the air and disappear. Two hours later, we lucked into a lonesome tom who responded to my calls, and once again my hunter managed to throw leaves in its face.

I knew the weight of his shotgun had taken its toll on my hunting companion. By the time the turkeys had come close enough to shoot, he had no idea about which direction the muzzle and front bead were pointed. I drove to another small woodlot and, after convincing my

Pennsylvania's resident turkey hunting expert Robby Rohm understands the importance of having all the right gear.

Being properly outfitted for turkey season means a lot more than having a box full of calls.

Three-dimensional camouflage patterns do a tremendous job in helping a hunter disappear in the turkey woods.

hunter to leave his 10-gauge cannon in the truck, took my 3-inch magnum 12-gauge pump instead. We had barely stepped into the woodlot when my call was greeted by a hearty gobble about 150 yards away. We eased down an old logging road for another 40 yards or so and called again. This time the bird was less than 50 yards away, just over the crest of a hill. A few minutes later, the tom strutted into view at the top of the hill. I purred and clucked a few times and the turkey slowly worked in our direction. A short time later, when it was only 20 yards away, the gobbler looked up in search of his hen, whereupon a load of No. 6s sent him rolling.

Most of us get by just fine by resting our shotguns across our knees while waiting for a turkey to show. However, I've hunted with a number of young hunters and a few women who've had real difficulty in holding up the muzzle of their shotguns for any length of time. And often when they do, it's like the hand of a conductor leading an orchestra. All of this can be eliminated by using a simple set of shooting sticks or a rest of some sort. One of the best I've seen is a set of adjustable shooting sticks from Stoney Point Products (New Ulm, MN). Their "Steady Stix" rest weighs less than a pound, and in the fully collapsed position it slips easily right into the game bag of any turkey hunting vest (it also comes with eyelets for easy attachment of a shoulder strap). In mere seconds, the legs of this rest can be telescoped out to any desired height, from around 15 to 35 inches.

Because the shotgun rests in a rubber-faced "V" at the top of these shooting sticks (instead of the rest being attached to the shotgun) the hunter can quickly adjust once a bird approaches one side or the other. The rest also allows the shotgun to pivot left to right, enough to provide several feet of sighting adjustment at 20 yards. Should a turkey suddenly appear off to one side, the hunter can forego the shooting sticks, lift the shotgun from the V-shaped rest, and swing the shotgun in that direction.

The more a hunter can hide his face with a good camouflaged face mask or head net, the less likely he will be spotted by the sharp eyes of a wild turkey gobbler.

These movements, of course, must take place while the tom is behind a big tree, or when it's head is hidden by a fully fanned tail. Other rests on the market will doubtless work just as well. One I've liked especially features a single telescoping pole which adjusts to the desired height. A plastic clip clamps onto the barrel, allowing the shooter to

A well-designed turkey hunting vest offers roomy compartments for calls, an extra warm jacket, possibly rain gear, a collapsible decoy, snacks and more.

timber binoculars are practically useless. But by relying on a set of lightweight, compact models, I can always carry them along with me; for example, when I need to determine what food source is growing in a distant field, or to identify a hunter at the far end of a pasture where I plan to hunt. In short, a good pair of binoculars can save a lot of unnecessary foot work. The ones I use mostly are a pair of 10x25 Nikon glasses. They are extremely lightweight—about half a pound—and yet they offer enough magnification to identify distant objects with clarity.

Turkey hunting decoys, which have been discussed in earlier chapters, are now quite common. Generally speaking, decoys are available in two distinct forms: hard-molded plastic or soft, collapsible foam/rubber/plastic. One advantage of the former is its realistic detail. It doesn't have to be "puffed" out or pulled into shape when the time comes to use it. The disadvantage of a hard-molded decoy, however, is that it can become tiresome packing one through the woods. It can also be dangerous traipsing around during turkey season with a full-bodied turkey decoy under one's arm. That's where the collapsible decoys have all the advantages. They fold up easily and can be carried in the rear game bag of a turkey vest. Some will even fit in a large jacket cargo pocket.

In recent years, decoys have become available in soft foam, rubber or collapsible plastic, each one looking as realistic as the best hard-molded plastic

pivot the shotgun from left to right while making sight adjustments for oncoming gobblers. Or you can simply cut a small sapling and trim a branch strong enough for holding a shotgun. A crude rest like that once enabled a small-framed 12-year-old I guided to keep the muzzle of his dad's 12-gauge autoloader pointed up long enough to make a great shot on a 23-pound Illinois gobbler.

Whenever I hunt turkeys, I pack a pair of binoculars (**photo p. 114**). More than once I've sat on a distant ridge and glassed a good gobbler far below, which otherwise I would never have spotted. I prefer using binoculars when scouting a new area or when hunting country that's relatively open. I'll admit that when hunting in deep, heavy decoys on the market. While slightly heavier than some lighter foam models, those produced by Carry Lite (Milwaukee, WI) look like the real thing from only a few yards away. Other companies, like Buck Wing Products (Whitehall, PA) have done much to eliminate the time spent trying to remove the folds and dents when setting up in a hurry. Each one comes with an internal expansion mechanism that works much like opening an umbrella. These decoys can now be set up nearly as fast as a hard-molded decoy. Two or three hunters together can pack a whole flock of decoys with comparative ease. A dozen or so placed at the edge of a field or pasture may well prove more than even the most reluctant old gobbler can resist.

Not all of today's decoys are hen decoys, either. Several manufacturers now offer lifelike gobbler and jake decoys, some in full strut. Others can even be arranged to look as if the jake is breeding the hen. This sight can really fire up a boss gobbler in a hurry. To lend today's decoys even more realism, most can be made mobile, powered by a string that runs back to the hunter, or by a battery-powered electric motor.

I've never been a big advocate of the blind, but I've seen how effective it can be, especially when left in an area that's frequented by turkeys. This includes food plots planted specifically to attract turkeys, known feeding areas, established strutting zones, along travel corridors, and (where legal) near feeders. Blinds are a great way to introduce beginning turkey hunters to the sport as

well. An inexperienced hunter's movements when using a blind are better hidden from a turkey's sharp eyes. I remember one Alabama turkey hunt that would have been nothing short of miserable if it hadn't been for a well-placed, waterproof blind. During the five-day hunt it had rained every hour of every day. After two days, I decided to swallow my pride and set up in a big, roomy blind. This heavily camouflaged nylon blind even had windows, or shooting ports, which could be unzipped on

Brad Harris knows the importance of being comfortable. Often a gobbler will run right in, while at other times the bird might take an hour or more.

all four sides. With all four ports unzipped, I was able to concentrate on several hen decoys that had been set up in front of the blind. That way, my calls extended in every direction. And so for the next two days, I sat in the blind,

can be erected by hanging the material between a couple of saplings, or tied to the trunks of small trees (using a dark-colored nylon line).

Following is a checklist of items I almost always carry with me when heading for the turkey woods:

1. *An assortment of diaphragm calls*
2. *At least one box call (often two)*
3. *A slate call*
4. *Shotgun (or bow)*
5. *Five or six shotgun shells*
6. *Head net*
7. *Camouflage or jersey gloves*
8. *Folding knife with 3" or 3½" blade*
9. *Binoculars*
10. *Small bottle of drinking water*
11. *Small "Mini-Mag" type flashlight*
12. *Small 35mm camera*
13. *Seat or pad*
14. *Fluorescent orange vest to wrap around harvested turkey for safety during walkout.*

Also, never forget to pack along a wad of toilet paper stuffed away in a cargo pocket or a jacket pocket. Depending on how long you stay out, carry a snack or a full lunch. And when hunting in unfamiliar country, especially if it's big and wild, carry a compass and perhaps a topographical map of the area as well. ■

An often overlooked accessory is a pair of pruning shears to remove brush that can prevent swinging the muzzle of a shotgun toward an oncoming gobbler.

calling several times every ten to fifteen minutes. Early in the afternoon of the second day, I spotted two huge gobblers strutting around my decoys. They had come in without making a sound. Quickly, I eased up my Remington 870 and fired. That gobbler proved the only one taken that week by all six hunters in camp.

When you know you're going to be hunting with an inexperienced turkey hunter, or when you plan to hunt in wide open country, you may want to carry along a seven- or eight-foot section of lightweight mesh camouflaged material. In a matter of seconds, an effective blind

Chapter 15

The Importance Of Safety In The Turkey Woods

WITH ■ Rob Keck, *C.E.O., National Wild Turkey Federation* ■ Harold Knight, *Co. Founder, Knight & Hale Game Calls* ■ David Hale, *Co-founder, Knight & Hale Game Calls* ■ Ray Eye, *World Champion Turkey Caller*

Right on cue, at the sounds of my owl hoots, two or

three toms gobbled back. I knew exactly where they were roosted, and in the pre-dawn darkness I slipped easily to within a hundred yards of their position. A few stars still glittered through the light of approaching dawn, and I knew it was going to be one of those days to remember--especially when the turkeys began to gobble on their own at every natural sound in the woods.

I waited patiently for the sounds of strong wing beats informing me they had landed on the ground. Fifteen minutes after setting up at the base of a huge old oak tree, I heard the birds sail down from their perches. At that exact moment, I purred lightly with my mouth diaphragm call pressed against the roof of my mouth and followed up with a few light yelps. When all three gobblers hammered back, slowly I eased the shotgun up onto my left knee.

A few minutes later, the tips of several fanned tails appeared as the turkeys slowly worked their way in my direction, about 50 yards away. As the light grew stronger, I realized I hadn't set up in the "ideal" position. There was a lot of underbrush between me and the gobblers, and after watching them strut back and forth for fifteen minutes or so, it became evident that those toms wanted the hen to come to them.

Ever so slowly, I reached down and lightly scratched the ground, then purred a few times, once more following up with a few light clucks and yelps. All three gobblers answered with deep gobbles--but they never made another step in my direction. Several times in the next ten minutes, the three adult toms would gobble in their attempts to lure that hen through the thick ground cover. Through it all, I remained quiet.

Always be sure of the target before squeezing off a shot.

Almost as one, the three gobblers dropped out of strut, and one behind the other, slowly walked in my direction, carefully picking their way through the waist-high underbrush. The bead of my Remington 870 followed the lead turkey as he inched closer. I'd already picked the spot where I was going to take him, and now I waited for that big tom to cover another 15 yards.

Suddenly, two quick shotgun blasts shattered the morning stillness. Instantly all three toms jumped into the air. I immediately rolled over and lay flat on the ground as all three gobblers flew over me. Three more shotgun blasts reached out in an attempt to catch the fleeing birds. I could hear the pellets zipping through the leaf cover, followed by bits and pieces of green foliage floating back to earth.

Quickly, I crawled around to the back side of the big oak before leaping to my feet and shouting, "Hold your fire, hold your fire!"

Even as I cautiously peeked around the oak, I heard footsteps running up the side of the opposite ridge. Two young hunters were covering as much ground as possible--but in the other direction! I sat down and tried not to think about how close I'd come to being the victim of a hunting accident. After collecting my thoughts, I made my way down the side of the point until I could see how the two men had slipped in so close without being spotted by the turkeys, or by me. Their footprints were clearly visible in the soft, damp sand of a narrow wash that ran along the side of the wooded point. Also visible were their hand and knee prints where they had literally crawled the last 50 or 60 yards. I picked up the empty shotshell hulls and have kept them for nearly ten years as a reminder of that morning. Fortunately, their first shots had been angled at some birds who were still 40 yards in front of me. The last three shots, though, were at turkeys 15 or so feet over my head.

A flash of white from an uncovered face is enough to trigger a shot from an approaching hunter.

What if those two hunters had come in from below and shot at the turkeys from the other side? Or what if those toms had decided to run instead of fly past my position?

I was supposed to have been the only hunter on that 400-acre farm in northern Missouri. The thought of another hunter being anywhere near me was the last thing on my mind as I concentrated on working those three birds.

THE IMPORTANCE OF SAFETY IN THE TURKEY WOODS

Packing out a gobbler by throwing it over the shoulder may be the classic end to a successful hunt, but the waving tail feathers are enough to attract a shot from another hunter.

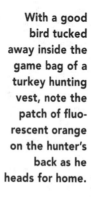

With a good bird tucked away inside the game bag of a turkey hunting vest, note the patch of fluorescent orange on the hunter's back as he heads for home.

It just confirms the fact that no matter where a person hunts, it's never wise to assume that no one else is around. The landowner and I later discovered that the two hunters were a teenage neighbor boy and his friend. They'd heard the birds gobbling and had tried slipping in on them from a pasture on the other side of the fence. What really upset me was the fact that they had run away when I yelled at them. What if I'd been hit by one of the pellets from their wild 60-yard shots?

It's unfortunate, but turkey hunting continues to suffer the highest rate of hunting accidents. Some can be attributed simply to ignorance about where other hunters are located. Then, too, successful turkey hunters must know how to conceal themselves from the sharp eyes of a wild turkey, which means other hunters may not spot them so readily. Add in the fact that your fellow hunters are making legitimate turkey sounds, to which you are responding in kind, and you have the perfect scenario for attracting other hunters toward a potentially dangerous situation.

David Hale admits that during his early years as a turkey hunter, he crawled a lot more than he does now. He remembers one morning in particular when he tried to sneak close to a gobbling bird and almost met his Maker. "I got on a turkey that was gobbling, but he wouldn't come," David recalls, "so I slipped closer until I could see him at a distance through the woods. Sure enough, there he was

strutting around a flock of half a dozen or so hens."

David figured he could crawl to within 40 yards of that gobbler and get a shot. But about halfway to where he expected the turkey to be, he looked up to see a hunter sitting against a tree, his shotgun aimed directly at David. It turned out to be a friend and a seasoned turkey hunter. Later, he and his hunting pal talked about what had happened. The hunter told David that the first thing that came into view was the floppy old hat Hale was wearing. To the hunter, the hat looked just like a turkey slipping along. Fortunately, the hunter held his fire until he was absolutely sure of his target. Had the hunter been someone with less turkey hunting experience, that incident could easily have had a tragic ending.

David Hale, who has had several close calls involving other hunters, claims no turkey is worth getting shot at or by accidentally shooting another hunter.

Decoys look like turkeys, so caution should be taken when packing them through the spring woods. Turkey hunter pro Brad Harris uses collapsible Feather Flex decoys which can be safely carried when folded in a vest pocket.

A flash of sunlight on ungloved hands (left and below) could result in a hasty shot from an approaching hunter who might mistake them for a gobbler's head.

Harold Knight recalls that "In 40 years of turkey hunting, I can't remember any close calls; but I've been stalked by other hunters. It's like driving a car. Once you've put 100,000 miles on it, you're going to have some close calls. So too, if you hunt turkey 60 days a year for nearly four decades, as I have, odds are you'll have more close calls than somebody who only hunts two or three times a year."

Harold adds, "If I see another hunter stalking through the woods toward me, I let him know I'm there. I whistle or speak out loud in a human voice, but I don't wave my arms or make a lot of movements, because I know that will spook the turkey. On the other hand, I can always go find another one!"

Knight points out that most turkey hunting accidents are caused by hunters who fail to identify their targets properly. Knight knows the importance of good camouflage. All hunters, he insists, should be fully camouflaged to eliminate the flash of exposed skin that might trigger hasty shots from other hunters. Knight is especially careful to wear dark or camouflaged gloves when walking through the wood.

"Most people swing their hands when they walk," he continues, "so even when you've got full camouflage on but your hands are showing, somebody might mistake that white skin for a turkey's head. I always avoid wearing colors that are the colors of a turkey's head--red, white or blue,"

Knight warns that a lot of hunters who claim to have enough sense to avoid wearing these colors will turn around and slip on a white T-shirt that shows at the neck, or a colorful long-sleeved shirt or a sweat shirt with slightly longer sleeves than the light camouflaged shirt or jacket worn over it. "I never take out a red handkerchief or anything else that's colorful," he concludes. "I'm even careful where I show white toilet paper. I take these precautions seriously and stay away from other hunters as much as I can."

Few hunters spend as much time in the spring turkey woods as Ray Eye. "I've seen thousands of turkeys and thousands of men," he says somewhat facetiously, "and I've never seen a man that looks like a turkey. There's no excuse for confusing the two, especially in the spring when a hunter ought to spot a visible beard before firing!"

Eye says that too many hunters actually lose sight of what turkey hunting is all about. They feel they **must** kill a turkey, no matter what the cost--as if harvesting a turkey makes them a hero in the eyes of their hunting buddies. They're not out there to enjoy the coming of spring, the companionship of close friends, the challenge of hunting a wild turkey gobbler **properly**, or to learn from the experience. They're out there simply for the sake of blowing a turkey away, and they really don't care how they accomplish it.

These hunters are the unethical few who will slip in and shoot a gobbler off the roost before daylight, or who don't mind shooting at a turkey from the window of a pickup truck. They're the ones

HUNTING AMERICA'S WILD TURKEYS

When making turkey sounds, hunters are also attracting other hunters nearby. Always be on the lookout for hunters who are trying to sneak up on what they think is a turkey.

Passing on the turkey hunting tradition to younger hunters includes teaching them the ABC's of safe turkey hunting. Here Bill Jordan and son Tyler proudly display the young hunter's first gobbler, a fine Georgia tom.

who slip between you and the bird you're working and ambush the gobbler, even when they know you're calling to the tom. In short, they represent those turkey hunting slobs who give hunting a black eye. They're also the ones you should avoid. They're so gung-ho they cause hunting accidents. In their zest to harvest a bird, in their minds they actually see a turkey when they take aim and fire at another hunter--like you!

David Hale feels strongly that there's no excuse for taking aim and shooting another hunter. There's always the chance that a stray pellet may strike another hunter who's working the other side of a turkey. The number one cause of turkey hunting accidents, though, is the failure to identify the target properly. "If a hunter holds his fire until he's absolutely sure about what he's shooting at," Hale advises, "and clearly identifies the bird and sees his beard, then he won't cause an accident. It's as simple as that!"

Harold Knight chimes in, "I think the danger in turkey hunting has been overemphasized. Lots of people who'd like to try turkey hunting are scared by all the negative publicity about how dangerous it is. Sure, accidents happen, and they're tragic and totally unnecessary. But statistically, turkey hunting is a lot safer than football or baseball or some other popular sports."

The National Wild Turkey Federation has established a Turkey Hunting Safety Task Force comprised of hunter safety instructors, wildlife biologists, legal experts, state agency administrators, conservation officers, representatives from the International Hunter Education Association, the outdoor product industry and the National Wild Turkey Federation. This group, which first met in 1992, has established a plan that addresses turkey hunting safety and complements programs already in place at state levels or through organizations like the National Shooting Sports Foundation.

"Although the Task Force is unable to gauge how much influence their actions have had in reducing turkey hunting accidents," states Rob Keck of the National Wild Turkey Federation, "numbers from recent meetings indicated that we are reaching hunters successfully. From 1992, when the group was first formed, to 1996, the rate of turkey hunting-related accidents was nearly cut in half. In 1992, statistics revealed that about 8.1 out of every 100,000 turkey hunters were involved in some sort of hunting accident. During the spring of 1996, the rate dropped to 4.6 incidents per 100,000. And the sport continues down that path, thanks largely to the efforts of the Turkey Hunting Safety Task Force and all the mandatory hunter safety courses now in most states."

STEPS AND WARNINGS EVERY TURKEY HUNTER SHOULD TAKE AND HEED

- **ALWAYS** identify your target as a legal turkey before firing.
- **NEVER** take aim at another hunter purposely.

When packing a decoy, especially a gobbler or jake decoy with red and whitish-blue head coloration, rely on a collapsible, fully concealed decoy, or carry a hard shell type in a camouflaged bag.

- **ALWAYS** make sure that no one is hunting or otherwise engaged beyond your target.
- **NEVER** attempt to crawl up to a turkey when other hunters are in the area.
- **ALWAYS** whistle or call out loudly at other hunters who approach you.
- **NEVER** wave your hands or arms at an approaching hunter.
- **ALWAYS** respect the presence of other hunters, and don't try to call away or ambush any turkeys they may be calling.
- **NEVER** wear red, blue or white (the colors of a turkey's head) clothing.
- **ALWAYS** use caution when carrying a turkey decoy into the woods.
- **NEVER** carry anything into the turkey woods that might be mistaken for a turkey head (a soda can, snack, handkerchief, etc.).
- **ALWAYS** place a piece of bright fluorescent orange material over a turkey when packing it out of the woods.
- **NEVER** walk though the woods while calling when you know others are hunting the same areas.
- **ALWAYS** wear dark or camouflage gloves when walking through turkey woods--and try to cover all exposed skin when setting up and calling to a turkey.

Turkey hunting safety begins with you. Always be on the alert for other hunters--those who've been attracted to your calls, or hunters you may encounter in the woods. Remember, no turkey is worth getting shot at, nor worth shooting someone accidentally. ■

Chapter 16

The Future Of The Wild Turkey

WITH ■ Ray Eye, *World Champion Turkey Caller* ■ Harold Knight, *Co. Founder, Knight & Hale Game Calls* ■ David Hale, *Co-founder, Knight & Hale Game Calls* ■ Rob Keck, *C.E.O., National Wild Turkey Federation*

My first turkey hunt took place back in 1972, in the

rugged Ozarks hills of southern Missouri. I hunted for four hard mornings before clearly hearing my first gobbles from a wild turkey tom. And it was three days later before I had a bird within range and hung my tag on the first of many gobblers. They have since made spring mornings in the turkey woods very special to me.

Even then, I felt privileged to have had the opportunity to hunt this magnificent game bird, which only a few decades earlier had been eliminated from most of its native habitat. I had grown up in neighboring Illinois, and while I was aware of several attempts to re-establish the wild turkey to parts of my home state, I had never once seen a turkey in the wild. In fact, the first one I ever saw was in 1972, when an obliging two-year-old strutted up to within 100 feet from where I sat on the side of an Ozarks ridge. Sec-

onds later, I hung my first turkey tag on that bird.

Most winter mornings, I can now look out the window of my office in rural Pike County, Illinois, and witness 20 to 40 birds feeding in the field next door. Most spring mornings, when I'm not already up and in the turkey woods, I'm awakened by a half-dozen gobblers sounding off from the ridge top overlooking my home.

During the first year of my turkey-hunting career, there existed only a million or so birds in the entire United States. Now the National Wild Turkey Federation estimates that at least $5\frac{1}{2}$ million turkeys roam our woodlands, swamps, fields and grasslands. The "good ol' days" for contemporary turkey hunters appears to be right now.

The National Wild Turkey Federation was founded the year after I began hunting turkeys. From the very

Millions of dollars have been spent to reintroduce the wild turkey into all of its original native ranges, plus those areas where the turkey was not found historically. (NWTF Photo)

Public interest has grown to the point where the restockings of wild turkeys have become media events. (NWTF Photo)

beginning, the mission of this organization has been: The conservation of the wild turkey and the preservation of the turkey hunting tradition. In that regard, members of the NWTF have done more for the sport of turkey hunting than any other conservation-minded organization that I know of. Still, we can't give this one organization all the credit for the growth of wild turkey populations during the past three decades. But without its support, management of the wild turkey population would be years, if not a decade or more behind where it stands today. Since 1985, this organization has helped by contributing more than $130 million dollars (including cooperative funding) to over 15,000 projects benefiting the wild turkey throughout North America.

The NWTF is a firm believer in scientific wildlife management and has worked with private, corporate, state and federal landowners to improve wild turkey habitat on a daily basis. Every five years, too, it coordinates a National Wild Turkey Symposia, which allows professional wildlife managers from coast to coast (including Canada) to review the various research and management programs taking place and gauge the effectiveness of these programs. More than 150 wild turkey management professionals attended the most recent symposia to review some 35 different research projects. All but two received at least some funding from the NWTF.

Years ago, one of my favorite turkey hunting destinations each spring was

the Quachita Mountains of west-central Arkansas. It wasn't because the region was overrun with wild turkeys, but simply a matter of how much my hunting partners and I enjoyed the beauty of this rugged land. We relished the opportunity to hunt deep into isolated areas, to work birds that more than likely were rarely called to. There were plenty of turkeys to hunt in those hills, but (depending on the weather) some years I would hunt an entire week without firing a shot, while at other times I'd quickly fill both of my tags.

During the first few years of hunting the huge expanses of the Quachita National Forest, we sensed that the timbering operations taking place there

Many wildlife professionals, including National Wild Turkey Federation Chief Executive Officer Rob Keck, have devoted their lives to the preservation of hunting traditions in America.

Rob Keck and daughter Heather pose with a South Carolina gobbler in front of the National Wild Turkey Federation headquarters in Edgefield, South Carolina. (Jay Langston, NWTF Photo)

ber of turkeys. Over a course of two decades, I witnessed one of my favorite turkey hunting haunts slowly being transformed into a "Great Pine Desert" of sorts, and as a result I have not hunted there in ten years or more.

One important program administered by the National Wild Turkey Federation is what it calls the "Pineland Stewards Project." It's essentially a cooperative endeavor involving the University of Georgia, Clemson University, the Georgia and South Carolina Departments of Natural Resources, the Georgia and South Carolina Forestry Commissions, and the Natural Resources Conservation Service. The goals of this program are to improve the management of pine stands for the benefit of the wild turkey and other desirable wildlife, to determine the costs of such management, and to get this much-needed information into the hands of private landowners.

Such programs are crucial to the ongoing management of the wild turkey, and other wildlife as well. Large stands of pines have proven beneficial for various wildlife populations, including the wild turkey, but only when the balance and quality of other habitats are considered equally important. The needs of humanity for lumber and paper products means we must adjust to the idea of extensive, slow-growing hardwood forests being replaced by faster maturing pinelands—that is, unless steps are taken to slow the trend. Unfortunately, even with programs like the Pinelands Stewards Project, the needs of the wild turkey and other

were actually having a positive effect on the turkey populations. Deep within the great expanses of those hardwood forests, several hundred-acre tracts of land were being cleared and replanted in fast-growing pines. While these new plantings by themselves did not provide much in the way of feed for the turkeys, the brushy clear cuts and two-to-four-year-old stands of young pines did provide an ideal nesting habitat for the hens.

Over the years, the balance between remaining hardwoods and managed stands of pines seemed to swing in favor of the softwoods. As these trees matured, we noticed a dwindling num-

HUNTING AMERICA'S WILD TURKEYS

wildlife will probably take a back seat to the needs of an ever-increasing human population.

The NWTF also administers several other habitat improvement projects. One, called "Making Tracks," is a cooperative initiative between the organization and state, federal and provincial wildlife agencies to ensure that the wild turkey will be successfully restored to its favorite habitats in North America. This program has so far witnessed a tremendous impact on the distribution of the wild turkey into areas where these birds had never been seen before. From 1990 to 1995 alone, the wild turkey in America increased its range by nearly 30 percent. Since its inception, the NWTF has donated more than 105,000 wild turkey transport boxes to various wildlife agencies and has assisted in the transport of more than 150,000 birds destined for new transplants. The organization has also worked closely with the National Forest Service in the improvement of wild turkey habitats on public lands, thereby improving the quality of turkey hunting for those who have no access to private lands.

Other habitat and conservation programs high on NWTF's list include "Project HELP" (Habitat Enhancement Land Program). It provides professional guidance, along with competitively priced seeds and seedlings, for private landowners who seek to improve the quality of the wild turkey habitat on their lands. A publication, called "Managing Openings for Wild Turkeys and Other Wildlife," provides practical, year-round regional habitat management information in support of this program. Other programs directed by NWTF include those which recognize landowners who've worked especially hard to improve habitat on their properties.

According to turkey hunting professional Ray Eye, "Just as turkey hunting needed help a half-century ago to get

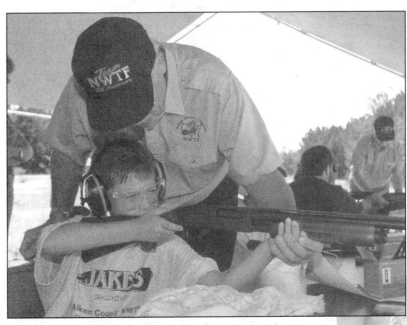

where it is now, the sport is going to need help in the next fifty years as well. It seems like every year we see more and more negative factors working toward taking the sport away from us. Such things as loss of habitat and groups supporting unrealistic concepts of animal rights and gun laws represent real threats to every sportsman. All hunters should join organizations like the National Wild Turkey Federation

Thousands of youngsters have been introduced to shooting and hunting through the JAKES Program conducted by the National Wild Turkey Federation. (NWTF Photo)

NWTF member landowners have done much to improve wild turkey forage and habitat on their properties. Such efforts often become family affairs. (NWTF Photo)

Women are now beginning to play an ever-increasing role in outdoor recreation, with interest in turkey hunting being no exception. (NWTF Photo)

and other pro-hunting associations. Not only should they join, they must become closely involved by donating both time and money."

Turkey hunting experts Harold Knight and David Hale agree. They attribute the successful re-introduction of the wild turkey to two main factors. One is that wildlife biologists have devised a

"Thanks to the dedicated work of thousands of professional wildlife managers and the support of tens of thousands of sportsmen and conservationists," states David Hale, "the future of wild turkeys in North America is bright. Flocks continue expanding into new areas. Each spring more birds and opportunities for hunting them are avail-

practical, highly efficient technique for trapping and restocking wild birds and establishing them in historic ranges. The other factor lies with a public that fully supports these efforts, primarily through the NWTF, which has consistently lobbied public and private wildlife agencies to expand turkey flocks and assists these groups in their efforts.

able, and more hunters continue to discover the pleasures and thrills inherent in this sport. These trends should continue into the next century."

On the other hand, warns Harold Knight, "There are some dark clouds on the horizon. Continued growth in human population, increasing loss of wildlife habitat, growing pressure from

Turkey hunting is a great avenue for building long-lasting bonds with sons or daughters. The author and his son Adam are shown with the young hunter's first gobbler, taken several years ago.

anti-hunters, all threaten our progress. That's why hunters should take an increasingly active role in supporting management programs, to keeping turkey hunting clean, and to spreading messages of conservation and the wise use of natural resources to the public at large."

But being the optimist that he is, Harold Knight adds, "I foresee turkey hunting in the next twenty years as being good. I really do. I don't think the continental turkey population is anywhere close to peaking. They say we've got a million more turkeys today than we had five years ago. If that trend keeps going, which it should, we'll have a lot of turkey in America's woodlands in the future.

David Hale agrees. "I think twenty years from now we'll have wild turkeys throughout America, wherever we can find them. Assuming we're still allowed to own and keep guns, and our hunting seasons continue, I think turkey hunting will be as popular as deer hunting. Right now the ratio is something like one turkey hunter for every six or seven deer hunters, but in twenty years it'll be closer to one to one."

But David sees a dark side as well. "I think the anti-hunting movement is part of a shift away from the conservative values on which our forefathers built this country, then fought and died for them. We hunters must spread the

message that, without our financial support, there won't be any wild turkeys or deer to hunt. Our dollars are what put wildlife in the woods for anti-hunters and pro-hunters alike to enjoy."

Harold Knight chimes in: "One difference between a hunter and an anti-hunter is that the hunter is lazy. He doesn't realize what he's got until it's gone. The anti-hunters may be small in number, but they get a lot of coverage in the media while the hunter lays back and says, 'Well, let them do their thing…they can't bother me.' Fortun-

A sign of the times! The wild turkey has become such a valuable and renewable resource that state wildlife agencies, along with the state chapters of the NWTF, are working together to stop the illegal harvest of these birds.

ately, a few recognize what's happening and they're moving to halt this anti-hunting trend."

Most veteran turkey hunters like Harold Knight, David Hale and Ray Eye all agree that the future of turkey hunting lies in maintaining interest among future generations in the wild turkey. If

we are to have a sufficient number of these great birds 50 or 100 years from now, it's imperative that we pass on the hunting tradition to our youth.

In that context, the National Wild Turkey Federation also promotes JAKES (Juniors Acquiring Knowledge, Ethics and Sportsmanship), a program that has introduced hundreds of thousands of youngsters to the pleasure of turkey hunting. For many of these youths, JAKES also represents their first exposure to any type of hunting. This program is more than just hunting and shooting wild turkeys, however. It started with a generous donation from John L. Morris, founder of Bass Pro Shops, stressing the importance of sound conservation programs and the need for wise stewardship of our natural resources. This educational and out-

reach program is for youngsters 17 and under; but the message it promotes goes much farther than JAKES' membership. For example, much of the JAKES literature is published by the National Wild Turkey Federation and finds its way into schools and other youth groups. Many state and local chapters conduct hands-on JAKES events, promoting special youth hunts that expose city kids to the pleasures of the outdoors and hunting. NWTF has also come to the aid of young college students, providing around $235,000 in scholarships, all with the intent of helping students in their pursuit of careers in wildlife conservation and related fields.

"We know that our children must carry on our legacy of hunting," comments Rob Keck. "Offering scholarships is only one way the National Wild Turkey Federation can ensure that we'll have enough dedicated conservationists in the future."

Recently, the National Wild Turkey Federation announced that it had pledged a million dollars to the National Shooting Sports Foundation's "Hunting and Shooting Sports Heritage Fund." According to Rob Keck, providing this funding is an important step toward conservation in general. "We must do everything we can to support the firearms industry, which has been so supportive of our nation's hunters and recreational shooters," he urges. "You wouldn't have hunting without firearms, and hunters are the ones who foot the bill for conservation."

The money provided by the NWTF and its more than 1,800 state and local chapters has been earmarked for funding a major public relations campaign designed to introduce to the general public the recreational and economic benefits that hunting and shooting provide for millions of men, women and children across the U.S. To date, the NWTF is the only conservation organization to have made this level of financial commitment to the Hunting and Shooting Sports Heritage Fund.

However, the National Wild Turkey Federation is not the only organization to promote wild turkey conservation and hunting in general—but it has definitely been the leader. In addition to the programs described here, the organization has devoted great amounts of time and effort in removing obstacles for disabled sportsmen, plus opening the door for more outdoor women to enjoy hunting and the shooting sports. While recent statistics indicate there are close to three million turkey hunters in North America, only ten percent or so are actual members of the organization. Those who are members represent the "cream of the crop" when it comes to turkey hunters. They are dedicated, hard-working people with one primary goal in mind: the preservation of our turkey-hunting heritage. Funding for all

NWTF programs comes from individual and corporate donations, membership fees, and other monies raised by thousands of banquets held across the country each year. Those who consider themselves dedicated turkey hunters owe it to themselves and the sport of turkey hunting to join the National Wild Turkey Federation and become involved with the many great programs it offers.

"We almost lost turkey hunting once," Ray Eye warns," but we were lucky enough to get it back through a lot of hard work. The next time we lose it could be our last." ∎

Thanks to the efforts of sportsmen across the country, this young wild turkey gobbler and future generations look forward to a bright future.

Chapter 17

Memorable Hunts & Other Turkey Tales

WITH ■ Rob Keck, *C.E.O. National Wild Turkey Federation* ■ Rick Story, *Vice President, Wildlife Legislative Fund of America* ■ Gary Clancy, *Outdoor Writer* ■ Ray Eye, *World Champion Caller*

"Why in the world would anyone in their right mind get out of bed at 4 a.m. and head off into the dark woods to hunt wild turkeys when they can run down to the super market and buy farm-raised turkeys on sale for sixty-nine cents a pound?" I was once asked that question by a man and his wife who had spotted me shopping in full camouflage.

I asked if they'd ever climbed a mountain, parachuted from an airplane or canoed down a whitewater river. As I expected, they answered in the negative. When I asked if they'd ever played golf, both admitted they had.

"Why is it so important to hit that little ball several hundred yards away," I asked, "and then try to knock it into a little hole in the middle of a nicely manicured lawn?"

"Why? Because it's a challenge, and it takes skill." answered the man.

"Exactly!" I responded as I took off down the isle looking for a few cans of beans and other ingredients for some chili I was cooking up for half a dozen hungry turkey hunters that night.

Trying to explain to a non-hunter why you hunt turkeys would be like trying to justify climbing a rugged peak to someone afraid of heights...or why one enjoys jumping out of a perfectly good airplane to someone who is afraid to fly...or the thrill of mastering a canoe or kayak down a stretch of rough water to someone who can't swim. Let's face it, challenge is the real reason why the vast majority of us look forward so eagerly to each and every turkey season. Sure, we enjoy the tablefare provided by a plump big bird, but that's not why we hunt the wild turkey. Most of us also like the opportunity to get back in the woods after a long winter, but again we could do that without hunting. We also enjoy the camaraderie of the other hunters who share our camps, but that's

Taking that first turkey is an unforgettable experience. It's even better when a parent is there to enjoy the event. Bob and Terry Weber proudly display 12-year-old Terry's first tom.

still not the true reason why we put up with long days and short nights, cold rainy spring mornings, or the buzzing of mosquitoes a few days later. The fine eating, enjoyment of the outdoors and spending time with good friends are all fringe benefits of turkey season.

To a true turkey hunter, every season is special in one way or another.

Special birds, including this five-bearded tom harvested by the author, will always enjoy a soft spot in our memory.

Hunt turkeys long enough and a few seasons will always stand out in your mind as being "extra special." Often it's the special challenge of hunting one particular bird, or perhaps it was the company of other like-minded people you've met during the course of a season or hunt. In the following pages, several highly respected turkey hunters have recalled some of the highlights of their hunting careers. Everyone has his

own favorite anecdote. Here are a few that stand out in the minds of these outstanding turkey hunters.

THE ZUNI HUNT
by Rob Keck

In which Rob Keck recalls his unforgettable experience with the Zuni people of the Southwest.

I arrived in Zuni, New Mexico late in the evening. Despite the late hour, the people of Zuni welcomed me with open arms and warm, smiling faces. We, however, didn't chat long, and I stowed my gear and went to bed, anxiously awaiting the morning and the hunt, which is a hunt I anticipated for several years.

The following morning was cool and crisp. The members of the Zuni hunting party Nelson Luna, Octavios Seowtewa, his son Alexander, and Pierre Bowannie—were all excited to be going. Pierre had the honor of been chosen as the hunter who would harvest the bird…and it truly is an honor because the wild turkey is very important to Zuni culture and is used in a number of Zuni ceremonies, including a rain dance and the making of prayer sticks. After a cup of coffee and discussing where we were going to hunt, we loaded up in the trucks and headed out to the woods.

Light had yet to crack the sky and the air was still cool when we reached the hunting grounds. We stood outside the trucks, breathing in the crisp morning air, waiting for a bird to gobble. We had been standing in the darkness listening to the morning sounds for about fifteen minutes when we heard what we had been listening for...a gobble. We looked at each other, as if to say,

"'Where did that come from?

The bird sounded off again and we decided on a general direction of the gobble and headed up the ridge.

By the time we topped the rise, darkness was giving way to the light and the bird gobbled often. We set up. When I started calling, more birds responded. From behind us and in front of us, birds gobbled, and it seemed the only question that remained was, which bird would come in first. Turkey hunts, however, rarely play out easily and we settled in for a duel.

Below us, in the dim light, we spotted a group of gobblers chasing each other. The gobblers readily answered my calls, but would not come up the hill. They simply continued chasing each other. The gobbling behind us slacked off, and we turned our concentration on the group of birds in front of us. After a few minutes, a hen started yelping. I yelped back at her. Irritated, she responded with a louder, angrier yelp, and in a few minutes we spotted her in a fast trot running up the hill to our location. I called, and she advanced toward us, not stopping until she was a mere 10 yards from us. Making nearly every call imaginable, she circled our position about 45 minutes. She offered

some of the most amazing hen talk I have ever heard.

The hen's incessant talk prompted me to sit quietly and eventually we heard another gobble behind us. The hen, however, had us pinned...we simply sat tight and hoped she'd stay with us. She continued calling and then, like a ghost, one gobbler, then another, appeared on the hill above us. Both birds wound their way slowly down the hill through the trees toward us. The birds broke from strut only to gobble.

As the gobblers approached, the hen made her way to them. I thought for sure she would lead them away, and sure enough, she pulled them to our right, away from us. I hit them with some light calling, and she turned into the woods, skirting our position. The gobblers continued to strut and gobble, working their way through the woods behind the hen. Fortunately, the hen led them directly to a clearing that offered a clear shot at less than 20 yards. The gobblers followed her right into the clearing, directly in front of us, moving to our left. The gobblers separated, and gave Pierre a clean shot. A blast rang out, a gobbler fell, and the hunt was over, but I had not yet begun to realize the impact of the fallen bird.

After the shot, the four Zuni men and I sprang to our feet and went to the bird. When we got to the gobbler, the men performed a Zuni hunting ritual...a ritual they perform over all harvested game. First, they cleared all the debris from around the turkey and faced him towards the East. Next, they

marked the spot where the bird's heart was on the ground and gathered around the bird and said a traditional Zuni hunting prayer. They then sprinkled a mixture of cornmeal and turquoise on the bird's head. The cornmeal and turquoise are significant because corn has been a major food source of the Zuni people for many years and the turquoise is a precious stone. When they had sprinkled the cornmeal and turquoise, the men would make a sweeping motion with their hands up the neck to the head and off the beak to their own mouths. This signified the passing of the breath of life of the harvested game to the hunters themselves. Then they said another prayer.

The hunters then gathered the turkey and moved to another site to remove the entrails. While cleaning the bird, they were very careful not to get any blood on any of the feathers. Once the entrails were removed the men took out their hunting fetishes, which are small stone figurines of different kinds of carnivorous animals, often black bears. The men placed the fetishes in the entrails in order to "let them feed." The hunters feed their fetishes whenever they harvest game in order to make them stronger for the next hunt. I put my fetish in the entrails with the others and was told that this would bring me luck on my future hunts.

After this, the four men cut a small piece of the gobbler's heart, a small piece of skin from the foot and pulled some small feathers from the birds leg, swabbed them in the bird's mouth to get some saliva on the items and took them to the site of the harvest. They buried them where they marked the position of the heart...something they did to ensure the future of the wild turkey for the Zuni people and their needs.

After the ritual, we gathered our gear and headed down the mountain. In town, we called a lot of different people, telling of our successful hunt. The people of Zuni were very happy that a turkey had been harvested. The turkey is well respected in the Zuni culture, and they use every part of the bird. The meat was to be used at a rain dance and the feathers, used primarily for prayer sticks, would be used for various religious ceremonies, which are very important to Zuni culture.

This without a doubt was the most moving hunting experience I've ever been a part of...and done without me doing the shooting. It touched me and connected on some of my own habits. I think every hunter has a little Indian spirit in his blood. This hunt brought that kindred spirit home to me," recalls Rob Keck of his unforgettable experience with the Zuni people of the Southwest.

A GOBBLER FOR FITZ

By Gary Clancy

I've shot my fair share of gobblers, but somehow the ones I remember most are not the ones I shot, but those my family and friends have taken while at my side. Among my most vivid turkey hunting experiences is the following story.

I parked my truck that morning at the same spot I usually do and stepped out into the black of pre-dawn. The smell of spring—mostly alfalfa hay and dogwood blossoms—was in the air washed clean by a light sprinkle. I tucked a couple of decoys in the rear pouch of my vest, grabbed my heavy pump gun and headed out across the new alfalfa. My hunting companion, Dick "Fitz" Fitzgerald, walked alongside me, clutching my arm. Even in a good light, Fitz couldn't see that well anymore. In near darkness, he was as good as blind. Thirty years of battling diabetes had taken its toll, but Fitz wanted to get a gobbler in the worst way, and I desperately wanted one for him.

We had hunted each of three previous mornings and each time it seemed that Fitz was finally going to get his wish. But each time, at the last instant, something happened and the gobbler emerged victorious. It was Sunday morning on Mother's Day, late in the season, and the gobblers had been hunted hard. I didn't know how many more chances we would get. It all started well when a jake came racing into my first series of calls, but the sun was not yet fully up, and in the dim light Fitz could not see the bird. The jake got nervous and left.

An hour passed and the only other bird we heard gobble that morning had long since shut up. It was time to take a ride in the truck. Usually I like to begin by hiking the ridges, cutting hard and trying to get a bird to sound off, but Fitz's legs could no longer carry him over the hills and valleys. At every high

For Rob Keck (center), CEO of the NWTF, his hunt with the Zuni Indians on their ancestral hunting grounds was an experience he'll never forget.

point we came to, I stopped, turned off the engine and listened. It was a calm, sun-filled morning, so any sounds we made carried a long way. I could hear the neighbor's cattle bellowing down by the creek nearly a mile away, while the new lambs in McCabe's pasture baa-ed for their mothers. We were halfway up a long driveway leading to Gordon's farm when I heard that wonderful sound. It was a long way off, but it was definitely a gobbler—and by the sounds of it, a lonesome one. I listened long enough to pinpoint the bird's location.

"He's in that strip of alfalfa on the far end of Gordon's east ridge," I said to Fitz, "over by those big white pines we hunted yesterday or the day before. It's a long walk, but I don't dare drive any closer. Are you up to it?"

Fitz shot me a "don't treat me like an invalid" stare, so I slipped into my vest, grabbed the shotgun and headed off in the bird's direction. It took us the better part of an hour to get into position. Fitz could only go 100 yards or so without stopping to rest. The bird gobbled the whole time, which is not unusual late in the spring, when nearly all of the hens are sitting on their clutches. If I'd been alone, the bird would have been a slam-dunk. I could easily slip down along the ridge in the timber, staying well below the bird's line of sight, then crawl up to the edge of the timber. From there, a couple of soft clucks would have turned that gobbler inside out. But Fitz was not up to hiking the woods and climbing the steep ridge, so we slipped into a little finger jutting out at the opposite

end of the alfalfa strip, where the bird was strutting. I could see the gobbler all fanned out about 300 yards away, but I knew Fitz wouldn't see him until he was much closer.

We sat shoulder to shoulder against the rough hide of a giant cottonwood when I began stroking the box call. The gobbler had been waiting to hear a hen yelp all morning and I really expected him to trip all over himself getting to us as fast as his long legs would carry him. But it had been a long season and the gobbler was in no hurry. I called just enough to keep him interested, mixing a few clucks with my yelps. Nothing fancy. Still, it took the bird 15 long, ex-cruciating minutes to top the last little dip in the alfalfa field. As soon as he topped it, I felt Fitz jump beside me.

"I see him, I see him!" he hissed.

"Just be cool...be cool," I instructed, realizing that asking Fitz to be cool at a moment like this was like asking the sun not to rise in the East. The gobbler, his head all decked out in red, white and blue, moved toward us with one agonizingly slow step at a time. The barrel of Fitz's old Mossberg pump was shaking like a sapling in a hurricane. I was wishing I had set up on the edge of the timber instead, where Fitz could have taken the bird in the wide open alfalfa field, but I feared we might spook the bird while we moved into posi-tion. As it was, the bird now had to make its way through 20 yards of timber before he'd be in range. As soon as the gobbler left the alfalfa field and stepped into the woods, Fitz lost sight of him. Now we had a serious problem!

The bird tip-toed to within 35 yards and stopped. For a minute or two, he stood his ground, his sharp eyes searching for the hen he knew must be nearby. By now, Fitz was shaking like a wet dog. Suddenly the bird gobbled and Fitz jumped like a frog crossing hot pavement. It's a miracle that the gobbler didn't pick us off, but miracles do happen.

"Just to the left of where your barrel is pointed...see his red head?" I whispered. I knew it was a dumb question as soon as I said it. Fitz was color blind too!

"I can't see him" Fitz whispered back. Just then, the gobbler took another step and Fitz caught the movement. "I see him! I see him!" he whispered excitedly.

"Then shoot him," I hissed back.

Before Fitz could pull the trigger, the bird took another step and disappeared behind some brush. A minute dragged by. I could picture that turkey standing there, tall and proud, but getting nervous. Then he began to strut...ppfftti-vvrrooom...ppfftti-vrooom. It's a sound like nothing else in nature. Fitz, whose hearing was excellent, homed in on the bird's location through sound alone.

"When he steps out from behind that brush, shoot him," I whispered.

The gobbler stepped out and was in the clear for only a brief moment. Before Fitz could line up the bead on his head, however, the bird stepped behind a clump of green ash and disappeared once again. I told Fitz to shoot as soon as the bird stepped clear of the green ask clump. Ever so slowly, Fitz moved the barrel to the right. The gobbler peeked around the clump, his long neck and head now in the clear. His body followed, barely ten steps away, and I was afraid to breathe, anticipating the roar of the 12-gauge.

"Shoot!" I implored Fitz.

"I can't see him," came his whispered reply.

The gobbler was on full alert. He knew something was wrong. In moments he would be gone.

"Lower your barrel," I hissed.

"What?" Fitz asked, wondering if he had heard correctly. I had noticed that when Fitz moved the barrel to the right, in anticipation of the gobbler exiting from behind the green ask, he had raised the muzzle slightly. The muzzle was now blocking his view of the red head.

"Lower your muzzle and do it real slow," I instructed.

"I see him...I see him." The rest of Fitz's reply was cut short by the "BOOM" of his Mossberg pump gun. Nobody was more surprised than me when that turkey went down. I grabbed the shotgun from Fitz (not wanting him behind me with a loaded gun) and ran to the fallen bird. It lay quiet in last year's fallen leaves. Fitz was totally unglued, leaping up and down and hugging me.

"I got a turkey...I got a turkey! I can't believe it, I got a turkey," he yelled.

Then, as they usually do, the turkey went into its death throes. Fitz never hesitated. He threw himself on top of

Challenge is one aspect of turkey hunting that makes some gobblers more memorable than others. Minnesota bowhunter Rob Evans will probably never forget the Merriam's tom he took with his archery gear.

the thrashing bird and implored me to shoot it again. I pulled Fitz off the bird, which resumed its wild flopping. Fitz, who was no quitter, climbed right back on. By the time the bird quit thrashing—and Fitz stopped hollering—turkey feathers were scattered everywhere and I was laughing so hard it hurt. I've hunted turkeys with dozens of fellow hunters over the years, but nobody has ever gotten as excited as Fitz did on that Sunday morning in May—and no one ever appreciated a gobbler more.

In the end, diabetes finally won the battle. We buried Fitz the following fall. I think of him often, which is as it should be. One thing's for sure: when I hike into the pre-dawn black next spring, my little buddy will be holding onto my arm, just like he did on that long-ago morning."

IT'S THE SET-UP, STUPID!

By Rick Story

Rick Story will be the first to claim that he's not a turkey hunting expert. Still, he loves the sport as much as any world champion caller or turkey hunting authority. Fortunately for him, his line of work with the Wildlife Legislative Fund of America has allowed him to become good friends with a few honest-to-gosh turkey hunting experts. Here's his "story."

When I began hunting turkeys in the mid-1980s, my goal was to transform myself into a crackerjack caller. After a ton of practice and consultation with some world-class callers, it became obvious that it wasn't going to work out. I sounded like a peacock with a val-ium habit. Next, I decided to become an expert woodsman. If I couldn't call turkeys, I sure could lay some wood-manship on 'em. Where I come from, woodsmanship is a fancy word for bush-wacking. Anyway, my best attempts at woodsmanship produced little in the way of a Thanksgiving dinner. It so happens that my friend, Ray Eye, is a world champion caller, guide, lecturer and outdoor video producer. Aware of my failures at calling and woodsmanship, Ray sat me down one day and gave me the facts of life.

"I don't know why you're always trying to make everything so complicated," he commented. "The turkeys are out there being turkeys. Find a good set-up, sit down and call to one that gobbles. In your case, call very little. Better yet, scratch the leaves and fight hard to avoid the urge to call."

Armed with this knowledge, I set out to become the best set-up man in the business. I eschewed fancy calling and gave up the woodsmanship in exchange for complex set-up theories. I further restricted a penchant for making things overly complicated. As for the fine art of the set-up, here is what I learned. Get on the same hillside as the turkey and set up on the same level or slightly higher. Try to have some cover, like a ridge top, between the bird and you so that he's in range the second you see him. Don't set up if there's a creek or fence between you and the bird. It took years for me to develop these complex strategies. And so it was that I traveled to Missouri with the

express purpose of showing off my detailed set-up tactics to my mentor, Ray Eye (whose own story follows this one).

"Park your truck by the steel gate," Ray told me. "Walk out the ridge top and wait by the tree line until you hear a gobble. Then call—but first scratch the leaves—until you see a turkey. Try to remember to shoot him"

Sounded like a plan to me.

I'm not really afraid of the dark. I'm just afraid of falling down and having some wild animal suck the life's blood out of me. I moved out to the ridge top quietly so as not to alert my presence to any creatures dwelling in the woods. At first light, a booming gobble caused goose bumps to rise on the back of my neck. I said to myself, "He's 250 yards at an angle to my left, on the far bank about half way to the bottom, about 30 feet off the ground in what is probably a beech tree. There's another turkey 20 yards behind him—a jake."

At the bottom of the ridge was a huge ditch, not unusual in the deep, highly erodable soil common to the area. I needed to go to the bottom, walk to my right about 100 yards, cross the ditch and move back to the left down the bank until I was 150 yards from him. Then all I had to do was sit down and start calling (so much for Ray Eye's advice). Twenty minutes later, I had traversed the ditch and was closing in on my set-up target. Meanwhile, the gobbler kept up his booming cadence. By the time I sat down, I had run two hen turkeys out of trees and terrorized four squirrels and two deer. Not a bad morning's work.

I sat facing the turkey, which had been quiet for a few minutes, and let fly a stream of my best rendition of dirty words in the turkey's language of love. He stood quiet for a few seconds, perhaps wondering if he was lonesome enough to consort with a hen addicted to valium. Sure enough, he came back at me, off to my left, still high in the tree, the same tree he'd been in all along, on the same side of the ridge on which I had started.

I called for a while, he gobbled for a while, and then I called some more. He was heating up nicely, but still sat in the tree waiting for a real hen to stagger her way beneath the tom's roost tree. There was only one way to break this standoff. It was time to make a move. Back up the ridge I went, retracing my steps, crossing the ditch and setting up at the edge of a honeysuckle patch less than 100 yards from the tree under which my prize now strutted. This time, I scratched the leaves as Ray Eye had suggested, causing the big bird to vow his eternal love for me, this time from the ground and on the same side of the ridge I had just departed. In fact, if I'm not mistaken, he gobbled from the same blow-down against which I'd been leaning some 20 minutes prior.

I stayed put for about 45 minutes, all the while scratching the leaves and heaving turkey calls in all directions. Still, my quarry kept moving further down the ridge, gobbling all the way. I raced to the top of my side of the ridge

HUNTING AMERICA'S WILD TURKEYS

**Young Zack Opel will always remember this early season gobbler,
which he dumped with his muzzleloading shotgun.**

and bolted out into the pasture on the ridge top, staying below the skyline and moving parallel to the turkey's line of travel. When finally I reached a line of trees jutting out into the field, I made my move, reentering the woods and crossing the bottom until I had effectively cut him off and ruined his entire day.

In an attempt to locate the turkey's precise position, I couldn't resist the urge to use my one remaining turkey call. I fully expected him to be 100 yards or so to my right, across the bottom on the far side. He answered from my right okay, but from some 350 yards back from where I had just spent the better part of an hour.

"This is real progress," I said to myself. "We're now both on the same side of the ridge!"

I continued moving down the bottom of the ridge in the direction of the turkey. The ridge featured a series of draws between small finger ridges at 75-yard intervals. At a point where I figured I was within 100 yards of the turkey, I moved toward the top of the ridge, using one of the draws for cover. As soon as I heard the bird gobble, I eased out of the draw, plopped down on the ground and unleashed a torrent of filthy turkey pillow talk. Intrigued by my call, the turkey appeared above me on the finger ridge, about a 45-degree angle to my shotgun muzzle. His little buddy, the jake, was tagging along behind. I sat still while the turkey made a complete circle around my position. He passed in front of me but offered no

shot, completing the circle and ending up back where he had first appeared.

"Settle down, keep your head on the stock, and swing slowly to your right," I lectured to myself.

For the first time all day, I did everything right. The shotgun boomed and the turkey fell, albeit after lengthening my shot by five yards in an attempt to retreat up the hill. Back at camp, I was the only hunter of our group who scored that day. When Ray arrived, tired and sweaty from drinking coffee and eating sausage and eggs all day, he looked absolutely amazed.

"I got to hear all about this," he said. "Tell me the story."

When I finished, Ray said, "I'm glad you're starting to learn how not to make things more complicated than necessary. For a while there, I thought you were going to tell me you and the turkey had swapped spots on that hill two or three times."

Well, perhaps I did edit the story just a bit—but only for the sake of brevity, mind you.

EUGENE, "THE NAME CALLER"

By Ray Eye

No one in the sport of turkey hunting has more "turkey tales" to share than Missourian Ray Eye. And while he is dead serious about hunting turkeys, there's no one else out there who has more fun doing it than Ray. I've known him for the better part of two decades and have come to respect him as one of this country's true turkey hunting experts. We've also shared many tall tales together, and one of Ray's best is about an Ozarks gobbler he became acquainted with back in the spring of 1983. Ray was doing some pre-season scouting in the rolling hardwoods near his boyhood home, hooting and hen calling in an attempt to locate some gobblers. That's when he heard "Eugene" for the first time.

"The gobble that came back from the long, high glade was like no other. It was...well, powerful!" Ray recalls. Every time the bird gobbled, all the other toms in the area went silent. And each time Ray returned to that same area to scout, the bird would answer from the same glade. It wasn't long before its deep, rattling gobbles began to bother Ray.

"I named him Eugene after a fat, smart-mouthed kid I knew in grade school. He wouldn't utter a peep when he was close to you. But let him get across the playground where you couldn't get to him and he'd call you every name in the book. Eugene the turkey was the same way," says Eye.

That bird became an obsession for Ray. It would stand at the edge of the glade, looking out over miles and miles of rolling Ozarks hills, gobbling at every hoot of an owl, every crow call and every yelp of a coyote; but the second Ray slipped near the edge of the glade and tried to call, Eugene went totally silent. When Ray couldn't resist the urge

any longer, he'd slip up to the edge of the glade for a look, and there he'd be—Eugene—looking as big as a pot-bellied stove. In a flash, the big gobbler would jump into the air and sail away.

"I didn't want to kill him as much as I wanted to fool him, reflects Ray. "I stud-

ied him every chance I got. I'll never know if Eugene was just plain smart—or just plain lucky. But something always kept him out of shotgun range."

All season long, Eye kept returning to the glade for another try at the big bird. During one mid-morning hunt, he and a friend had moved to within calling distance of the glade when they got a response. The calls came from two gobblers, not just one. Some excited calling had gotten the birds all fired up, and soon the two hunters witnessed a full-scale gobbler fight. The eventual victor was, of course, Eugene. Ray continued calling to the old gobbler, but

Wise old gobblers, like this "limb hanger" with his 1¹/₂-inch spurs, can challenge even the best of hunters and callers.

nothing worked. With that, the two hunters went after the bird who had flown off, and a short while later Ray's friend tagged the bird—a fine 23½-pound gobbler with a 12-inch beard and 1½-inch spurs.

He'd been beaten bad," Ray recalled. "His plumage was raked and his breast was scarred with deep gouges from Eugene's spurs. Ray continued his pursuit of Eugene right up until the last day of the season, when he and three others returned to that Ozarks ridge for one last try. They worked in and around the glade all morning, but the gobbler never answered to any of their calls. It had rained hard off and on all morning and it was during a brief lull in the weather that they got themselves a trio of gobblers to work. One of the hunters dropped the lead bird, and a split second later came the sound of a second shot. One of the other hunters, noticing a slight movement to his right, turned just in time to spot Eugene, who stood easily a foot taller than the other birds. The hunter tried to snap his gun up, but Eugene ducked and flew off into the rain.

"That was the last time we saw him," Ray Eye reminisces. "He wasn't there the next spring. Turkey hunting in those hills just hasn't been the same since."

Yes, it's the challenge that keeps us going back into the turkey woods each spring, along with unforgettable places, special friends, great experiences, and gobblers with real personalities. I could share a hunt or two of my own, but I trust the preceding tales from four highly respected hunters have conveyed the message of just how special turkey hunting can be.

Should you ever run into me, don't be afraid to ask me about the time I guided a novice hunter who tried to reload his over-and-under shotgun with a Chap-Stick, or the time Gary Clancy let me hunt with a muzzleloading shotgun with no shot charge, or the time a "dead" gobbler came back to life in the back of my Jeep, or....... ■

Index